Reading
the
Marseille Tarot

J-M. David

Reading the Marseille Tarot

Copyright © 2009

J-M. David and *Association for Tarot Studies*

Association for Tarot Studies bibliographic detail:
Author: David, Jean-Michel
title: *Reading the Marseille Tarot*
date of publication: 2011

ISBN: 978-0-9757122-3-8

image credits:
Jean Noblet tarot - Jean-Claude Flornoy
Nicholas Conver tarot - Kenji Ishimatsu
other images electronically edited by J-M. David

Association for Tarot Studies
A 0044941 T

PO Box 4013
Croydon Hills
Vic., 3136, Australia

ATS
ASSOCIATION.TAROTSTUDIES.ORG

FOREWORD

Foreword

This book arises out of an online course I prepared during the period of a year spanning across 2007-2008 following previous requests that I provide something of the sort for online users. For the participents at the time, what they obtained was (precisely) a six-page document for each of the thirty chapters that forms this book. At the time I had no intention of transforming the material into bookform, though was encouraged to do so from its onset – and this encouragement, from both various participants, friends and those closest to me could not be unheeded.

So allow me here the usual author's prerogative to at least acknowledge a few people who have made this document a 'completed' work-in-progress. Firstly, everyone who participated in the very first course during those thirty weeks spanning across two years. I never asked for their permission to name them, so they shall remain anonymous. Some were simply encouraging (something an author always needs), others took the time to write lengthy suggestions for improvement (something else an author such as myself needs), yet others offered alternative views to some of the ones I offer (and, of course, this allows for the currently unquestioned to be brought to reflection). Without their support, assistance, enthusiasm and criticisms, I doubt I would have taken the ongoing time to complete the task I set myself.

Once I made some (very minor) revisions, Shane Kendal took the time to go over most of the manuscript and sensitively, with 'my voice' remaining with all its peculiarity, make numerous suggestions to clarify the text. Most of his suggestions I happily took, and some I stubbornly, and no doubt to my future regret, simply read. Once the book was completed – though that's a term that I frankly feel I cannot yet fully apply – Robert Mealing, who had similarly and from the start encouraged me to write it in the first place, designed the cover. Though even there he did not have *carte blanche*, but was rather restricted to my demand that it have a white background and that it 'match' the other *Association for Tarot Studies* covers. He also did not recall that the very title is something he suggested during a conversation we had some years prior.

The online course completed, it also motivated me to again locally organise a year-long course, using the text as its basis. The participants of those two courses I also sincerely thank – not only for their deepening feedback, but also from the friendship that has resulted out of the sessions, the wonderful delicacies brought for the tea-break, and the community we effectively formed during that time.

On a personal level, and apart from those already mentioned (Shane and Robert), others deserve especial mention. Con Margaritis, Judy Ratz, Vicky Spanos and Paul Martin have been particularly valuable in my striving to bring this to some kind of 'completion'. As have Lyn Olds and Fern Mercier. In fact, without their enforced deadline, it would likely still remain on my computer... more or less 'nearly finished'. A further special mention should be made here: Jean-Claude and Roxanne Flornoy have not only shared their hospitality, but without their own determination in bringing forth this deck from semi-oblivion, we would all be so much the poorer. The Noblet is a deck that truly deserves its rank amongst but few as one of pre-eminence.

There remains many details in the book I would have liked to have altered a little – mainly for clarity and due to not earlier on taking some of the suggestions made. I am also certain that errors remain to be corrected, and trust that it remains, nonetheless, well received. The book remains, however, as it stands for this edition, and I intend clarifying, adding to, and subtracting from various sections with forthcoming revisions.

Finally and, to be sure, also firstly, as any author in an intimate relationship will attest, all too many 'free' days and times are taken with the writing of the material... to have the support for not only its first writing but also the persistent encouragement to bring it to birth in this form, I deeply thank Pauline, without whom, none of this would have been feasible.

INTRODUCTION

Welcome!

This book is set up as a self-study course. If you are using the electronic version of the book, please note that hyperlinked words, images or sequence of letters will show in deep blue.

In these chapters, I will presume that you already have a basic idea about tarot... but only basic. At the very least, you have the 1650 Jean Noblet tarot restored by Jean-Claude Flornoy and available from tarot-history.com in Europe and tarotgarden in North America. In addition, I shall consider that Alfred Douglas's *Tarot*, or an equivalent introductory book, has been read – howsoever briefly.

But let's get started...

Why the Marseille?

For those who have chosen this book because of the style of deck, this may seem rather obvious. Yet, I would suggest that the question may similarly be put to you: why even study this deck?

And in any case, what *is* the Marseille!?

We'll return to this second question after we have briefly looked at the first.

The Marseille style of deck is central to the development of tarot. Most 21st and 20th century decks take as their base either a Marseille, or another deck that is itself based on the Marseille. If I can use a metaphor, the Tree of Tarot has large and numerous branches, and strong and deep roots. Its branches are the various types of decks that grow out of the Marseille-type trunk. To study tarot, then, one may indeed look carefully at one of its offshoots, but a better and fuller understanding comes from having a familiarity with the Marseille. So...

What is the Marseille?

The term appears to derive from Paul Marteau[1], the former owner of one of then largest card makers in Europe at the turn of the 20th century. His interests ranged from card play to tarot's divinatory uses. In many ways, he was the one who put this style of deck back into the public arena.

---

1   Papus used the term earlier in 1889 in his book *le Tarot des bohémiens,* though it was undoubtedly Marteau's release of the Grimaud 'Marseille' deck that caused the term to become widespread for the *style* or *type* of deck.

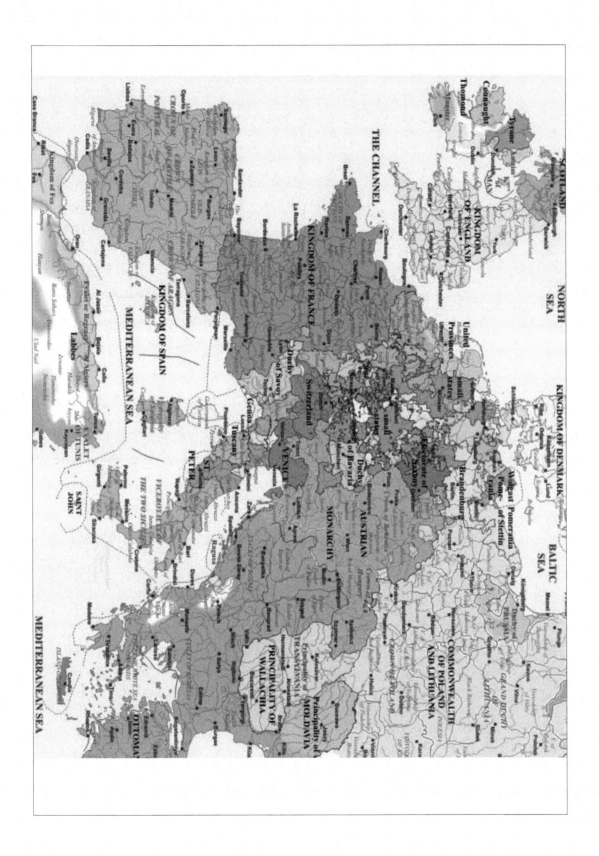

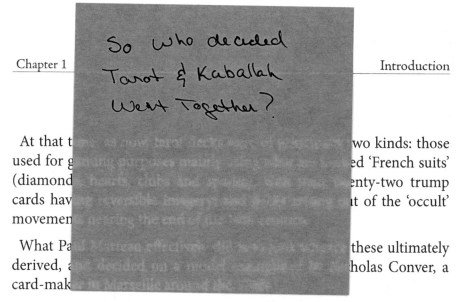

At that t[...] as now tarot decks [...] wo kinds: those used for g[...] purposes mainly [...]ed 'French suits' (diamond[...] hearts, clubs and spades, [...] enty-two trump cards hav[...] [...] t of the 'occult' movemen[...] nearing the end of the [...].

What Pa[...] Marteau effectively did [...] these ultimately derived, a[...] decided on a model [...] [...]holas Conver, a card-mak[...] [...] Marseille around the [...].

Until Marteau, these decks were simply called that: tarot decks – or in French, *'jeux de tarot'*.

Types of Marseille

But let's pause a second and reflect on what we already have thus far, for *two* Marseille-type decks have so far been mentioned (the Noblet and the Conver), and though similar by quick perusal, the same they are not.

The deck we shall be using as our basis, the 1650 Jean Noblet deck, is not even from Marseille, but rather from Paris. The Nicholas Conver deck from Marseille just mentioned emerges over a century later. These are, to my mind, the two markers that delineate the Marseille-type. In between these two is a third deck of the same general type – though again with significant differences, exemplified by Payen in Avignon and Dodal around 1710 in Lyons.

Four different locations, different dates, five (and more!) different decks... yet we tend to call them each 'Marseille' – or, as I prefer to call them, 'Marseille-type'.

How one specific deck influences the other is hard to tell. What is important, however, is that by noting subtle differences, details that may be ambiguous or missing in one deck may suddenly become obvious by having recourse to others. And for this, we may at times move to similar but non-Marseille-type decks. We'll get into that as we go along. For now, let me just mention two of the more important 'cousins': the Bologna and the Besançon. This might be a good time to have a look at a map and see where are key locations: Lyon; Paris; Marseille; Avignon; Milano; Bologna; Schaffhouse; and Genoa – only some of these are clearly visible on the above 1600 map!

In the context of the times, these are virtually exclusively Christian locations: Jews were repeatedly expelled from various areas over the centuries; other religions were usually simply not tolerated; and individuals who had a more liberal orientation would generally couch their works in such as way a to maintain their own relative safety.

This did not prevent divisions of viewpoint – some which will emerge as we begin to look at individual cards. Nor did it prevent the Reformation; counter-reformation; various religious wars (1648 ended the 30 years war); and the later revolution that swept France, that in part mirrored in a far more brutal form the American War of Independence – and the colonisation of Australia – these last occurring immediately after the period we are considering.

On other trends, 1650 was seeing the full effects of the printing press having had its birth a mere 150 years earlier, the domination of the Abbey at Cluny was already well into its death throes – though its influence still felt, and the Sun-King was exhuberant in Paris as to be expected.

The socio-political landscape in Europe and the world was about to radically change by the end of the 18th century, yet the influences on the formation of the Marseille deck is of the period.

It is also during this period that Freemasonry undergoes a major alteration with the formation of rival Grand Lodges in London – something that will eventually transform the Masonic landscape. And also during this time that the Royal Society (1660) and the Academie des Sciences (1666) are formed. The UK only became a union in 1707.

The Rosicrucian movements and countermovements were active in Germany and the lowland countries, and the tensions between the Huguenots – or basically, Protestants – and Catholics remained high... all with a strong undercurrent of a secular and liberal worldview.

This course, however, is not about history – yet even the snippets mentioned have much to add to an understanding of the times in which this deck bursts into a field of blossoms.

Let's get back to the *decks* and make some remarks as to their differences and nomenclatures.

TdM I and TdM II

'TdM' simply stands for 'Tarot de Marseille'. What various historically oriented researchers have noted is that many Marseille-type decks can be grouped according to characteristics found in a small number of cards. TdM-I has exemplars that predate TdM-II, but they also are found concurrently.

The 1710 Dodal is TdM-I variety, and the 1760 Conver a TdM-II - both key identification decks.

I should note that this nomenclature is not the only one used, and Michael Dummett and others use alternatives based on patterns and their likely origins (hence, 'Milanese', 'Bolognese', etc). For our current purposes, however, TdM-I and -II seems not only apt, but provides for a basis from which to cleanly make distinctions of *image* design without getting into more controversial problems of *origin* of design.

I will here only mention, for the sake of interest, that the earliest cards found of the TdM variety possibly date from around 1500 - unfortunately, only a few cards and parts of cards have been found in a well in one of the Sforza castles, their dating remains problematic, and whether or not a few cards can be claimed to be a whole deck of *this* or *that* pattern similarly inconclusive. We'll return to this when we look at card XXI – the World, towards the end of the 30 weeks.

Let's briefly look at some of key characteristic differences between the TdM-I and TdM-II, and compare these to the Noblet. When we get to individual cards, mention of other decks that highlight the Marseille will also be made – as an example, the Schaffhouse, which has recently been packaged and marketed as a 'Tarot de Marseille'.

Let's briefly look at four TdM-*I* and TdM-*II* cards: VI the Lover; VII the Chariot; XVIII the Moon; and XXI the World.

L'Amoureux

The title as 'The Lovers' we'll also consider in due time – I simply note here that I translated it above as 'The Lover' intentionally.

If we look at the image of the 'cupid' aiming an arrow, the TdM-I Dodal (1710) has its body presented in the opposite direction to the TdM-II Conver (1760), and whereas TdM-II can *see* where his arrow will strike, TdM-I is blinded for *fate* to decide, or for the *heart* to see.

Comparing these with our Noblet (1650), is it of the TdM-I or TdM-II variety? or neither!?   TdM -I

Those two images are on the next page.

Vanden borre - TdM - II
        JV   - TdM - II

The Chariot

Again, let's look at the top of this card and note the differences in the fabric that is depicted on its roof: the TdM-I Dodal (1710) has what Robert Mealing refers to as 'scallops' – they remind me of the bottom of Roman blinds – quite distinct to the 'pulled sideways' curtain effect of the TdM-II Conver (1760).

Nloblet also has Scalops TDM-I
Ha Vandenborre – Profile w/ No canopy
JV - - Scalops TDM-I

The Moon

The *Moon itself* presents face-on in the TdM-I Dodal (1710), and is in profile in the TdM-II Conver (1760):

Noblet - Face-on
Other Decks Face on but Totally Different Scene

Finally, let's look at the World

The World

Here it is the central figure that is to be noted: in the TdM-I Dodal (1710), a cape is worn, and the figure appears masculine, whereas in the TdM-II Conver (1760), the figure appears feminine with a cloth-as-ribbon being 'worn'.

There are of course other differences of note in especially this card – but again, we'll leave that for now.

Noblet & JV - TdM I

The Noblet

What the above shows is that first and foremost a careful attention to detail needs to be paid. Also, even if you decide to not persevere with this course, these cards alone will normally enable you to identify the *style* or type of Marseille being considered.

From this consideration, we can probably classify the Jean Noblet (1650) as an early TdM-I.

Let's look at these four details on our cards – I'll display the originals, and suggest that you look at the restoration copy you have:

Contemporary Marseille decks

Many, but not all, of the Marseille-type decks created over the past century have been of the TdM-II variety, though some are also showing TdM-I influence. Yet it is upon the TdM-I that TdM-IIs are themselves likely based and from which they are modified – no matter how 'better' these may be judged to be.

I would suggest throughout the duration of this course that ongoing comparisons be made between the Noblet trumps and not only any other Marseille you may have, but any tarot to which you feel drawn.

Tarot, of course, is not simply about getting a sense for its history, but also about the deck itself. Let's now look, then, at the deck as a whole, and from next week begin with individual cards and groups of cards.

Groupings in deck: Atouts/Trumps

Unless already familiar with tarot, 78 cards can at first appear a little overwhelming. Yet these can easily be seen to be in major groups of five suits: trumps (or atouts, words I occasionally interchange in this course), batons, cups, coins and swords.

Let's briefly look at these separately, at this stage simply carefully observing whatever relations appear to emerge.

(Please note that the Hare indicates a practical exercise) Let's begin with the atouts, and line them in sequence, from I-XXI. Please take the time to do this before proceeding.

A question that immediately comes to mind is where to place the un-numbered card titled *Le Fou*. We'll leave that for now, putting it aside as though outside the series, and simply note two important features: the first is that all the cards except for this one are actually numbered, and that this numbering is in the additive Roman form – ie, four is IIII, as 'IV' in the additive Roman would make one and five, in other words *six*. The additive form was in common usage throughout mediaeval and renaissance times - it is more our modern age that has half forgotten its use.

The second point is that similarly, each card has a title (in French – though a style of French that is a little equivalent to Chaucerian English). It should here be noted that *most* TdM (both type I and type II) do not actually name card XIII - here titled 'La Mort' (Death).We'll have a look at possible reasons for this in week 19.

Looking at the sequence, does it seem to make 'sense'? Are there kinds of cards at the beginning of the series that seem to be more or less naturally grouped, and cards towards the end that appear to likewise bear a similar kind of grouping?

To my eyes, an example of the former is that the Papesse, Empress, Emperor and Pope – all figures of worldly power, are there as a bunch, and not distributed. Similarly for the celestial bodies near the end (Star, Moon and Sun).

Next, let's look carefully at the direction of gaze of any main character in the cards in relation to adjacent cards: do they look *towards or away from the next (or previous) figure*?

This may have importance, though again will point out two considerations: some decks appear to be mirror images of other decks, as though the woodcarver or artist simply took an existing model and effectively stenciled the image onto the wood, making the 'stamp' or woodblock inverted in relation to the original image. Secondly, in terms of the cards you currently have in front of you arranged in sequence, is card IIII the Emperor looking at III the Empress or V the Pope?

Most other Marseille decks, incidentally, have the Emperor card facing the other way, towards our left as viewer. Yet this was not the substance of my question.

Chances are, being English readers, we each placed our sequence thus:

I; II; III; IIII; V; VI; VII; VIII; VIIII; X; etc

but what is there to indicate such a direction?

why not, indeed, from right to left thus:

etc; X; VIIII; VIII; VII; VI; V; IIII; III; II; I

We may yet have reasons to favour the former over the latter. What we nonetheless need to be open to are considerations that may at first be counter-intuitive.

I would suggest to re-arrange them from right to left for the remainder of this lesson.... even though I should mention that I normally arrange them from left-to-right. Remember, this is an exercise to open to consciousness certain relations that may come to light, not an intrinsic part of the deck.

Let's now begin a few manipulations of these cards and see how groups may reveal different aspects. Firstly, pairings, being guided in the first instance by the Roman numerals:

X; VIIII; VIII; VII; VI; V; IIII; III; II; I

XX; XVIIII; XVIII; XVII; XVI; XV; XIIII; XIII; XII; XI

There are here some qualities about each card that seems to mirror or provide a complement to the other in the pair. I shall briefly go through these, the top layer suggesting an outer manisfestation to the inner life suggested by the lower layer. Please note that though I suggest these for ease of becoming familiar with the set, it should be remembered that there is little from history that suggests that pairings are warranted. Still, of related interest is the manner petroglyphs are carved *in pairs* on *Lumiere* (ie, 'Gothic') Cathedrals and churches. For example, a whole series of virtues and vices, seasons and activities, and scenes from the life of Jesus are depicted as *pairs* on Chartres, Paris, and Amiens (amongst many other) Notre Dame Cathedrals. Below is an image of such from Amiens, to which we will have occasion to again refer to over the ensuing thirty weeks.

So let's look at our pairings:

I/XI in order to manipulate the elements, an inner strength and dexterity is required;

II/XII inner light of initiation requires sacrifice;

III/XIII fructification and life is mirrored by death;

IIII/XIIII a ruler requires inner moderation;

V/XV religion points to a blessed life, its structures to a binding;

VI/XVI the arrow of love is the thunderbolt to the established home;

VII/XVII the victorious leader has allowed himself to be guided by the flows of the waters of destiny;

VIII/XVIII the law reflects justice through understanding;

VIIII/XVIIII the inner light of the individual shines as the Sun;

X/XX a turning of the outer wheel is mirrored by an awakening to the spiritual;

as for XXI and the Fou, I shall leave these for now in this pairing.

These are *not the only possible pairings*: going from I to XI and immediately returning (XII under XI; XIII under X; etc), or yet other means, also result in useful reflections. After all, our intellect is able to weave stories and relations between *any two or more concepts*, and it is this ability that allows us to build a meaningful narrative when using tarot for readings and insightful excursions or reflections.

Groupings in deck: non-Atouts

Two similar excercises can be made for the four other suits, each bringing to light various details and insights. The first is to place sequentially cards 1-10 for each suit, carefully observing the qualitative differences that differentiates batons from cups, coins from swords, cups from coins, etc.. Are the floral decorations symmetrical? do they suggest particular plants?

Similarly placing the four court cards sequentially, and comparing one suit to another (for example, the backgrounds, or stances, or general features), as well as paying particular attention to the implement depicted – of clear note of 'worked craftsmanship' is the change in the batons held by each court in ascending order. Which direction is each facing in relation to the other? what of the ground – does it suggest an indoor or outdoor setting? is the clothing a preparation for battle, work or social event?

The other is to compare how, for example, each of the four aces, or each of the four sevens, are depicted (and this for each of the pips). For example, there may be some obvious practical reason to present the six swords and six batons as given, but what of the six cups and coins? they could have easily have been presented in each case as two columns.

By this stage, you will also have noticed that the sword suit has stylised scimitars – except for the odd-numbered (and two in the ten card) sword. From a visual perspective, this certainly allows for instant recognition and differentiation between the suit of batons and of swords that using glaives or straight swords would otherwise mask. When we look at the suit in more detail, we shall also have a closer look at the Mamluk influence, and simply mention this here for the sake of acknowledgement.

This week

If taking this book as it was originally intended – ie, each chapter as part of a weekly course – I would suggest repeating the above card manipulation a number of times, and *selecting a regular day and time each week.*

Please note that we will revisit each trump, and that a number of chapters will focus on various aspects of both the pips and the court cards, so the above exercises are meant only as beginnings in discovery.

I - LE BATELEUR

Le Bateleur

As will generally be the case throughout this course, I will first and foremost presume that the card (if we are looking at one card) or cards (if we are looking at a group) is or are in front of you.

Imagine yourself standing in front of this character, in open air, with perhaps a dozen or more people also observing the event. This is an important skill to develop, and one used for centuries in order to all the more grasp a text, image or allegory that one desires to better or more fully understand. In fact, it forms the basis of Ignatian Meditation: placing oneself in the place and time on which one is meditating. In the case of strictly Ignatian meditation, of course, there are preparatory prayers, a select text, an active feeling of *being present*, and a closing prayer. There is something of similar notion here: there is a select 'text' (the image), a preparation (which may, if you are so inclined, include a prayer or similar), and importantly, allowing a sense of *being in the scene.*

Perhaps a way to describe this is to imagine you have been on holiday from which you are returning with a series of photos. To a casual observer, they are static and relatively meaningless images. To yourself, they are a reminder of a scene full of vitality, movement, smells, actions, feelings – whether of the day, and other events of the day not captured by that single image that nonetheless it calls to mind as one reminisces and contemplates the photo: by having been there, the image is but a snapshot of a scene full of vitality.

The imaginative faculty slowly builds a similar meaningfulness as the image of this card is progressively entered, each time, and with each reflection, re-membering the image that initially may need to be *dis-membered* to its elemental building blocks, and rebuilt in its meaning afresh and anew.

So let's do the latter a little as well – let's dis-member the elements of the card and observe its several parts.

Rogue performer

I'm not sure how many of you have had a close rapport with a presti-digitator, but the essence of the work is not only to be swift and dexterous with the hands, but also to shift the focus of the viewer away from what is actually taking place. This is done in two especial ways: the first by having the hand that is not actually involved in the deceit act as a visual attraction (or distraction); the second by word and head movement. This is similar to being drawn to looking in the same direction you see another person look (for example, upwards at the sky, or to the left over a bridge, etc.).

Observe the Bateleur as not only an image that captures all the details of the instant, but as moving actor. His *raised hand* holds the magic wand – what observer would not pay attention to its action?... but wait... where is he looking, and at what?

In the meantime, the other hand, with little movement and partially obscured by being in front of his own body, moves that small item.

Here one is distracted, or rather the attention is sought to be guided, to both the right and the left... and in case it falls near the other hand, there is enough on the table to cast more visual disarray!

Rogues and Magi

I have described above very much the image of the Bateleur as rogue, yet so many modern authors speak of him also as Magician. Even in the 18th century, however, there was a clear connection between these two concepts.

Allow me a quote from *Magister Pianco's* 1782 *Der Rosenkreuzer in seiner Blösse*[1]:

> *"All Magi at all times were either Professional Performers or Rogues.*
>
> [...] They [various famous individuals mentioned] either knew the natural and mathematical magic, and were high-class jugglers, who made their living before the eyes of the world with their arts, and practiced openly for money, without passing off their knowledge for anything more than natural, and therefore were professional performers: or they made out their Science to be Black Art, or White Art, or even like yourselves, Divine Magic, by means of which they wanted to rule the devil, the stars, the good spirits and angels, and finally God Himself, and these were cheats, rogues and blasphemers; [...]"

Within this same portion of text are mentioned Albertus Magnus, Paracelcus, and Simon Magus. To jump from one type of 'magician' to the other is therefore not simply a modern tendency: the usage of trickery can be practiced intentionally, and to be sure may also be attributed to those who perhaps intended no such lie.

Just amongst these three individuals mentioned, we have a bishop in Albertus Magnus, a medical founder in Paracelsus, and reference to the Bible with Simon Magus. In each case, also, we are in some ways lead to consider alchemy and the transmutation of one substance to another... and again, by the same token, to the various accusations of foul-play and delusion by purported alchemists.

A rich beginning to the tarot's atouts or *trumps* if ever there was any doubt about its intrinsic wealth!

In fact, in the times we are considering, the only legitimate type of 'alchemist' (or transmuter of substance), and hence the only legitimate type of 'magician', was the priest as celebrant of the mass and the transubstantiation of the bread and wine to body and blood of Christ, and images can indeed appear similar to the card we are considering.

And even then, Catholic priests were at times considered by various people as, similarly, swindlers.

---

1   *Ancient Texts of the Golden Rosicrucians vol 1*, 2007, isbn 978-0-9734424-6-5, pp 71-72

Contents

The table is of great interest: I have always struggled to determine not only what is, but what *may* be intended. It's actually the priestly image above that leads me to consider this as our next step.

The items on the altar are clear and recognisable (or able to be recognised by a little research in the implements of the mass). The items on the table of our Bateleur should similarly be recognised by considerations as to his *implements*. The situation, however, is unfortunately not as clear as one may hope, or as some have written.

Let's take a look at not only our Noblet, but also the TdM-I and TdM-II examplars, as well as a Visconti and a couple of others. Comparisons may at times clarify the possible intent of the design.

Nearly a hundred years earlier than the Noblet, Catelin Geoffroy shows a number of onlookers (and possibly a losing gambler) on his card:

Though it is quite distinct to the Marseille, the Geoffroy has aspects reminiscent of Marseille-type depictions. So let's have a look at the Marseille in light of these details, and see if the items on the table can better be identified. Again, I am here going to presume you have your Noblet handy, but have also above the original more indeterminate model with which Jean-Claude Flornoy had to work.

What we have are some pretty standard conjuror's – or rather street performer's or prestidigitator's – tools for tricks: the dice and cups-and-balls.

The rest is not as clear. But let's focus first on those just mentioned.

The dice are interesting in that the woodcarver has gone to the trouble to carve out 'standard' values on many faces: 1, 2, 3 on the right-hand one, 1, 2, 3 (or 5?) on the middle one, and 1, ?, ? on the left-hand one (Flornoy sees 1, 3, 4 on this last). In any case, we can presume, given the context, that these are not regular, but rather regularly loaded!

The cups-and-balls are actually quite accurate and standard, even though the one on the right appears a little smaller than the other two. Accurate in the sense that, firstly, there are precisely three. Standard in that they each have a ledge around their rim, though very early as by the beginning of the 1700s the cups started having a 'shoulder bead' or rim to aid manipulation. The first set below show the earlier design, and the second set the later one, standardised with 'shoulders' later than our card design.

According to cupsandballsmuseum.org, the first publication explaining how to develop the trickery was written in *Hocus Pocus Junior*, in 1634. This, however, does not mean it was not known before, as Seneca's letter to Lucilius *circa* 65 C.E. mentions the trickery of a 'conjurer's cups and pebbles'; and possibly the 'first description of an actual performance of the cups and balls that has survived is from Alciphron of Athens, who, in the second century C.E., described a performance of the cups and balls by a man using *"a three-legged table, upon which he placed three small dishes, under which he concealed some small white pebbles"*.

That there are precisely *three* cups, then, is perhaps to be expected. Perhaps, to also question the intent, we should wonder why the cups are not depicted mouth down, but rather as recipients. Here of course, the bateleur perhaps shows us why: he is still holding, in his right hand, the token – described as perhaps a pebble, a rolled piece of bread, or the common use of balls made of cork (also mentioned in the 1634 *Hocus Pocus Junior*).

The 'linked' three 'balls' to the left of the cups I am frankly unsure about. Certainly in later decks these appear as separate balls - but then, numerous later decks also tend to depict the most central cup as more or less spherical and having lost its intended depiction. Perhaps those three are not balls at all, but rather another version of the three cups: three shells (usually walnut halves) and a pea.

The items on the table to the (viewer's) right *appear* to be some kind of knife, a pencil, and another item we'll get back to shortly. I realise that within a couple of later deck designs in the Marseille-style, these will will have more definite delineation (I am always hesitant to be so definite!) with, for example, a knife and its sheath. I do not think that on the Noblet it is at all clear, and the elongated items may have been various types of *wands* used for different purposes (silk disappearance comes to mind – especially in light of the ambiguous item on the Visconti-Sforza card imagery).

The larger item to the right of the card has often been claimed as a bag. Though likely, there are other alternatives that have to be considered, amongst these a book – and the Noblet, of all decks, makes this perhaps more possible than most other deck depictions.

Prestidigitation – a trick

Let's practice a quick prestidigitationary trick with three small cups or glasses and a small rolled piece of bread.

To stay in the time-frame, I'll also use a visual explanation from Diderot's *Encyclopædia* of the 1750s, and consider what is actually being done to the poor viewer who simply cannot win, unless decided by the sleight-of-hand (overleaf).

In my personal view, there is nothing like adopting some stance in each of the cards we shall consider. Not only will a deeper understanding of the card develop, but often unexpected insights arise, even forewarning what may otherwise be misguided by one's unaccustomed imagination (an at times all too fertile imagination that may beguile).

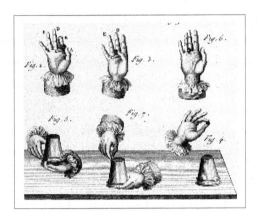

And here, of course, is precisely one of the key and important factors of this card: is one going to be deluded by appearance? will one develop the requisite skills to not only undertake the dexterous activities, but also to understand the actions one observes in the world at large?

The trump sequence, thus, presents us with a beginning that both cautions and instructs, and asks us to look below the appearance of events, to seek to understand the world's manipulation, to seek to uncover the elements at play – to develop what I consider the mind of the scientist who seeks to hold both an attitude of healthy scepticism, with a passionate curiosity for the world around.

To develop the dexterous skills displayed, he must also, of course, develop an appreciation for the tools of his trade, and through habit, regular practice, trials, and thoughtful reflection, become adept at effortless skillful manipulation.

In fact, these are often some of the concepts that come to mind when this card is randomly drawn for either reflection or narrative (ie., reading): becoming a master with the tools of his trade (whatever these may be) by first developing an understanding of the basics or the elements in whatever is being considered, carefully avoiding, on the one hand, rashness, and on the other, fear of engaging what must at first remain unknown.

Astrological considerations

It is inevitable that considerations other than what the imagery on its own presents will emerge. With the Marseille, however, we must be particularly careful to remain in the depiction as presented, and avoid temptations to assign to cards more than they present. Many modern decks of course incorporate in different ways astrological considerations, and we shall return to astrological and astronomical considerations much later (specifically in week 23, but other chapters will also touch on some aspects when relevant).

With the Bateleur, there is no obvious and direct relation that holds... save by comparison to how the various trades were seen to be under the influence or protection of one or another of the seven then known planets: Saturn, Jupiter, Mars, the Sun, Venus, Mercury and the Moon. Etymologically, incidentally, each of these is correctly termed a 'planet', in that the term refers to a heavenly body that though regular (unlike the portent or omen of meteors and comets), each appears to move or meander against the 'fixed' background star formations.

Let's return to the Bateleur image: I once thought that I had identified a definite astrological association by reference to an astrological book (or astronomical – there was not such a distinct difference in intent at the time) made for the young Sforza duke[2]. Have a look at the top of this depiction of the Children of Mercury.

---

2   *De Sphæra*, late 15th century and attributed to Cristoforo De Predi. We'll return to another brief mention of this book in chapter 23 on Astronomy.

Here one could expect that the table and activities thereon are quite reminiscent of the Bateleur and that, therefore, Mercury can be somehow attributed.

Approximate similarity of overall design, however, does not mean that such would have been seen in a similar manner. In fact, the very same book shows another planet (in this case the *Moon*!) that depicts our familiar Bateleur in a more apt fashion. The activities are always shown as an image in a *pair*, in this case with that of the Moon as depicted to its left (in smaller rendition and above its activities on the adjacent page – though in the original they are each of equal size)

Here[3], again, it is the *Moon* that is represented, not Mercury. And whether we prefer one planet or the other, we cannot neglect that numerous other depictions represented in a similar manner – including, of importance, a Bateleur figure – the orbit of influence of this astral being (ie, the Moon, and not Mercury). Here are a few other images to further whet the appetite. Note especially the page overleaf.

---

3   Except for Hieronymus Bosch's 'Conjuror' painting, shown overleaf, that does not necessarily have any particular astronomical connotation – except that for the period it *would have been seen*, if the question had been asked, to be under the rulership of the Moon, as is the purse thief displayed thereon.

We should pause here a moment and consider these images especially and look at their overall depiction in light of other cards, for one thing is certain: if we wish to find similarities, we often can by the simple gymnastics the mind is able to perform when considering any two or more concepts, images, or ideas. It is, after all, precisely this ability that permits us to string together sentences, weave stories, and collate images in meaningful ways... and be both enlightened and deluded by the magic these weave on us. The 'trick', therefore, is to develop discernment between that which is pertinent, and that which is only superficially similar. Is there a card which is more directly pertinent given considerations of the respective imagery?

Having briefly mentioned possible astrological (in its broader sense) connections, let us also at least mention two others: alchemical and kabbalistic.

Hebrew letters

Perhaps to the dissapointment of some, I will here suggest that if any Hebrew letter correlation was intended, it is not obviously apparent in the set, even though some cards, such as the Bateleur, appear to display elements worthy of note.

Mark Filipas, some years back, suggested that perhaps some early decks, specifically including the Marseille, may be considered as an *abecederium* – a sequence imaging in order the alphabet. This is still possible, but if so, remains well hidden or well lost in intent. Still, it may be worth noting that Mark's *Alphabetic Masquerade* is well worth considering in light of further considerations of the Marseille. There are only three cards to which I shall make mention of his suggestion: the Bateleur and the Hanged Man especially because they can each be seen to reflect, respectively, the first and twelfth letters of the Hebrew alphabet, and the World for reasons I shall mention in our penultimate week.

Alchemy

It is easy to see similarities between this card and that of an alchemist: alchemists have often been accused of duping those around them; of performing what are considered acts of 'magic' and transformation; and of manipulating the elements at hand. Perhaps more importantly from an image perspective, they can often be depicted with a table laden with cups (*ambix*) and other bits and pieces at times rather difficult to properly identify.

Still, I would suggest that here in the Bateleur is not an intended alchemist – except in the broadest and indirect of sense.

After all, the very opening of this week's study has already shown that many and diverse relations *can* be made, as has been made in the past, between the trickster prestidigitator and Magi.

The subject of alchemy and tarot in general will also be re-considered later (chapter 20).

Setting: Outdoors

Unlike the ensuing card, he is definitely outdoors. Again it may be worth noting here the different *settings with each successive trump*. Though we are in some ways beginning, we are also not dealing with any card in isolation, but rather a card which in each case is very much part of a set, of a sequence, that may reveal in their order more than when singly considered.

In this context we must also recall that tarot is composed of not only the trumps, but also of four other suits consisting of implements variously used. These shall be the focus of next week.

The top of the card

We've focussed especially with the central region of this card, and made mention that the ground appears outdoors and therefore in passing referred to the lower region of the card.

The top region also, of course, is quite peculiar. Not only is his head facing *away* from the actions of his raised hand, but he appears to display an inner calm. Or is that another deception?

His raised hand – which is, incidentally, his *sinister* (meaning 'left' in Latin) – is peculiar to this deck. From my point of view, the deck shows that the woodblock used was damaged prior to this imprint, with the top fingers and upper portion of the bauble broken off (showing that perhaps this imprint may have been made many years later than the 1650 dating of the design, in a similar fashion to Camoin using 18th century woodblocks for a Conver imprint made some 200 years later). How appropriate that this possible illusion of date be brought to reflection with this card!

The lower portion of his bauble does look rather phallic. I remain to be convinced, however, that this was the original intent. If 'intent', perhaps no more than as a image now broken that showed more vague signs of similarity between a *legerdemain*'s 'magic wand' and a phallus.

The Bateleur's face is young, he appears strong and we could expect him to be agile, as were many who performed multiple skills on the streets for the amusement of all.

His hat is possibly far simpler than has been latched on over the course of the past couple of centuries: it is broad-breamed, but simply and cleanly so. That we have later seen it to be lemniscatory shows as much how we seek to make meaning of each and every detail, in the process giving ourselves a Midas touch and transforming that which we touch into living *aureole*.

If I compare his hat-rim with many other Marseille, we can see that our Noblet has a simplicity that remains just that: simple, yet wide-brimmed and relatively, it appears, new or fresh and young. This is something that the whole image itself reflects, down to the shoots growing from the Earth shown through both his and the table's legs.

Combining cards

Looking at the Bateleur, allowing the image to be considered as mere photographic snapshot of an event, draw another card at random, and *imagine* the depiction of the other incorporated within the first – not as an image, but as an *event*.

For example, a card of coins may easily be imagined as the Bateleur slowly filling his coffers by his skill; a swords card by his dexterous manipulation of the repertoire of his tricks with sword swallowing or juggling; a knight as coming to the fair; a queen as she to whom the event is in honour; etc..

Again, here it is to bring to imaginative life the second card *within the context of the first*, in a manner that both become, in imagination, part of the same overall 'story'.

Once this is relatively easily imagined, add more than one card, the third as either to the Bateleur, or as 'part' of the second – or even as a *shifting* card of movement between the two. Again, the image is but a snapshot of a scene that becomes animated with what Goethe called *precise active imagination*: precise because bound by (in our case) the image, active because alive in action.

Moral Development

Finally, there is something of this card that speaks very much of the need for moral development; for ethical conduct; for appropriate action in the situation at hand. Even the thief, to be successful, has to develop a sense for what is apt, and what may be considered at the very least as the beginnings of the stirring of moral conscience.

There is a deep aspect about the whole card that calls morality to mind, even if only because so many aspects of his caricatured demeanour speaks *against* this same. He would soon be run out of town were he to simply and without charm dupe one and all. Thus, this charm that has its own potency must, together with the intelligence he needs to simultaneously develop, be balanced by disposition to ethical action.

As he develops discernment for what he may be able to manipulate, to dexterously manifest, and cunningly invent, he similarly and allegorically develops discernment of spirit and a bravery to engage in just the right fashion at just the right moment with just the right inclination and just the right movements.

A Bateleur we shall have cause to undoubtedly re-encounter in various ways over our 30 weeks!

THE PIPS

The Four Suits

Even the very heading with which I open this chapter is questionable. Are there in fact four suits? or are there five? are the trumps not a suit?

Though I personally prefer to consider tarot as having five suits, there may be various grounds for considering the atouts or trumps somewhat distinct to a 'suit': these considerations include their distinct grouping; that they may be *additions* to an earlier deck having only four suits; and that as they *trump* any *suit* in the gaming version, they somehow stand outside the suits proper. There is also the additional consideration that links the trumps to both the festivities involving pageantry procession of *triumphs* on the one hand, and on the other various imagery and card sets outside of tarot.

Throwing cards onto table cloth

I would here suggest, to also show how clearly the difference between especially pips and trumps is visually obvious, to place a cloth on a table and 'flick' or 'toss' in the air one card at a time until a nice broad spread manifests. Some cards will fall face down, some face up, with various relations and distinctions becoming rather obvious – we shall return to this exercise further down, at this stage, simply quickly look for overall *patterns* and especially observe how pips are differentiated from court cards and trumps.

Four suits

So what are these four (other) suits, and what of them?

They have at times been referred to as the 'Italian' suits, in contra-distinction to the 'French' suit that has become the dominant form in standard playing cards. The latter is formed by the black spades and clubs and the red hearts and diamonds. In the former is, alphabetically by the common Marseille appellation: Batons, Cups, Deniers (a Roman coin value), and Espées (swords). Whether there are definite correspondences between the Italian and French suits remains at best unclear. Certainly the English names *suggest* a connection between, at the very least, 'clubs' and Batons; and between spade ('*espade*') and swords. Yet clubs is generally considered the (visual) cognate of *Coins* (or Deniers) in France!

We therefore need to be careful to not make assumptions about supposed intrinsic correlations. On the other hand, this does not preclude personal preferred connections based on visual (as is commonly done for clubs and coins in French books), linguistic (as is commonly done for clubs and batons in English books), or 'mediated' connections based on a third aspect (such as a preferred elemental attribution).

Ten + four Courts

Again, let's look at the cards.

For those relatively unfamiliar with tarot, these four suits should prove the easiest for which to get a sense (assuming a standard pack of playing cards is already known). Similar to standard playing cards, tarot has four suits of ten pips (Ace through to ten) and a number of court cards in each suit. The difference is that tarot has *four* courts per suit instead of three: the Valet; the *Cavalier*; the Queen; and the King.

Let's hold back on any possible *meaning* of these for a while, and simply note their form and their composition. We'll do this by first placing, as we had done in the Introduction (chapter one), the cards sequentially, in four rows, one per suit: Ace-10 followed by the court cards.

Again, I would suggest arranging each row not only from left-to-right, but also from right-to-left, and afterwards alternating the rows: left-to-right for the first; the second row right-to-left; the third, left-to- right, etc.. Looking at the pips independently to the court cards, not only may some patterns become apparent, but also that each suit appears to grow or diminish in a manner that is distinct from suit to suit.

For those unfamiliar with the Marseille pips, it should quickly also become apparent that the suit of swords is easily and quickly recognisable by its curved sabre-like (or, more properly, scimitar-like) stylised blades.

It is very likely that these suits derive from earlier playing decks such as the Mamluk cards – to which we shall return in a short while.

Looking at our sets, there are various ways we can consider the sequence, for not all that has the *appearance* of increase implies a larger amount. For example, let's consider a cake: it can be given in one piece, or cut in two pieces, or four, or five, or six, etc. (up to ten for our purposes). Similarly, the effects of consuming a bottle of wine by either one glass (and one drinker) or by ten consumers will result in quite distinct consequences!

Let's therefore look at the four suits and specifically consider the implement of each suit and its uses, and how an increase in the *number* of implements may nonetheless be considered as potential *diminution*.

Batons

It perhaps should be noted that of the four suits, Batons is the only one that results from the growth of a living being, namely a plant. To be sure, there are design details in the arabesque of the other suits (and this one) that present to our consideration flowers and vines. As an *implement*, however, only the Baton suit is taken directly from the natural world. Also, unlike the other three implements, no fire is needed for its formation, except the 'living fire' flowing through the sap of the plant prior to its cutting.

Taking its nature into consideration, we can view the growth from one through to ten as also an increase or growth in *propagation*, where from one many arise: a plant has that as its nature, whereby even a cutting may be used for either germination of new roots or even grafting, and of course transplantation.

Here then, we may not even be dealing with a dead branch, but something that within itself may still have living sap, and from which, despite all odds, it may generate forth new stalks. Looking closely at the batons through the sequence in this manner will prove, I would suggest, highly instructive – not stopping at the ten pips, but also carefully noting the distinctions that arise in the four court cards.

Looking at the cards, which appear *living*, and which not? how can the floral details be seen as somehow intrinsically connected to the implement? and what of the nine!?

Cups

In contradistinction, the suit of cups is one that requires a quite refined skill in order for the item to be crafted – whether it be from wood, stone, metal, or glass. It's as if its essence lies not so much in its material composition, but in its potential *usage*.

Comparing this to the Batons, which bear (or would bear had the cut not been made) flower or fruit of their own nature, Cups have a different 'nature': they are made to contain, to hold, and to be held. Yet, unlike the Ace of Batons, the Ace of Cups is not held.

In fact, the Ace seems to be a very specific kind of cup: the type used as a sacred chalice in Church services, in this instance covered, crowned with a representation of the *New Jerusalem*. I'll reference here *Revelation 21:2*

> And I saw the holy town, new Jerusalem, coming down out of heaven from God, like a bride made beautiful for her husband.

This 'holy city' coming down upon the Earth can also be seen as occurring each time with the act of the Host's Consecration and transubstantiation in the Catholic (and equivalent) Mass – the point here being that the container, the *ambix* or cup, will hold its content in a form that is often transformed – whether it be wine, host, juice, etc., into a sacred or divine substance.

If we look at the sequence of card imagery, we are also faced with the only suit that has a clear and totally uncontroversial uprightness for our modern eyes: the other four suits can be reversed (except for some individual cards) without significantly altering their detail.

What of this suit's 'growth' or increase? Here let's first consider, again as a first step, the Christian sacrament. One of the popular criticisms the Cathars had of the Catholic Church was that if the transubstantiation of the host is the body of Christ, he must have been larger than a mountain. In other words, by adding all the bits of bread and wine that were supposedly the body and blood of Christ as had already been given out by even the 12th century, an enormous *volume* results. Never mind any theological point-scoring or mis-representation here, I mention this more as a reflection that the Ace brings to mind these considerations, especially in the context of the times.

The increase in the number of cups is perhaps not, however, to be understood as mere multiplication, but rather increases as force-fields. Let's reflect for a moment on the manner in which homoeopathy works, considering not so much the 'signatures', but rather the medicinal modes or methods of preparation, giving the product its *potency* by its 'force-field' ('force-field' being a more modern equivalent appelation to what traditional homoeopathy terms 'memory'): vigorous shaking or pulverisation or dissolution in a liquid or inert substance, repeated a number of times, may leave no traces of the *substance*, yet its *power* is increased by presumably being 'released' from its physical chemical compound, resulting in what is called a *tincture*. I should point out that homoeopathy was developed by Hahneman just outside the 1650-1760 (the Noblet-Conver) time-frame.

The cup (or rather, the *tincture* it may contain) can be multiplied indefinitely without its content diminishing in potency. Rather, and with even greater power than the bit of dough put aside for its yeast to grow and be used from day to ensuing day, the tincture not only maintains its power, but connects its partakers across time, whether this be days, weeks, or even centuries.

This is also a good time to begin to consider the arabesque or curlicue ornamentation, for the two cups is the only pip card that appears to reference *animal* life, and that as emerging from a floral base. These are not peculiar to tarot, as the following petroglyphs (below and in the next column) from just north of Paris made *circa* the 13th century show:

There are of course hundreds of similar depictions throughout cathedrals – buildings that are rather stark and can be considered 'bare' and unfinished were it not for these and the numerous more elaborate images that the iconoclasts later decided were too... well, idolatrous.

Let's return to our main discussion and visit the other two suits.

Deniers (coins)

With Coins, we are again dealing with an item that is manufactured by, in this case, a very specific process, rather than either carved or cut. Also, unlike the other two implements discussed thus far, not everyone is permitted to mint coins, and these had to, traditionally, have a precise weight and be made of a determined metal (usually gold or silver). Without the legislative authority of the city or nation *as well* as its acceptance by its citizens, a coin is worthless. Even as *gold* or *silver*, it is of no *use*. It is only by mutual *symbolic* value that it may be used to facilitate and calibrate exchange. This is something that we can often forget, yet made poignant when travelling abroad and returning to our

own country of residence with a pocket full of now 'useless' foreign coinage.

Unlike the other two implements thus far considered, the more coins there are, the less value they may individually have. For example, as symbolic of the wealth of a nation, each can only have as much value as being a symbolic fraction of the whole. In the days when the coin was minted in the value of the metal (gold or silver), each was at least worth its weight, and each increased or decreased proportionally with either the scarcity or ease of access to these metals. Even from early times, however, coinage had also symbolic value against a reserve or treasury of gold, or the twins of gold and silver. In such cases, if 200 000 pieces are minted, each is worth 1/200 000 of the whole. If a million are minted, each is worth only 1/1 000 000 of the whole. What the latter also permits, to be sure, is an easier means by which to *distribute* wealth: the greater the desire for wealth redistribution or means of exchange, the more the need for relatively small incremental value.

In the card sequence, the Ace may be also considered as representing the whole, and each subsequent card to be various ways in which this same single value is divided. If considered in this light, each card is of equal 'value', in a manner similar to ten successive images in which a cake is shown progressively divided into ever smaller pieces (none so far eaten!).

I am not suggesting that this was the intent of the depiction: instead, I am rather confident that ten coins would have been considered as having *greater* value than three. What I am rather suggesting is, on the one hand, to consider these as points from which to reflect on meaning *starting from the implements themselves*, and on the other to consider the various ways in which 'increases' can be variously and differently considered given the suits.

What is also fascinating – perhaps only to myself – is the design found at the centre of each coin on the Noblet (though this detail is *not* depicted on Marseille decks in general). All coin cards, with the exception of the Ace, depict what is commonly referred to as a Cross of Malta, emblemetical of the Knights Hospitallier or Knights of Malta[1], the successor order of the Knight Templars after these were officially destroyed and dissolved between 1307-1312, the Templars of course famed (or infamous) for their power through their acquired wealth.

Two pips especially also distinguish themselves: the two deniers and the four. The first of these, the two, has become the standard bearer of the details of the house manufacture: who and when. This is usually the first card that will be sought by anyone wanting to check what deck is at hand[2]. The other card, the four deniers, has what appears as a shield, or

1   the Hospitallers became known as the Knights of Malta following their settlement there when given the island by Charles V, a figure to which we shall again return.

2   two other cards are also usually used for identification purposes, being used by either the artist, woodcarver or 'publisher': the two cups and the Chariot. The Noblet deck, amongst others, makes use of all three: the two coins, two cups, and Chariot.

emblem of a shield, within the centre. Again, this appears as something that has remained in most other Marseille and cognate decks. It would make for interesting research to see if the shield depicted in numerous decks somehow reflects a specific heraldic emblem and whether this therefore had (and has since lost) any connection to any deposited mark and specific locality; or whether there is simply copyist's modification without any obvious meaning.

Espées

With this spelling as 'espées', used on the Noblet, it should be noted that a number of words have seen changes between the French of the 17th century and more modern times: many instances of 'es-' have become 'é-'. In this case, '**es**pée' becomes '**é**pée' (on the court cards, 'DESPEE' would, in lower case and apostrophe, become "d'espée", ie, "of sword").

Let's, however, again look at the set of pips and note how they 'increase' in the context of the implement. The implement, here being the *sword*, is an item designed specifically for human combat, unlike the spear, dagger, arrow, or even gun, these latter also finding their use in hunting and hence food acquisition. Also, unlike the other suits, the sword is often made from separate parts: the blade is forged separately to the hilt (even when the two are metal), and the instrument requires constant attention, or its blade will become blunt.

As an instrument of warfare, it generally increases in power proportionally to its number: ie, the greater the number of swords (and thus presumably sword holders), the greater the power depicted – assuming other things are equal, of course. Also of interest, from a military perspective, is that units are (or at least were) usually broken up into smaller factions of ten[3]. So here we have not only an increase in number, but a proportional increase in power.

You may also notice that I have ensured that all the odd numbered sword cards online have their point down. Today we are no longer accustomed to viewing the sword in imagery. If you go back and observe the two swords on the petroglyph previously shown, you will note that they have their point down, as do all images I have seen from the period – unless the sword is held by a hand.

---

3   or at least, that was my experience when doing compulsory military service in France during the 1970s. Such a unit of ten had its roots, so I was told, in Roman times.

Here again is another carving, this time from the 15th or early 16th century, antedating the Noblet by over a century. Whatever you decide is viewed as 'right side up', this is one specific orientation that will have its proponents, and it has taken me some time to 're-learn' to see the cards as naturally presented when the straight sword is downward-pointing (unless hand-held).

For the swords in particular, it may be worth also having another look at the exercise given earlier whereby the *sequence* is looked at. Note that *circles* are produced from the stylised scimitars of one card visually 'connecting' to adjacent cards. It is also rather intriguing to place the ten-swords card in the centre, and on one side placing all the odd and on the other the even numbered cards, then imagining these as a single strip or band joined at the back with the Ace opposite the ten. Also note the relative size increase (or decrease, depending on the direction of attention) that the central sword displays.

Hilts

From a design perspective, the depiction of the hilt (or lack thereof) is one of the few areas I personally consider the Marseille designers could perhaps have taken on those of Bologna or Schaffhouse, which seem to retain something earlier intended and depicted: a distinction between the hilts and blade-tips. Furthermore, the Bologna appears to *explain* how the small curlicue on the 'corners' of the TdM arose. So let's have a look at that.

We'll also take this opportunity to briefly look at what is undoubtedly tarot's precursor for the pips in the Mamluk deck.

Let's however move to the seven swords of the Bologna deck.

Bologna

Below is a design that clearly marks the Bologna (right-hand image) as a transition between the pre-tarot Mamluk cards (left-hand image) and the Marseille, with visual elements of each in evidence. Compare the Bologna to both the Mamluk and to the Noblet.

It should be noted that the proportion of the The Bologna is reminiscent of the Mamluk, and quite elongated in comparison to the Marseille in general, and even more so when compared to the Noblet! It should be noted that the Noblet has one of the smallest elongations of any early deck.

Looking at the Bologna, we have the hilts of the scimitars at the bottom, with the blade tips depicted at the top, and the large green straight cross behind, point down (in this image), showing its cruciform.

Explaining the sword decorations

Note well how the Bologna's hilt-ends forms those small triangular-like shapes, and now carefully look through the Noblet in light of this. Looking through the apparent development of numerous decks, this seems to be one of those details that can be accounted for by simple image evolution and the 'misguided' work of the copyist: the central sword shrinks in relative proportion, and the hilt-ends somehow get copied, but now sit without reference to the implement they once depicted.

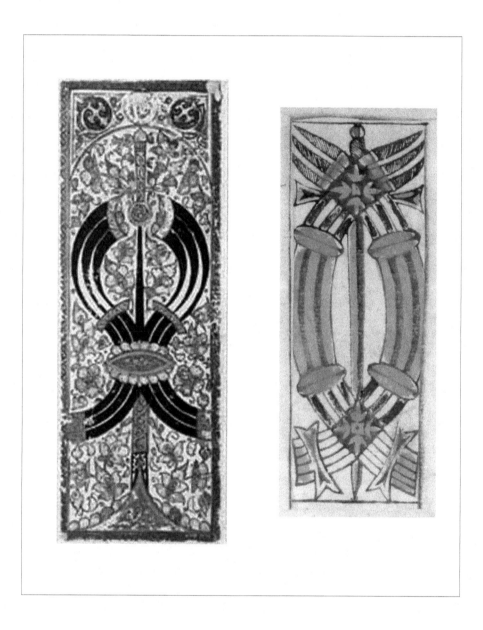

Let's also take a closer look at those droplets on the Aces of Batons and of Swords. In heraldic device, a number of implications are indicated by colour. For example, were they to represent tears, there would have been blue '*gouttes*' (droplets) – but we find silver, gold and red, indicating gold, water and blood (neither tears nor oil is represented). These three colours used, by the way, are also the ones used for the tuft of grass under the Bateleur's table. Yet colour remains one of the least likely to have specific symbolic intent (at least judging from the variety of colours used across a multitude of deck design) without, of course, preventing *us* from assigning specific mood or tone based on the colour of the specific deck at hand.

On the subject of heraldry, the Ace of Swords is also particularly interesting, in that the crown is of a specific type – neither royal nor ducal as may be expected, but that of a marquis. Admittedly, these did somewhat vary from region to region. What we here have, however, is a crown typical of the marquis variety, and this appears so across Marseille decks in general and not just on the Noblet.

From its crown emerges two different plants: that of the palm and the laurel. Perhaps I should here mention that Michael Hurst notes that Gertrude Moakley, in her trailblazing 1966 book[4], had already made "observations of Milanese heraldry in her investigation of the Visconti-Sforza deck. Among them, she noted that 'the crown of Milan encircling the palm and laurel branches' was a heraldic device".

---

4   *The Tarot Cards Painted by Bonifacio Bembo for the Visconti-Sforza Family: An Iconographic and Historical Study*

In any case, here we have what is most likely palm (branch) and laurel (wreath), with crown, with all its symbolic meaning of triumph, glory, and nobility.

Holding hands

Both the Ace of Batons and that of Swords are held by a *right hand*, yet the image is depicted from a different perspective, and can, at first glance, appear as though one is held in the right, and the other in the left.

Looking through the four suits *and trumps*, determine the hand holding key items: not all items are held with the right.

The implements and social division

We cannot complete our discussion of the four suits without reflecting on which social groups are likely to have been implied by each suit and consider their modern equivalents.

This division into four classes goes back to at least the *Pahlavi Dînkard* of Zoroastrianism[5]. In book VII, it was said of Zoroaster that:

> [...] there is manifested in him a mind which is more capacious than the whole world, and more exalted than every worldly possession, with an understanding whose strength is perfectly selected, an intellect of all-acquiring power, and a sagacity of all-deciding ability; also with the much heedfulness of the kingly glory, and the full desire for righteousness, the efficacious diligence and authority, and even the superiority in mightiness and grandeur of strength which are in the character of these four classes of his, which are **priesthood, warriorship, husbandry,** and **artisanship**; besides a perfect friendship for the sacred beings and the good, and an awful enmity for the demons, and the vile.

Let's reverse our alphabetical order of discussion and proceed from Espees to Batons.

Swords were the province of the nobility. Pure and simple. In modern day equivalent, the nobility can perhaps be considered as those involved in the legislative powers and its representatives and employees, from government, courts of law, to the police force and military and their various branches.

Deniers were the merchants and, I would suggest, also the guilds of various crafts, who were distinguished from the land-tillers and

5   Quoted in E. M. Butler's *The Myth of the Magus.*

peasants. In modern terms, where this level of industry has become so prominent, it may be more difficult to also differentiate between these and those formerly considered of the 'peasant' class. Perhaps of difficulty in placement are the artists, who seem to cross over between this aspect of crafts-people on the one hand, and learned creativity on the other. In modern times, these are not only bankers and those directly involved in financial markets, but also those involved in retail, transportation and distribution of goods, and most professions dealing with crafting and movement in our richly gadget-ridden society.

Cups were undoubtedly associated with the Church, and hence also with all levels of learning. Personally, I would also here consider artists who's creative work can be seen to be reflected in this suit. Yet, as mentioned above, they seem to cross over a little with the previous group. The cups as related to the educational, religious or spiritual and artistic sphere seem to be relatively easily brought to the modern era in similar tones, including here authors of various kinds (whether by works of the pen or of the brush).

Finally, *Batons* were likely to be associated with not only the peasants who worked the land, but also vagabonds and beggars – the latter two being far more common then contemporary experience suggests. In modern times, these may be considered as not only farmers, but also workers of the landscape and a whole broad base of work in myriad fields that includes what is still often referred to as 'blue-collar' positions (including cleaning and assembly-line factory work) as well as various mining and building or construction endeavours.

It may perhaps be worth reflecting on how we are (likely) each involved in each of these four areas in our personal lives.

I have to admit that in terms of more modern equivalents, I am personally more influenced by Rudolf Steiner's socio-political ideas as found in, for example, his *Threefold Social Order*. I mention this not to impose upon the deck modern considerations but, rather, if the suits are taken as reflecting social engagements, then not only do we need to reflect upon late mediaeval social conditions, but also upon modern equivalents, with due consideration to both advantages this brings as well as less apparent connections.

This also brings us to some considerations pertinent to the art of reading, whether used for the purposes of *dialogue* in a psychological, reflective, or narrative setting; or alternatively used to guide or inform someone else or oneself; or, indeed, used for artistic creativity.

Spread and reversals

The exercise we introduced on the first page of this week's work will here be taken a step further. So let's again take our cards and 'flick' them one at a time onto a covered surface until a broadish number have landed thereon.

Now simply looking at the 'spread', begin to discern patterns. For example, are there recurring cups, *directions* of gaze between figures, cards that seemingly 'flow' into one another or form a flowing 'stream' (even with cards face down)?

Personally, I tend to look at the cards as neither upright nor reversed, but rather see them as though looking at the ceiling painting of renaissance artwork: any individual figure can be seen as both (upright and reversed) and as neither, and this simultaneously.

Modern equivalents may be found in some modern artists, or as in the following image, created by a number of young people working simultaneously and cooperatively on the same canvas (or cardboard in this case): there is no upright, nor reversal, as each paints from their seated perspective around a large table.

Similarly, I would suggest stepping away from the 'spread' that is flicked into random positions and observing it from a variety of distances, as well as from the left, the right, and moving to the other side. Are there links that appear to be made between the cards that appear more strongly connected or natural? Are the cards somehow creating a dialogue that, using the previous two weeks' exercises, gives a hint as to the living scene from which such a combined image may have arisen?

Taken the time to undertake this a couple of times, if you have a digital camera, take a photo from above (standing on a chair if necessary), and periodically, through the week, revisit that image as a meaningful tapestry, observing that even a quite small movement in some cards may hint at strikingly different connections.

In all this, it's not so much either using or of not using reversals, but rather of seeing the cards as they arise, neither forcing nor not forcing a 'reversed' presentation. This is the purpose of the image shown above: to show not so much that inverted images are precluded, but rather that they become seen and understood as part of a whole *weaving* of

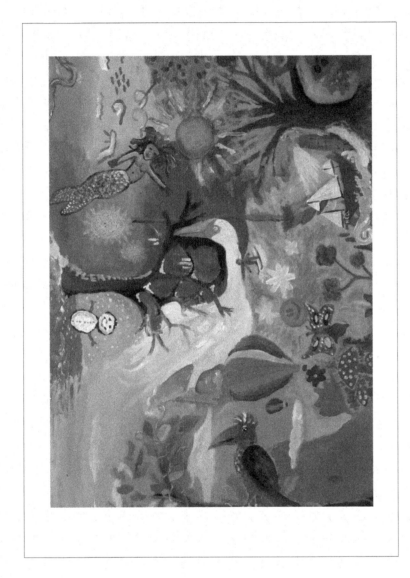

inter-relations that interacts amongst itsef. In essence, it is more along the lines of allowing the cards to fall in any manner, and permitting a combined tapestry to begin to unfurl its own story.

II - La Papesse

Quietude

The previous three weeks have been rather active. In the first, simply as an awakening to the differences between deck types, and an observation by deck manipulation. Similarly, chapter two, focussing on the Bateleur, saw an outward activity and handling of the elements, further worked in chapter three. Even the end of that last chapter, however, suggests a slowing quietude and time taken to *discover* the possible patterns suggested by the 'random' throw exercise.

This card of the Papesse, in contradistinction especially to the card that precedes it, has no festival nor street activity, but rather a seated meditative quality.

Observing the image, she is likely seated indoors, shown by the seat coverings and overall posture. Seated, not standing as in the previous card. On her lap is an open book (or so it seems - we'll get back to that later). Open, though in other decks there is ambiguity as to whether it is open or not. In the Noblet, however, the wavy lines seem a clear indication that thereon is writing.

Both by title and period, it is likely that the book is the Bible, and that she is practicing one of the habits (if you excuse the pun) of the times, *viz, Lectio Divina.*

Lectio Divina

A modern mystic, Thomas Keating, notes of *Lection Divina* "what use to spend your time in reading or listening to the deeds of the Holy Fathers, unless we bite and chew on them through meditation, and draw out somewhat and swallow it and send it to the heart?".

So what is required of this type of meditative practice? Firstly, and though there are various types and descriptions, I want to here focus on the form as it may be reflected in the card image itself. Looking at her, we can perhaps see how, to paraphrase again Keating, she may be listening to how God is addressing her in a particular text of scripture. This is the essence of this meditative practice: to take a sentence, and repeating it, allow each part, each parts, the whole, the arrangement, the point, the comma, the closure, the opening, to slowly speak itself to us, and, in the religious context, to enable the Divine to speak directly to our hearts via the precision of the words rendered and torn asunder.

How can this help us in understanding the card image, for there are no words (except for her title, on which a little more later)? by actually *doing* as she may be: taking the time to sit and reflect.

Four stages

Lectio divina is traditionally described as having four stages: the *selection* and reading of a section of text; reflection and its *personal relevance*; an *opening of the heart* to the substance of the text; and finally a *hearing* or 'contemplation' (in an older sense of the word).

So let's take the time to do this later during the week. For now, simply select a *short* passage of text you personally highly value: whether from sacred text; from poetry or lyric; literature; philosophy; ritual; or even sporting or political commentary if you are that way inclined!

Now stick to it. A choice has been made. Another time may be for another passage – whichever is chosen for this time will work.

When the time comes to undertake the exercise, finding a quiet place to sit, with the passage selected on paper on one's lap, read it a number of times, until its words are memorised. Then allow it to reveal its *connectedness* to yourself. How is its message useful to you at this time; what are its meanings; are there words that can be deepened in connection to yourself and to other words? Allow this part sufficient time to play itself out. Then simply feel, in one's heart, the substance of the passage selected: its weight, its form, its burden, its levity, its freedom, its shapelessness, its yoke, its bonding, its pull.

The final part, the *contemplatio*, is a deep inner 'listening' that follows all of the above.

I would suggest undertaking this exercise at least three times, with the same selected text. If you have difficulty finding a passage, here's one:

> Each human has it in them to be a free spirit, just as each rose bud has it in it a rose.

But why a Papesse?

Let's imagine going back in time.

If we were faced with creating a set of trumps to be added to a deck having pips and court cards, we would have to decide how many cards to make to the set, and what to include thereon. The *number* of trumps may have been decided for a variety of reasons. Whichever was considered, however, would have to be *functional* in terms of both its intended uses (which may have been simply for reflection) as well as any other uses that developed, including various rules that arose in games. Here, it *may* be that early models – what I would call 'proto-tarot' – had other than *twenty-two* trumps.

Having arrived at twenty-two, its imagery would need to also be selected. If we look at the set, we can begin to surmise why many of the images would have been selected: they seem to represent aspects of the socio-political spectrum; virtues and allegories in more or less common use; and eschatological and metaphysical considerations.

There were Bateleurs around, there was Empress, Emperor, Pope, Hermits, Death, hangings around, and there were images pertaining to the Devil, Temperance, Fortitude, Justice, and the like. These seem to be *explained* by the times. But the Papesse?

Here we must also be careful not to be lead to consider only the first couple of considerations that come to mind or that inevitably surfaces with a little study, but to also seriously consider their historical implications. The first that is at times mentioned is the legend of Pope Joan. Though it is unlikely to have been as an intended model, it is also possible that from an early time the card may have been used to mention the tale. Despite this, I frankly do not consider that the card *depicts* the legend: apart from the title 'Papesse', ie, 'female Pope', the card has none of the usual representations of the image of Pope Joan as current before or during the development of the Marseille deck prior to 1650 and 1760 (or, indeed, after).

Moakley, in her important 1966 book on the Visconti deck, mentions that the 'popesse' figure thereon (remembering that no titles are on that deck) was indeed elected Pope of the Gugliemite sect. It is possible that the image as it developed was causally related to this 15th century deck, and acquired new shape and form out of this early and historically semi-forgotten Visconti figure[1].

This Gugliemite Papess, for whom the "most enthusiastic of her followers believed that she was the incarnation of the Holy Spirit, sent to inaugurate the new age of the Spirit", had by then already been half forgotten. Such results in later carvings and copies of any imagery being understood in perhaps quite different ways to what may also have been originally intended.

---

1   Cf. Moakley, *The Tarot Cards Painted by Bonifacio Bembo*, 1966, p.72.

If Luther can mention (albeit in critique of the then Pope's) comparisons of Christ to the Sun and the Church to the Moon, then there is also a similar reflection in the Pope, ie, Christ's representative on Earth (from the Catholic perspective) having its allegory mirrored in representations of the Church as Papesse. As allegory, Stuart Kaplan in vol. II of the *Encyclopedia of Tarot*, and Ross Caldwell, mention a number of such representations that are well worth a look. Yet, there is also something distinctly *lacking* in these representations of the Church: the book (or item) clearly and consistently presented on her lap in card depictions.

Papesse as Mary

The Popesse as allegory of the Church should not be dismissed, and we shall return to that in a short while. One of the common and popular mediaeval and Renaissance depictions, however, is also of the Annunciation. And here we see Mary usually depicted as sitting *with a book*. To be awake to the details we are observing, there are also clear and distinct differences: the papal crown is missing on Annunciation depictions; conversely, Mary is usually depicted, following the Gospel text (Luke 1:26-28) with an air of surprise.

Despite this, the seated figure, 'rightfully' crowned, bears some striking similarities to the Madonna and, more importantly, has some element of merit to consider it as such. Let's rather quickly have a look at a few more famous ones and suggest that the card, for this purpose, is placed next

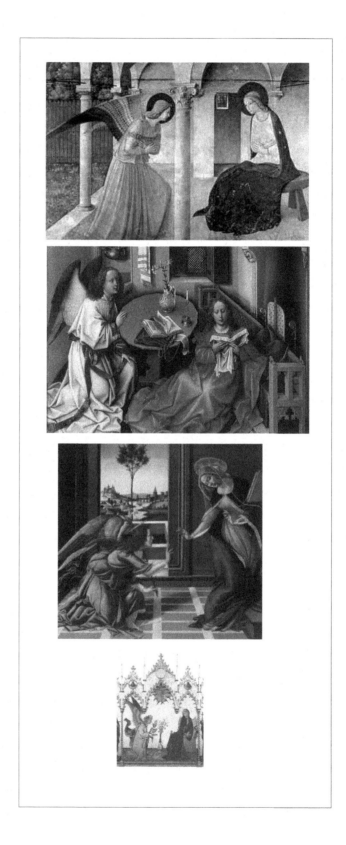

to the following. With this in place, imagining that the card depiction is only but *part of the scene*, calling to mind the exercise undertaken with the Bateleur (though in his case with regards to street scenes).

The following are from the works of Fra Angelico, the Merode Altar piece, Botticelli, and Martini. Hundreds more, including some by other well known artists such as Leonardo da Vinci, can also be found. What they usually have in common is a seated Mary with Gabriel to the left of the image, more often than not also represented with a book.

As I was making some revisions to this chapter, I happened to find another depiction of Mary, this time as crowned Queen of Heaven importantly, it should be noted, *triple* crowned[2]:

The Message

Let's go back a little to the opening of this chapter and reconsider for a moment the exercise of *Lectio Divina*. The purpose of the exercise is not for mere connection of word to word, or idea to idea, but rather for a *revelation* to open to an opening of the heart and an annunciation to be made: in the context of the period, and well within the mystical

2   there are inevitably thousands of images from the period that have yet to come to light in further studies pertinent to tarot. This is but one of those examples that is of significance. Source: Kings College, Cambridge University

tradition of the epoch, for our own heart to become pregnant with the indwelling living presence of Christ.

This aspect seems to me to also be quite consistent with considerations of the Papesse as allegory of the Church.

Here, then, and in contradistinction to the card that precedes it, we have an *inner* movement of spiritual revelation, of *intuition*. Even though no angelic being is presented on the image of the card, the crown and the title both appear to suggest that the mundane is transcended, and that the spiritual is sought.

Direction of gaze

In previous exercises, we have generally also looked at the direction of gaze. Yet here, when comparing our Papesse with our Bateleur, something other also comes importantly to the fore: both *look in the same physical direction*, yet we can distinguish that there may be quite important differences as to why the look may appear similar. The Bateleur may be looking at nothing, rather looking to divert his onlooker's attention. The Papesse may be looking at that which the Bateleur and others are oblivious to: an angelic or spiritual being. The gaze of the first is distraction; of the Papesse, attention.

Conversely, the Bateleur, as master of the elements of his trade, is utterly effortlessly focussed on his dexterous activities. In contrast, the Papesse may be utterly oblivious to the physical to which her awareness may be temporarily as asleep. In *his* hands the Bateleur exercises his will, whereas in her hands the Papesse allows the will of the Spirit to move.

Clothing

If we look carefully at her clothing, she appears to be wearing a warm mantle clasped at the front, perhaps indicating that though indoors (from the seat), the weather is not as clement as may be at first imagined. Again a distinction to our Bateleur who, though outdoors, appears to be comfortable in far less. Here again looking through the deck at the various layers of depicted (or indeed omitted!) clothing may bring to light new considerations.

Or is that mantle one of modesty, somewhat similar to those shown above in the images of the Annunciation? If we take the Annunciation to have taken place nine months prior to Jesus's birth, and we also take his birth-date as Christmas (which, in the Western Church at least, was generally considered to be correct), then the Annunciation would have taken place in late March (which coincides, of course, with the the Feast of the Annunciation celebrated on the 25th of March)[3].

Returning to the card, I have often been fascinated by the apparent loss of detail occurring near her feet, and will here bring other Marseille images to attempt to shed light on what appears to be more than simply items of clothing. But first, let's have a look at the original as well as Jean-Claude Flornoy's reproduction – the latter on the assumption that you have a copy of the card. Whether on the original or the reproduction, the intended depiction is not, to my eyes, clear. Certainly they may 'just' be folds in clothing, but I suspect otherwise.

This rather rough ambiguity recurs in many Marseille-type decks. Of note is the Dodal (Lyon) from 1701 (reproduced below). Here, the detail is more distinctive, and very similar to the (Avignon) Payen (named, as with most TdMs, 'La Papesse') deck from the same pattern and period.

What both the Dodal and Payen details resemble is somewhat reminiscent of the wheel of a spindle – quite an astounding instrument of transformation, literally spinning loose threads into a continuous whole. In other words, changing a mass of somewhat loose material into a form that gains incredible strength, and from which may be woven garment, tent, or further spun into rope.

3   Incidentally, this feast marks one of the four points on the (northern) solar calendar (out by a few days as are the others): Gabriel's Annunciation to Mary with the Spring Equinox; St John (the Baptist) with the Summer Solstice; St Michael with the Autumnal Equinox; and Christmas with the Winter Solstice.

Two images, from the 15th century, are the following:

The card image is also consistent with a shift from Virgin with spindle to one with Book... though where is her right hand on the various cards, whether on the Noblet, Dodal, or Payen?!

And is it book, or is she weaving a tapestry? in which case her right hand may be actively engaged in passing the thread from underneath.

As I have shown the Marseille type-I Dodal card earlier, I shall also briefly make a passing remark on its title thereon as "La Pances", which is *olde* French for "the paunch". If there was any historical connection to the Annunciation, this title would certainly have additional relevance.

The Crowned Feminine

The Papesse is *crowned*. How does her crown compare to any and all other feminine figures within the deck? Do they appear a similar age, or rank? Of the crowned women in the deck, and only of those who look in a similar direction to the Papesse, what is it that is common and what is it that is markedly different?

Both the Pope and the Papesse have *multiple* crowns: triple, though hers seemingly not as clearly represented near the top of the card, perhaps the space for the number preventing a full rendition. Her crowns are also distinct to those of the Pope's: whereas his are three 'solar' rays, hers appear more as stylised *fleur-de-lys*. These are important distinctions, yet they are also details that, with our 21st century *zeitgeist*, have been stripped of commonly referenced symbolic value.

We shall again revisit the crowns in a couple of weeks. At this stage, let's simply carefully look with attention at the crowns as they are presented in this deck. The previous page shows the images from the original Noblet, and I would suggest looking at these in conjunction with the Flornoy reproductions. Also, look at these in light of the facial expressions and pose each figure adopts (when the crown is on a figure), as this may bring to light other important distinctions.

The One Cup's (ie, Ace of Cups') 'crown' (not included) is also worth a look *as crown*. I have included as well the 'crowning' by laurel and flowers for this comparison, but have *excluded* non-crowning head-coverings, such as the Bateleur's.

Let's remember that these are woodcuts that, had they been instead drawn, would have greater detail and finish. That is, of course, on the one hand part of the frustration at not being able to clearly identify

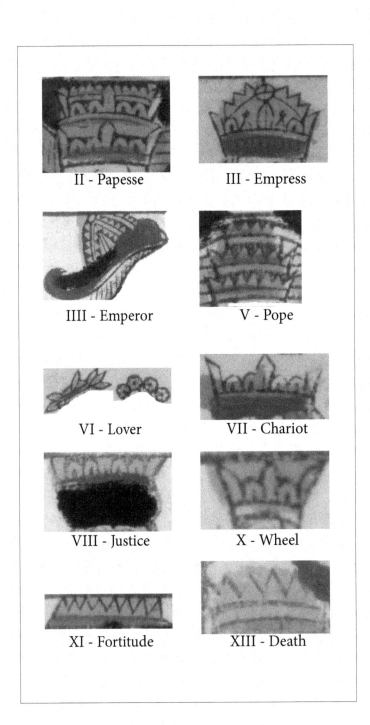

II - Papesse

III - Empress

IIII - Emperor

V - Pope

VI - Lover

VII - Chariot

VIII - Justice

X - Wheel

XI - Fortitude

XIII - Death

certain objects or their detail; and on the other the wonder provided by the ambiguity or unclarity.

Observing, Reflecting

The term 'intuition' is used earlier in this chapter, yet it is a term often used with rather ambiguous meaning. At one level, it appears to refer to an insight gained without reasoning consciously involved. It requires an engagement of deepened observation and reflection, and it is to these two aspects that even the presentation of the crowns seeks to point.

By observing and reflecting, however, we are also led far beyond the initial point of departure, yet our inner journey remains connected thereto. It is a little like one of the exercises Rudolf Steiner gives in *Knowledge of the Higher Worlds*, in which a seed is held in one's palm, and the imaginative faculty is allowed to unfold into the seed and perceive not only the tree, but its life cycle. In other words, even by entering the reflective state, instructed by careful observation and reflection, we are lead to a direct apprehension or grasp or insight into not simply a static, but rather a living and engaged imaging.

Another aspect of both intuition in general, but also with *Lectio Divina* and care-filled observation and reflections, is the necessity of patience... and *trust*. Trust, in that what we are observing or upon which we are reflecting is worthy of the same, and patience that it will, with time, unveil its own character: that it will grace us with its own living presence.

This is one of the aspects of this card in particular that I consider the feminine quality as entirely apt, and quite distinct to the previous masculine card of dexterous engagement. I mention this as perhaps some early depictions were not intended as feminine. If we look at the Cary Sheet dated, with some uncertainly, to *circa* 1500, it is possible to see the figure that may be the cognate of the Papesse as a younger bishop, clean shaven Roman fashion. Something that time would easily alter to a feminine representation.

This partial uncut sheet, incidentally, remains one of those important finds that can assist us in understanding the images of not only tarot in general, but specifically the Marseille-type decks. We shall return to it at various times through this work.

Though I show this Cary Sheet image in this chapter on the Papesse, what is not unequivocal is whether it is, as I here suggest, the cognate of the Papesse, or whether, perhaps and instead, it is instead cognate of

the Pope. If it is masculine, this and the other partial card on the sheet may indicate bishops of, respectively, the Western (Rome) and Eastern (Constantinople) Churches[4]. What remains astounding with the Cary Sheet and other very early renditions is the precision of the woodcut, showing that, perhaps, with time, the interest of the image *qua* image diminished in importance.

Also of interest is that, unlike nearly all later decks, these very early ones remain both without title and without number.

A question, then, worth considering at this point in time: *Are the titles and number an intrinsic part of the deck, even as Marseille-type?*

Ordering and Chess

Of all the deck sequence, the four cards starting from the Papesse have a notionally popular reflection in that they reflect precisely the four central chess characters of *bishop, queen, king,* and *bishop* (as viewed from the player when white, and *queen* and *king* inversed when black

---

4   Of course, having pointed to the earlier Visconti Gugliemite Papesse, we should remember that a feminine figure was clearly intended in the Visconti-Sforza type decks, and may also therefore have been so for the (later) Cary Sheet.

– in other words, as *right-to-left* in that latter case, something that also reflects the direction of writing between European scripts and that of, to use the common appelation of the times, the Moors):

Chess was not only known and popular amongst the nobility, but also amongst knightly orders within the Church, such as the Knights of the Temple of King Solomon (ie, Knights Templar).

With this, we move towards the ruling class...

III - L'Imperatrise

LEMPERATRISE

What an amazing presence the artist has been able to convey despite the crudity of the woodcut. Here is a card – one of only two – that faces us square on. It's actually quite astounding that of the whole set with figures, *ie*, of the 22 trumps and 16 court cards, the only two cards that directly face us are the Empress (card III) and Justice (card V-III). Looking directly at the viewer, we in turn look directly into *her* eyes. It is, however, relatively rare for images of the period to depict the character facing the viewer in such direct fashion.

The 'presence' is undoubtedly produced by this orientation: an orientation that is rarely observed when looking at another person, except in the context of looking at oneself in a mirror. So let this be our first exercise: to sit, look carefully at our mirrored image and observe how another person who may not know us *see* us, for that is what we are also doing with each card, not only discovering what each has to reveal, but also getting to know ourselves through this very process.

Social and Self

We left off last week with a careful *looking* at, in that case, the crowns, and now with this card we observe that the very top of the crown appears to be cut off by the included section left for the numbering. If we again look carefully, it seems as though the crown's top mimics incompletely her sceptre.

Together with the shield, both crown and sceptre present us not so much with a person, but with a social position. It is as though there is a tension inherent in the image between, on the one hand, the emblems of office, and on the other her very direct gaze that only an actual and real human being can carry. The *personæ* as opposed to the '*De Re*' or '*De Se*': the mask of social convention instead of the individuality of the person herself.

And yet, she looks. Even through the highest office, her very *I* or *ego* cannot be contained, but is instead vitally expressed. The word 'ego', by the way, is used herein in its Greco-Latin sense as simply and yet deeply "I" (εγω), rather than in its 'diminished' Freudian sense which has gained widespread currency.

Loyalty

As I was striving to find the right word to bridge this divide between the *personæ* and the *ego*, various terms emerged, but none that seem to me so apt as that of 'loyalty'. Interestingly, this is the term that has close etymological connections with the other card that faces us straight-on: Justice.

The Empress needs to both evince, and also herself have, loyalty. She is loyal to her subjects, and in turn her station bears the burdens of loyalty.

Looking again at the image, we can enter it and wonder about the accoutrements that she holds: neither hand is free, her right upon the shield, her left holding the universal sceptre; her head crowned with the emblem of office; her very pose seated on what must inevitably be a throne.

Does she have the worldly experience to bear the burden of office? Or does the station itself and its attendant servants carry the office of which she remains titular mask?

How *old* is she? In both senses of the word: from which period in history does she arise; and what is the age of the individual depicted – is she adolescent or crone?

These are questions that can, perhaps, not only help in identifying who may in fact have been depicted, but also speak to us of something that transcends individuals and rather portrays a quality that may be found at different periods – even in our own times.

Age

The more I look at the image of this Empress, the more I am struck by her apparent youth – though admittedly this may simply be a reflection of my own aging! It is as if the image depicts a relatively *young* empress or wife to emperor elect. In contrast, I call to mind the Empress whom Eleanor of Aquitaine had to endure in her youth (her mother in-law) – I doubt *that* Empress would have been depicted in quite the manner used on this card.

Which Empress?

Over the past number of years, I have at times tried – as others too have – to identify a particular individual that may have been implied by the Marseille depiction. It is worthwhile to remember that the individuals on the earlier hand-painted Visconti-type decks did indeed depict various members of the Visconti and Sforza families. Even if those decks are a direct antecedent to the Marseille-type decks, I would suggest that it is likely that (other) individuals are *implied*.

Also, it should be recalled that these Marseille, whether the Paris based Noblet or the myriad others made in Lyons, Avignon, or Marseille, would likely not represent insignia that would be at odds with the then French monarch.

It is these mixed considerations that make it difficult to identify likely individuals, and yet I am personally repeatedly lead to a specific couple: the Empress Isabel(la) of Portugal, and her husband, the Emperor Charles V (*aka* Charles I of Spain).

We shall return to Charles V when considering the Emperor. For now, let us remain a little more focussed on our Empress.

By the time of Noblet, Isabel of Portugal had been dead for just over a century. Yet, it seems, her memory in popular culture appears to have remained rather strong, perhaps in part due to some of the religious changes that the couple oversaw or immediately inherited. It was their predecessor that saw the expulsion of non-Christians from the Iberian peninsula, and they presided over the council that legitimised the German Lutheran reforms.

Though the crowns of both Empress and Emperor supports such attribution, the shield and its emblems do not: by that stage, the *double-headed* eagle was employed as Imperial emblem. Yet, the single-headed would have been politically far more astute and ambiguous, for it would have called to mind the Frankish first Holy Roman Emperor who at least shared his namesake – Charlemagne – and avoided the rivalry between Charles V and the French king (who had disappointly and in vain hoped to have been elected Emperor).

Shields and their difference

If we closely look at the shields of both imperial monarchs, they depict a different kind of eagle: both are 'eagle displayed'. In other words, both are single-headed eagles with legs and wings outstretched, and in each case the head faces *sinister* (to the left of the shield as held by its user).

This should perhaps alert us that the woodblock has been made as a reverse image of an original, for the eagle is *normally* depicted facing *dexter* – to its right.

In addition, we would normally expect the sceptre of office to he held with the right hand, not the left, and instead reasonably expect the *shield* to be left-held.

If we compare the shields alone, there are key differences. Similarly, there are differences with the crosses above the orbs topping the respective sceptres of Empress and Emperor. Let's stay with the shields and their emblem first.

Not only are the shapes of the shields distinct, the eagles are different from a heraldic perspective: the Empress's has its wings raised; the Emperor's has its wings 'inverted'.

The spread wings has been claimed to allude to protection, and the eagle is (*or was*) the dominant insignia of power on the continent of Europe[1].

Sitting as Empress - Mirroring

Carefully looking at the Empress, develop an *imaginative picture* of yourself sitting as the Empress, looking in a panel-mirror. Once the position is checked for relative accuracy (including crown, throne, sceptre, shield and robes), look at yourself in the imagined mirror as if *that mirrored* position is the card image, and then observe your own reflected eyes, and note the holding of the emblems of office. Allow that active and very precise imagination to develop the pose and image. Give

1　　The Roman Eagle appears to be the precursor of the Imperial Eagle, and continued to be in use in transformed ways by dominant military nations, including the USA.

time to permit various thoughts to arise, rather than completing this too quickly.

As Empress, what needs to be done, said, thought, felt, and *how* do these need to be done?

I am reminded here of various social graces that formerly formed part of the education of especially the nobility, including rhetoric and what still exists as 'finishing schools', where 'social graces' and cultural subjects are deemed of primary importance. Certainly the social expectations of various ranks would require a sense for etiquette and appropriate tact (ie, appropriate to the social rank and gender). Again, the tension between the individual on the one hand, and the station or masked *personæ* one occupies on the other. To be able to make these function efficiently together!

Personal Identity

The Empress is empress in large part because of 'who' she is. This 'who' revolves around not so much intrinsic *ego* (in the sense earlier mentioned), but rather in terms of the biological and familial connections to a whole network of others also in power.

Certainly with the birth of tarot (let us cast a broad net within century of 1500), individualism appears to take its rise[2]. Yet, this individualism still operates within very strict social and familial ties.

The Empress, I would suggest, is not only well connected, but also best establishes herself by learning to work within this network. By working *with the network, the network works with her*. In modern terms, this may be described by 'social' and 'emotional' intelligence, and by the myriad works that have appeared dealing with improving these aspects of social life – something that, with the diminishment of broad social ties, has for some centuries been increasingly neglected.

Not only '*who am I?*', but '*how do I belong?*', '*what are my roles?*' (yes - plural), and '*how to be myself within the roles I take on?*'. To let one's face (*personæ*) clearly shine through despite the accoutrements of the stations she occupies.

Empresses

Though I suggest a connection between our Noblet Empress and the Empress Isabella of Portugal and between the Noblet Emperor and

---

2   Cf Taylor's *Sources of Self* as an excellent study.

Isabella's husband Emperor Charles V, this should not be taken without serious questioning. After all, the *office* or *station* or *allegory*, appears to be of more import for most cards, and why assume otherwise for this card?

Looking through lists of empresses does make one realise that numerous individuals have occupied the position in history. It is also something that we very much appear to have long forgotten its value or its significance.

To gain a sense for the prevalence of the position, peruse through a list of Empresses, and note in particular the Hapsburgs, both in terms of their Sforza Milanese connection, as well as the Hapsburg crown-form: clearly our Noblet Empress is represented as of this era by the crown alone.

Card details

Let's take another look at the card and try and identify various of its other details, for quite a few remain rather difficult to clearly see.

As mentioned, her crown is reminiscent of the Hapsburgs', and her sceptre, distinct to the Emperor's, is topped with what appears to be replicated atop her crown.

The back of her chair seems to be, as to be perhaps expected, covered with cloth, suggesting perhaps her status as not only married, but also as wealthy.

Her shield bears hallmarks that this may have the remnants of a tournament shield, with, as seen even more clearly on the Emperor's, 'cuttings' for support of the lance, these called '*bouche*'. If we compare, for example, the shield (here flipped) on the Visconti-Sforza deck of the 15th century to this deck, we can see how the image may have altered, though but a little, with time:

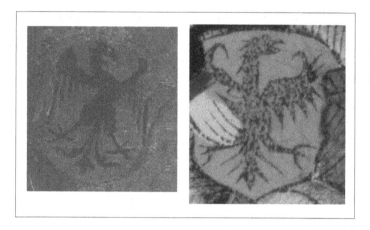

The most intriguing detail, however, has remained, for not only myself but for others in many discussions I have had over the years, as to what could possibly have been intended by the rather strange details that may have been copied without understanding the intent. These details also appear on all subsequent Marseille-type decks (whether type *I* or *II*).

So what are those things she appears to half-sit on, below her left elbow? They have at various times been described as a wing (poor bird!) next to an inverted 'umbrella-shape'.

It is only during the early phases of the preparation of this very course that I believe some of those details to have finally been identified – in this case by Robert Mealing. There remain many wonderful mysterious details within this and other decks that time will undoubtedly unveil to those who not only carefully look, but also *compare* imagery with still earlier decks and other artwork of the period.

This comparison to other decks has a quality that reflects the Empress herself: her identity is connected to her past, to her peers, and to her descendents – yet remains singular. Traits, however, may at times be more clearly identified by representations on her forebears... so let's have a look and compare this descent of card imagery.

First, the detail of the card itself:

Let's here simply observe the transformation as it manifests over a mere 150 years.

From *circa* 1500, the Cary Sheet shows a sleeve of the period, allowing the arm either to make use of the length of the cloth, or to emerge mid-way within the sleeve itself.

By the time of the Vieville (below the Cary Sheet), which is a distinct and significantly different pattern to the TdM that appears to nonetheless retain some early details, and in many ways connected to (and also, incidentally, contemporary) with the Noblet, the 'sleeve' is barely recognisable.

Note that in this image, the crown is distinct to the Cary Sheet, and similar to the Hapsburg imperial crown as also found on the Noblet. Also, similarly to most other depictions, her *right* hand holds the emblem of authority and power. Her shield, more closely resembling the Visconti-Sforza card, has the *bouche* more prominently rendered, and we can here easily see how, with time, such may degenerate mere curvy lines without clarity of the detail depicting a *bouche*.

Her waist-line cord or 'belt', as on so many depictions, is characteristically and fashionably high, tying around her just below her breasts and above her abdomen – the fashion of the times appearing to favour maternity-like beauty.

What is here interesting are those lines descending below her elbow towards and ending with *something* that suggests a loss of understanding, that only the Cary Sheet, approximately 150 years earlier, nonetheless clearly renders.

Also note that though we now call this card the 'Empress', neither Cary Sheet nor Vieville bears a title, and though the latter, by crown, is clearly Empress, there is no reason to assume that the figure was originally

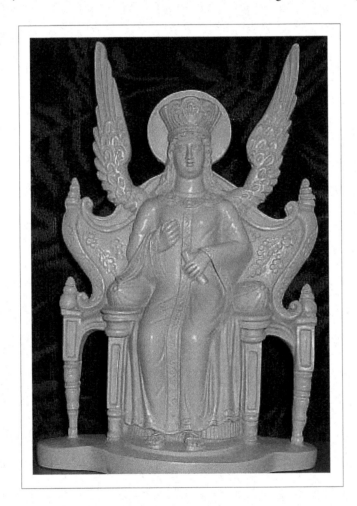

intended as Empress. In fact, in both Visconti-Sforza and the Cary Sheet, she seems to depict a local Milanese duchess – and here again the shield and its emblem, as well as the depicted crown, bear this out: the *single* eagle.

We have weaved back and forth across cards and details, yet the 'three points' or 'bird-wing' below the upturned umbrella-shape, that can be seen as her sleeve extension, is something that still requires explanation.

I *suggest* that this is to be explained as a similarly half rendered and misunderstood detail that perhaps in early depictions (now lost) may have more clearly shown to be the ends of a long pillow-cushion on which she sat. One closely similar image that mimics this aspect is the following, a reproduction of *Sophia* from what is claimed as 6th century from Constantinople. Observe specifically the cushion emerging from the side[3].

Perhaps what we have in our card detail are the confused remains of a combination of extended sleeve and seat cushion, jumbled and copied at first without much attentive care to detail, and later faithfully reproduced without understanding.

Adventures in imagery

Having mentioned *Sophia*, let us also take a brief excursion into the vast reservoir of the broader European cultural heritage by travelling across the sea into a brief Egyptian tour.

These are interesting excursions, especially when considering similarity of imagery or iconography. Nonetheless, what is perhaps of equal importance is to remain awake to and aware that *similarity* **is not** *identity*.

When beginning to investigate claims made for tarot many years ago, I was struck by two recurring statements: on the one hand, the diversity of views each at odds with the other yet each clearly stated as 'truth'; and, on the other hand, with what appeared as unchecked repeated statements that, if repeated often enough, would support its own claim.

One of these was the near constant identification of the *Papesse* with Isis. Reflecting on the imagery of the Papesse, I can and do see how such an aspect can be reflected therein. Reflecting an *aspect* is not, however, identity.

---

3   We'll again see similar depictions towards the end of this work.

One of these similarities that, with active imagination, can be transformed, is Isis's head 'crown', the raised throne, being imaginatively seen as triple crown. In terms of *imagery*, there are even more similarities between representations of Isis over centuries and the *Empress*. These visually closer similarities are again, to be sure, *similarities*, and not identical representations to the Empress.

For example, Isis's son is Horus, represented as eagle, who as a child is seen seated on her knee, finger to its lips as sign of silence (often his youthful name of Harpocrates used instead of Horus). If we observe the design on the shield of the Empress, we can observe one of the wing-tips near the beak in a similar gesture[4].

In later depictions, during Roman times, imagery of Isis and Horus will call to mind for still later Christians the Mary and Child image. An example of this is the following unexpected representation of not Mary and Jesus, but rather of Isis and Horus. The image is unexpected not only for our modern eyes, but also for *mediaeval* Christian eyes.

From here it is not such a huge leap to combine this Isian model to Mary mother of Jesus, whose other representations are as Queen of

---

4   on some TdM-derived decks, the wing-tip *just* touches the beak.

Heaven, and intimately connected to various allegories of *Sophia*[5].

For the sake of calling to mind the child Harpocrates's more familiar representation as Horus, below are two. It is but a simple imaginative step to substitute the child for the falcon representing, after all, Horus, and the falcom to become embedded in the shield's emblem.

These imaginative exercises can allow connections to be made between images that share similarity. What is to also be kept in consciousness, however, is that *any two or more concepts or images may be linked in thought and in imagination*. Again, and though useful to reflect on these in that light, *similarity is* not *identity*.

Land as representation of Empress

Returning to Europe, other similarities arise, in this case to assist the art of geographical memory, whereby various continents and places are represented as animal-like or as people. I recall as a young school-child how I saw France itself reminiscent of an elephant. In former times, *Europa* has been represented as 'Empress':

In this representation, the crown is over Spain, and the orb over southern Italy (ie, Naples).

So let us return to a European map and consider for another brief moment the context of the times, albeit a little before the 1650 Noblet was created. At the end of the reign of Charles V, parts of northern Italy formerly under the French Crown were now part of the Imperial Crown, including the important Savoy-Milanese area. Our Empress, Isabella of

5   This close connection is even more pronounced in some languages. For example, the Russian appelation for Mary as 'Our Lady' (*Vladychitsa*) implies or connotes 'empress'-like characteristics or rulership. Similarly, we should take care to also consider representations, as in some Russian icons, that differentiates *Sophia-as-Holy Spirit* and Mary.

Portugal, had died earlier, and much interchange of ideas, pilgrimages, images, and intermarriages within especially the nobility meant that it was a Europe far more 'unified' in terms of its inter-influences than has at times been claimed or is popularly considered.

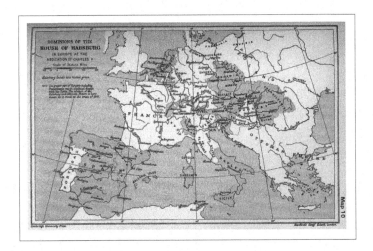

In 1547 and in the years that followed, the Hapsburg empire not only straddled France, Italy and Germany, but also included domains in the newly conquered lands of the Americas. This breadth is something we shall again mention when considering the Emperor in a couple of chapters.

Identity

The concept of identity has recurred a number of times in these pages, and the very mapping above also reminds us that personal identity is often also connected to national and regional identity. We do not simply identify as individual, but also often as part of a social group, as part of a nation, and linked to others by genetic connections (or, to adopt the language of former times, by blood).

Gnothi Seauton – "know thyself" – was said to be inscribed in the forecourt to a temple at Delphi. To know one's own self, amongst other considerations, is the need of increased familiarity with the conditions we not only face, but carry within as our own impulse, as part of our individual unfolding, in meeting one's destiny through deed and action in the world around us. Taking on the accoutrements required of us, yet meeting the tasks truly and authentically. This appears part of what makes an Empress excel in her roles.

....and yet, personality is not denied. Nor is it subsumed.

THE COURTS

ROY·DE·DENIER·

Reading tarot

What is the difference between reading with a Marseille-type deck and various others available (whether tarot or not)? The answer depends in part on methods one prefers to employ when reading, and to what purpose the reading is put. One thing ought to be clear by now: when spreading cards, the atouts (or trumps) and court cards are visually distinct and of a different nature to the pip cards. There is power in the distinction as visually presented.

This is also an opportune time to mention a few points directly pertinent to reading. In the first place, a reading may (perhaps obviously) be undertaken in order to gain insights into a situation. The manner in which it 'works' will undoubtedly be explained in different ways, very much reflecting our metaphysical and epistemological views, in the same way that 'brain-storming', free-form writing or talking, and doodling will also be differently explained. In each case, what tends to occur when a specific situation is given attention is that subtle aspects begin to emerge and the 'space' necessary for the mind's *creative* insights to arise freed. Attention to the situation at hand takes a similar form to the exercises we have already encountered – the difference is (in part) that we may not consciously be awake to its subtleties.

Let's briefly revisit the exercises we have so far undertaken.

Past exercises

the sequencing of cards

pairings

Ignatian imagination

prestidigitation

image comparison

incorporating two cards in imagination

card-flicking spread

pip card sequencing

living batons and arabesque details

sword 'circles'

looking for the implement-holding hand

directions of seeing spreads/reversals

Lectio Divina

image as depicting *partial* scene

comparing detail: crowns

asking whether titles/numerals are intrinsic

seeing oneself as others may see us

mirroring of Empress

researching (list of Empresses)

Let's undertake another exercise.

Place the court cards *face down* in groups of four: Valets together, Cavaliers grouped, Queens combined, and Kings likewise.

Take two of the listed above exercises, one amongst your preferred and one amongst the less successful. Take the time to apply those two exercises to a *Valet* randomly chosen from the Valets group; then (perhaps on a different day) to a Cavalier randomly chosen *but of a different suit*; to a Queen randomly chosen from the remaining two suits; and to the King of the suit not yet selected.

Personalities

If we look at the sixteen court cards, what we are faced with is, effectively, a bunch of people. What differentiates them are a number of factors: their gender, which is at times ambiguous; their age; their social station; and their 'trade', emblem or held implement.

Here we have all the hallmarks of personality seemingly manifest, combining the workings on the individual of not only the external world (*via* socio-cultural influences) and the internal world (*via* familial genetic traits, personal health and temperament), but also how the individual is able to express his or her *ego* (ie., εγω) across time – even over the course of one's life.

We can imagine, to use an example, that the King of Batons senses and acts into his environment in not only different ways when 25 and 75 years old, but that the ways he responds is also influenced by his characterological dispositions that have in part been shaped in a more or less consistent manner by his genetic makeup as well as by his experienced environment. The same applies for each of the sixteen cards.

This manner of considering the court cards as reflecting personality is not new. In standard playing cards in France, for example, many decks are still obtainable with the names of historical figures included thereon to which the cards are supposed to either depict or allude. For example, the Kings are often named after Charlemagne, Alexander the Great, Julius Caesar and King David – each of these personalities *still* having recognisable aspects that many of us may identify (even if that is no longer the case for the named Queens and Valets).

What is striking is that as soon as one names these Kings (or Queens, Cavaliers or Valets), we move them from abstract form to individual characters. Or perhaps, more accurately, caricature or stereotype, for it is not even the fullness of the individuals that is brought to mind, but rather characterological dispositions or individualised caricatured stereotypes.

Boiardo poem

One of the earliest tarot related writings to do something very similar is the poem by Boiardo, dating from the 15th century. Therein, admittedly, we have not the four suits as we know them, but rather the suits of *fear*; of *jealousy*; of *hope*; and of *love*. Also, unlike the standard four court cards for each suit of tarot, they are given – and this is the point I wish to here raise – the names of famous people, heroes and heroines, or gods and goddesses; in other words, individuals with stereotypical characteristics:

Phineas, Ptolemy, Andromache, Dionysius; Argus, Turnus, Juno, Vulcan; Horatius, Jason, Judith, Eneas; Cyclops, Paris, Venus, Jove.

In the context of the times, these evoked far more living qualities than they now carry. For most of us, Andromache, or Turnus or Eneas are but names that we would need to look-up rather than names that evoke specific characteristics.

So *what are the characteristics* that may be reflected in the court cards? Again, let's look at the cards themselves and the implements they hold.

Suits vs Rank

By placing the sixteen court cards in a four-by-four grid, we can simultaneously compare not only the differences across suits (for example, Valet with Valet), but also across rank (for example, Valet with Queen).

Where does each figure face? re-arranging the court cards by placing, for example, all the Valets in the top row, then the Cavaliers in the second, etc., do different suggestions arise? what about re-arranging the

same by figures that all face the same way in each row; and those whose body faces differently to their eyes; grouping those who look at their implement, and those that seem not to: do all these different arrangements suggest ways in which each figure is either engaged with the *implement*, with the *viewer*, or with another card in visual *arrangement*?

How and in what manner is each Queen image similar to the *Empress*? and each King to the *Emperor*? and in what manner is each Valet similar to the *Bateleur*? and to *Death*!?

Personality revisited

In a similar manner that calling to mind or assigning a person (whether from fiction, legend, or fame) to reflect a sense for particular characteristics can assist, it may also lead us away from the card at hand.

Without looking at the title given to the cards, how many of the figures are clearly masculine or feminine? Or, perhaps suggesting this in a different manner, let's look at each and every card *as though it was a man,* and then *each and every card as though it was a woman.* Each can be seen as of either gender. Literally.

The kind of person that we begin to see goes beyond names that have perhaps been associated in stereotypical fashion. Yet, their implement points to their suit, and the suit is symbolically also meaningful.

Valets

We tend to think of 'valets' as servants, yet a better term would probably be 'personal assistant', with much of the actual work carried out by servants that do not even form part of the court cards. In that sense, valets are more likely to be of the similar social class as those whom they assist. The valet, nonetheless, will generally be part of a household removed from his (or her) immediate family, yet often connected.

A team of valets may be at the service of the more wealthy amongst the nobility, yet each qualitatively different to the domestic servants, gardeners and other labourers.

Cavaliers

The valet may not only be of service to the ruling crown, but also to the cavalier, perhaps hoping that one day he (and I am here using the masculine pronoun exclusively) too will achieve that rank.

Yet, 'cavalier' has not quite the same singular connotation as 'knight':

the former is perhaps better rendered as 'horse rider'. As horse rider, he *may* be a knight, or instead simply that: a rider (and for this latter, irrespective of gender).

The use of a horse suggests that either distance needs to be covered, or alternatively that a processional show is implied – still, some wealth and independent means is implied.

Queens and Kings

Kings and Queens harken back not only to rulership in particular geographical areas, but also regions and *peoples*. For example, the king and queen of the 'little people' in not only Irish and Gaelic myth, but also its equivalent in German mining mythology.

What is also brought to mind is not only the 'midget king' – even if only king for a day, but also that each profession has its crowned figure. The 'king' and 'queen' of bakers, for example, as symbolic of winners of recognition by their peers... and of course, this recognition by their peers is precisely what needs to similarly take place for the crown to be able to be legitimately worn.

Yet there are also often competing claims to the throne, with deposed rulers being perhaps acclaimed as the 'legitimate' ones. Unlike cavaliers and pages, it seems that this question of 'legitimacy' has important consequences for the woman or man who would be king or queen.

As we saw in chapter four, many crowns are represented, to which let us briefly return.

Crowns

Below's depiction of European crowns shows from whence imagery such as the various types displayed in the deck may have their origin. Whether or not the cards intentionally depict certain specific forms, or whether instead the woodcarver may have surreptitiously or even unintentionally included a form visually close to a specific crown, is unknown. Still, what we have are standard representations that may assist in identifying the type of crowns represented and to which comparisons may be made.

Sequence of courts

In the sequence from Valet to Cavalier to Queen and King, another aspect that comes to mind is the sequence of professional life that may

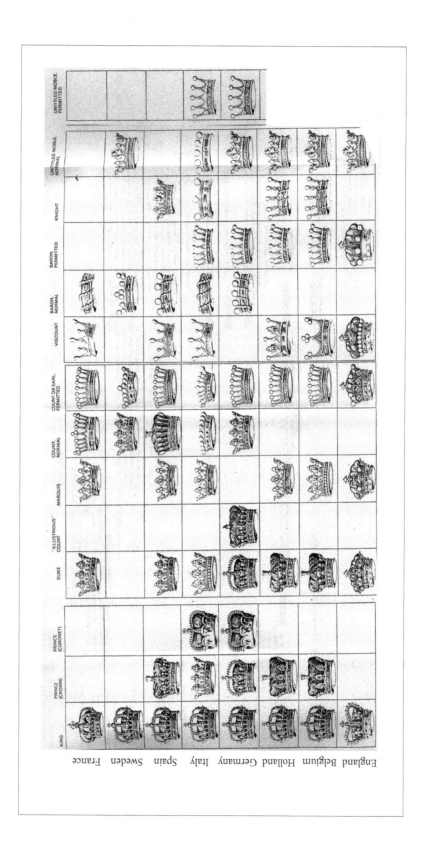

be apparent in any profession – whether it be through accession by inheritance or by increased mastery of a craft.

The Valet as apprentice *becomes* journeyman (literally) or 'companion'. In some parts of Europe, and undoubtedly elsewhere, even today the journeyman is expected to travel through regions to various masters in order to increase his or her proficiency – and only thereafter settle to both the profession as master as well as to establish home and family.

Conversely, the master is expected to both take on apprentice and to employ journeyman, as well as see to their professional improvement, all the while also paying attention to their own familial engagements.

The courts, as a group, reflect these combined aspects in discrete economy.

Suits

We cannot forget, of course, that each court sequence is also of a suit, and that each suit can be considered from various perspectives. On the one hand, as mentioned in chapter three, each can be seen as reflecting professions or areas of life: swords the judicial-political spectrum; deniers the financial and artisanal professions; cups the educational and religious sphere; and batons the peasant and menial labours. All are required, and all are dependent one each on the other.

In addition to considering these as various *professions*, they also reflect part of our lives, for we each inevitably engage in every one of these four areas of life.

How we *engage* in these may also be reflected in any of the courts for each of those areas. For example, I may have 'Queen-like' characteristics when it comes to matters of learning and education, and be far more 'Valet-like' (or apprentice) when attempting gardening (without any implied diminishment of the pleasure I may obtain from the latter).

Even when considering my own garden-work, I may approach it from any of the afore-mentioned four suits: am I considering the selection of plants from a social perspective (irrespective as to rank from Valet to King); or from an economic perspective; or one of delight and upliftment; or as toil and maintenance?

Drawing a court card in relation to my garden engagement may perhaps not simply reflect something of the way I am, but perhaps also guide me to consider it from the perspective of the card drawn.

Reading exercise - one card

Let's consider something that each of us engages in: washing the dishes. Even those amongst us who may have domestic staff contribute to the dirtying, and hence to the cleaning, of tableware.

Mixing the sixteen court cards only, randomly select a card and reflect on considerations of the cleaning of dishes from that perspective.

To be sure, the same can be repeated with all sixteen court cards. I would suggest, however, to allow a single card to be given the time to unveil its own value over a few days rather than attempt to quickly pass through all sixteen.

Realism vs symbolism

We have already looked at the cards side by side by placing them in a grid form. Let's now also carefully look at each one with one very specific consideration in mind: making allowances for poor representation because of the woodcut, is the depiction as presented on the card realistic?

To give one of the more extreme examples from the sixteen cards, look carefully at the Cavalier of Deniers. Not only is the floating coin far too disproportionate relative the figure, but can a horse move in the manner depicted? If so, is its gait in gallop, canter, trot, or walk, ...or is it pacing!?

What kind of horse rider would sit comfortably and hold the various implements as depicted? and of the various gaits, which are depicted across the cards?

Looking at each horse, we are also faced with, possibly, different *types* of horses, with perhaps different uses and, likely, different costs. The type of horse that is used as battle horse seems different to the Batons horse, and different again to the Deniers horse. Each is not only dressed differently, but is also perhaps of different breed.

Is the horse and rider looking in the same direction, or is one seemingly at odds with the other?

Symbolic representations

We have already considered briefly various aspects of the court cards, including personality characterisation. Symbols may at times also be used in ways far more metaphorical. As an example, let us briefly consider the *Grammatica Figurata* of Matthias Ringmann. Here, we have both King and Queen representing grammatical figures. Ken Mayer, on trionfi.com, translates the Latin for these two in the following manner:

> The Verb is the Third Part of Speech: It is what signifies to do or suffer something or neither. It has tense and person, but not case, and is represented by a King. Which the figure below and the adjoining distich expresses clearly enough:

> The king symbolizes the Verb, by acting on and being acted upon by enemies,
>
> And sometimes by doing neither, when peace is strong.

and:

> The fourth part of speech is the adverb, which added to a verb explains and fills out its meaning. And it is represented by the Deacon preaching in lieu of the Curate. And indeed it is symbolized by the Queen, which can be seen from the following figure and distich:

And the Queen herself represents adverbs to us. Explaining, elaborating, and loving the particulars of the King

The Queen who moderates the king connotes the adverb, or rather the social bonds of a legitimate marriage: She explains and elaborates all things at her beck and call (just as an adverb explains and elaborates the meaning of the verb).

Though the *Grammatica Figurata* is meant as a pedagogical tool from the beginning of the 16th century (about 150 years before the Noblet) and does not contain court cards across suits, what it shows is that though symbolic meaning may meander from the literal, it also, I would suggest, also remains closely bound to it.

Symbols, though having no fixity in meaning, do not lack precision: it would be inept for the adjective to have been said to be King. It is because of the characterological personality of kingship that the *Grammatica Figurata* works – even if it now seems somewhat strange and distant.

Allow me here to also share a personal journey of insight from the 1980s, when striving to deepen my own insights into the deck and, specifically, the court cards.

Personality types

What struck me then – and much of what follows I still at times use in either reading or personal reflection – is that the court cards (arranged in that four-by-four grid makes it easier to see) have, in each suit, two decision makers, and two others finding, taking or bringing things into the world.

Also, there appears to be withdrawn, introverted or melancholic tendencies in the valets and queens, and, conversely, extraverted or outer-world oriented tendencies in the cavaliers and kings.

When I came across the work of Myers-Briggs in *Gifts Differing*, what struck me is not so much that these could be correlated (any similarly numbered sets can be quantitatively correlated), but that at least in terms of orientation (inner and outer), decision-making (judgement), and engaging in 'finding things' or perception, something of the kind was similarly expressed in the court cards.

In addition, both Myers-Briggs and the court cards in general do seem to 'speak' of distinct characters reflecting personality typology – and it is this latter aspect that bears the hallmarks of human diversity, a diversity that may be grouped by similarity of *tendency*.

With the court cards themselves, however, we perhaps need also to take care to look at these as presented. To superimpose on the imagery another framework, no matter how satisfying – as this happens to be for myself – may also take us in distant fields without properly reflecting the cards at hand.

For the sake of showing my preferred MBTI correlations[1] with the court cards, this summarises to the following:

	P	J
I	Valet	Queen
E	Cavalier	King

Arm and hand movement

Let's return to the cards for another observation, this time *disregarding*

---

1   note that I do not here provide suit attributions.

all but the position of both arms of each card and the implement(s) being held.

Also, let us imagine that each successive card within a suit is the same person who has simply been captured by successive photographic image. In imagination, let us move the figure's arms and implement in order for the Valet's to become the Cavalier's, and from thence to the Queen's, and henceforth the King's. Now reverse the order, from King to Valet. And *alter the order*, from Cavalier to King to Valet to Queen... and other permutations.

For the purposes of this exercise, the location, posture, and other important details of each figure are *not considered*: only the motions of arms and hands, and implement held (or aloft).

This exercise, though focussing solely on the arms, can also be applied to any sequential cards. We had, in chapter two, the active inclusion of multiple cards as scene. Here, instead, the imagination is called upon to *transform* one card image into another.

Virtues

Another question that can be asked is what particular qualities are especially being developed by the court cards in their respective suit. We shall return to consideration of virtues in more detail in a few chapters. If we briefly take into consideration the cardinal virtues presented in the deck and, for our immediate purpose, look at another deck from the 15th century and its images, a natural relation emerges. I first came across this in Gareth Knight's *Magical World of the Tarot: Fourfold Mirror of the Universe*[2]. In the incorrectly named Charles VI deck[3], there are, of the cards that remain, precisely four that have figures with stellated aureoles: Justice, Fortitude, Temperance, and the World. The first three are clearly cardinal virtues, and the fourth only so by far more indirect considerations, though as 'Soul of the World' and 'Sophia' can

---

2   I am indebted to Stephen John Mangan for reminding me that John Shephard's earlier *The Tarot Trumps: Cosmos in Miniature* also mentions these as the *four cardinal* virtues. Where Gareth Knight remains unique is that he takes these four as central around which the rest of the deck is positioned, and hence also makes a direct connection between these four cards as cardinal virtues and the four suits.

3   'incorrectly named', as the deck is from the 15th century. This deck was at one time thought to have been the (non-tarot) card gaming set made for the French King Charles VI. The name 'Chales VI deck' has since stuck.

be considered as Wisdom, alternatively named Prudence.

Looking at these four cards, we can see that, *unlike the TdM*, visual iconographic connections can be made to the four suits: Justice holds (as is standard) a sword; Fortitude a pillar; Temperance cups; and the World stands upon a circular depiction. These can *visually* be seen as reflecting the suits – and hence also specifically the court cards – of swords, bastons, cups and coins respectively.

In terms of their worldly uses, these do present us with useful considerations. Prudence connected to coins certainly brings forth one aspect of the implement; as does temperance in relation to cups; the usage of brute force in considerations of bastons; and justice before engagement of swords.

Regions

Finally, let us also call to mind that by the very fact that various royal houses are depicted, and though they can be considered, as earlier mentioned, as representing not only personality, but also professions, the most literal and direct manner of playing with these is to consider that they rule over different regions.

The world not only was, but also is, divided into various geo-political regions, and then as now each exemplifies certain traits and characteristics with differing socio-political orientations. So let us, as a final reflection, consider how each individual court card may reflect the political landscape, for which I would suggest considering the model provided on www.politicalcompass.org.

'Mapping' each court card, relating their characterological dispositions to personality type, considering their relative maturity in various professions: each provides rich materials by which to read the courts and, importantly, to develop in us an increasing understanding of the forces at play in the developing individual as he or she interacts in the world.

IIII - L'Empereur

Political Power

To look at the Emperor without considering political power structures would be to overlook the main role of the depicted figure. The same, of course, can also have been said of the various court cards and the Empress we previously considered. The Emperor is here especially important as without the political hierarchy in place which creates this position, there is no emperor.

An 'empire' makes a number of assumptions, one of which is that various states are unified more or less under a common rulership. Conversely, there is thereby a hint that though unified within a common empire, *differing* and somewhat autonomous nation-states co-exist. If I consider various world orders, the closest that comes to mind is the current European situation: independent nation-states within a union at whose head is the modern equivalent to the imperial court – a parliament. Yet, each of its member nation retains an autonomy that is not similarly reflected in other modern 'unions' of states, such as Canada, the USA, or Australia. Perhaps other examples that *did reflect* the 'imperial' form include the former British Commonwealth at whose head was a common Crown, or the former USSR... with, of course, their peculiar differences.

Additionally, unlike a *royal* crown that had far clearer lines of filial descent, the *imperial* crown was one to which the emperor was *elected* if, to be sure, suitably qualified. The relationship that ensued hence had greater reciprocal ties than that of vassals of any crown – though even therewith, reciprocal obligations enforced the division and distribution of power.

This reflection of political structures in place would, I suggest, have been brought to mind in the 16th century as it now does, and though the creation of the Noblet is approximately 130 years prior to the French Revolution, political struggles and changes are ever-present. Even the position or office of Emperor alters with time: from the extremes of near absolute political autocracy to that of mere figure-head, with or without legislative powers.

Certainly in the France of the 1650s, ruled by a King who appears to display an absolutist hand and having been involved in various wars on all sides of the kingdom, political considerations towards an emperor, who by that stage had lost effective power, would have meant something rather different to what it meant for both rulers and the populace under

Charles V some hundred years earlier, or what it would mean again much later under Napoleon.

If one compares the reigns of Ferdinand III (Emperor at the time of the Noblet's creation) with that of Louis the XIVth ('Sun'-King of France at the time), there is a stark contrast that one feels: the loss of imperial power on the one hand and the absolutist rise of the king.

This is one of the considerations that, we can surmise, may already have been at odds in the minds of the general population between the political powers of the day and the image depicted on the deck[1]. Today, we are possibly more prone to see in the Emperor something closer to that intended than some of Noblet's compatriots for whom the Emperor, though an actual person, was relatively powerless. A situation unlike the memory of Charlemagne which would evoke fondness, or the memory of the then quite recent Charles V – the Emperor perhaps actually intended in the depiction and to which the rival French Crown had at that time expected to have been elected in preference to Charles.

Politics and Power

Despite the political powers of the day, much of our modern era arises from writings that see their light at precisely the time of the Noblet's creation: Hobbes's *De Cive* and his better known *Leviathan* dates not only from this time, but from his time in Paris as Noblet (or the carver in his employ) would have been shaping the woodblocks from which is imprinted our deck. That Hobbes's political views suggest that an absolutist monarchy is desirable not only reflects well the then political situation of Paris but also, I would suggest, a view of the idealised position of Emperor.

His contemporary and fellow Englishman James Harrington (who also wrote and published within a few years), by contrast, advocates redistribution of both wealth and power amongst the *body politic*.

These writers, of course, take much of their thoughts from a combination of the political theories descended from the Aristotelian and Platonic works, as well as from contemporary considerations – perhaps also of political writings of early but more recent times, such as Machiavelli's *Prince*.

What seems an important reflection is on the role of supreme power:

---

1   and indeed throughout the period in which both types of TdM developed

'supreme' not in the sense of 'absolutist', but in that of 'ultimate' and whether or not a crown figures therein (whether by name or not). In this, the Hobbesian division seems apt as a good overview of the three modes of political view: power in the hands of one (the monarchy); a few (aristocracy or oligarchy); or all (democracy).

Imperial powers across politics

In practice, each of these three forms of political governing *could* have an Emperor as 'head' of political state. I would suggest that this also has important ramifications in interpreting the card in any situational reading, so let us consider what such Emperor would be within a *monarchy*, within an *oligarchy*, and within a *democracy*.

Within each of those three political forms taking shape in imaginary states, what would be the differences of *tyranny* without an Emperor, and how could an Emperor either *alleviate* or *worsen* such a situation.

We shall return to explorations of these points in a short while, but would suggest taking the time to reflect on these thoughts prior to reading further.

Looking at the Card

In contrast to the direct glance of the Empress, the Emperor is shown in total profile. There are indeed very few cards on which a person is depicted in such total profile. Of the trumps, Death is the only other cards that has the main figure similarly oriented, and thereon it can be surmised as depicting intended motion – unlike the Emperor.

If we look through the whole set, only IIII the Emperor, one of the smaller figures on V the Pope, one of the figures on VI the Lover, XIII Death (already mentioned), the two figures on XVI La Maison Dieu, and, from the court cards, the Valet of Bastons and Queen of Deniers are so depicted.

Let's take a look at these and notice that perhaps their *attentiveness* may be entirely different. To accentuate this, I would suggest using one of our previous imaginative exercises, and placing ourselves within the depicted scene (but not the figure itself). In such an exercise, we would normally imagine the setting to include other figures and a wholesome scene, even though not captured by the card's imagery. For our current purposes, however, imagine only the image as presented on the card and oneself.

So taking these cards, how is the Emperor's engagement different to each of the others *in relation to ourselves* as present?

Profiles compared

Within the scenes, some profiles do of course make for important considerations. For example, we should be rather surprised if the figure shown in profile on card VI was to instead face us. Nonetheless, simply looking at the profiles below brings out other aspects of their individual feature that, combined with the above exercise, enlivens those differences.

Looking at these, another question that arises is how facing right or left makes a difference, and whether there is iconographic significance to this.

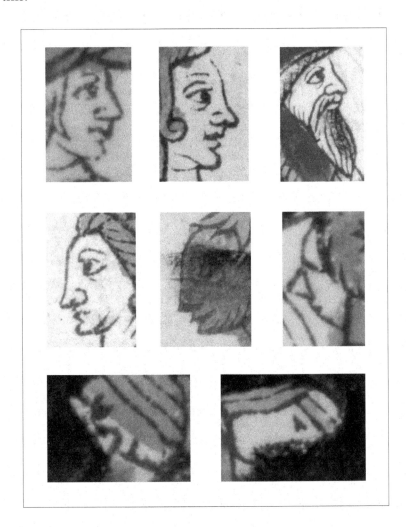

As I have listed the cards from which the figures arise (in the previous section), I randomly present these here from the original cards rather than Flornoy's wonderful re-creations. I suggest to simply look at the figures before looking again at the cards from which they are taken and see how different they may appear in context.

The profile calls to mind earlier depictions that appear to be made purposefully showing only one side of the face, as in some Assyrian royal carvings, as well as some Jewish references to YHVH (or Jehovah). This latter may also be called to mind by the profiled beard, something that has also been of significance in Kabbalistic writings.

In terms of the Noblet there are also, as for the profiles, precisely seven cards that depict bearded individuals:

Of these, the last two are the only ones possibly without a moustache – or if these two have a moustache, it is not prominently depicted. Of interest as well is that only the two *Kings* have beards that show forked growth.

Irrespective of the connections we can make between beard and Kabbalistic considerations, what is evident with the depictions is, I would suggest, threefold. Firstly, in general the beard will depict that the individual is masculine – this is perhaps only important in XX the Judgement card, as the others are 'obvious' in themselves; secondly, there is a distinction that is implied between youth and age – this is perhaps implied in the difference between the two other Kings without beards, as well as the numerous other masculine figures in the deck, whether it be on the Pope, the Lover, or Chariot (and we shall also consider these as 'feminine' in later chapters); thirdly, however, there are also location and political considerations that may be indicated or hinted, such as the differences between eastern and western, or indeed northern and southern, European preferences.

It may be called to mind that only some centuries earlier, stone-masons had threatened to burn all churches in France – both the hundreds that were under construction as well as those completed – if an ecclesiastical edict for them to shave was not rescinded. Beards won out – perhaps the first instance of the equivalent of a trade union speaking collectively on what are effectively employment conditions.

Let us return to the overall card image.

Overall image

I made reference in chapter five in regards to the Empress that perhaps the woodblock was mirror image to what we may expect, in part because we could expect of the staff that it be held by the right hand, and that the eagle on the shield face *dexter* (its own right-hand side).

With the Empress, it should be noted, we nonetheless have a consistent, even if counter-intuitive, representation across many decks of the period – except for the far earlier Visconti types – in that her shield is held with her right hand and her staff with her left. Certainly TdM-*I* and TdM-*II* decks both depict her this way.

With the *Emperor*, however, the Noblet image is shown mirror-image to what is generally the case for TdM-*I and* TdM-*II*. In fact, the depiction of the Emperor in this left-to-right inversion of what became standard later can be seen as either being a peculiar instance to this very specific deck, or an indication that though an early form of TdM-*I*, it isn't quite that yet.

Personally, I consider the image *mirror* to what was likely intended, with the image producer 'mistakenly' or carelessly drawing the inverse of the intended Emperor on the woodblock – though of course correctly engraving the title.

Let us look at the Cary Sheet, the Dodal and the Conver by way of contrast, and then also have a look at what the Noblet would have looked like in this inversion. The Dodal (a TdM-*I*) is on the left, the Conver (a TdM-*II*) on the right, with the Cary Sheet and the flipped Noblet below these:

Excluding the Cary Sheet (third above), the three cards are J-C Flornoy reproductions from those respective three decks. What is perhaps surprising, but also justifies the *Empress*'s left-hand holding the shield with her right hand and staff with left, is the Cary Sheet Emperor (in black-&-white outline).

Mirror imagery and drawing

What would each card in fact look like if mirrored? With the Empress, we imagined that the image was as our own reflection. Here, I would suggest taking a small mirror and randomly selecting twelve cards, looking at each through a mirror. The *drawing* part is directly on the mirror: using either a small paint-brush or wax crayon, select a card from the twelve and simply – actually, it is not so simple – imprint on the glass surface the image seen.

The image drawn, if in outline only, is the equivalent to what the woodcut artist would have to produce for the block.

'Universal Rights of Nations'

In *Der Rosenkreuzer in seiner Blösse* ('The Rosicrucian Exposed') of 1782 (that I have already quoted in an earlier chapter), it is stated that:

> It is one of the most important axioms in the rights of all States that the regent, or those who wield supreme authority in the State, make it one of their first duties to procure, spread, and maintain inviolable the tranquillity and safety and general welfare of the community, and of all members of the State, jointly as well as separately and individually.

> [*Ancient Texts of the Golden Rosicrucians*, vol 1, 2007, p. 78]

Perhaps this, more so than similar statements of the times, is a reflection that – at the very least – the cardinal virtues are implied in the effective social fabric, with its 'supreme authority' having specific 'duties' – these words as used in the above quote.

In considering such, we are lead also to wonder at the religious wars, massacres and revolts that marred and marked the periods of tarot's development. By the 1700s the number of Huguenots that had been banished or killed throughout France was immense, and one of the country's most popular (but now nearly forgotten) philosophers was Pierre Bayle, himself a Huguenot who spent most of his life in exile in the lowland countries to the north.

His poignant arguments for *tolerance* can perhaps describe a most important aspect finding itself differently expressed in the quote above. His concept of the 'rights of conscience' entails that a ruler must act so as to prevent persecution – and in that he specifically referred to religious persecution. Here we have, in a similar manner to Locke, a first and clear distinction between this card and the next, for Bayle sees in the secular ruler a duty to perhaps even mitigate against the truth that the Church or religious innovator may legitimately have.

Here, the ruler or political laws designed to protect "the tranquillity and safety and general welfare of the community, and of all members of the State, jointly as well as separately and individually", needs, in essence, to do something we may perhaps not expect: *disregard* conscience – so that an individual who, for example, is called by his or her conscience to kill another may have no choice in carrying out the act dictated by conscience, but similarly, the ruler may prosecute punishment without regard to the conscience of the individual but rather to the *act* as carried out.

This aspect plays, I would suggest, a very large part in the changed representation of Justice around this time: from having open eyes to being blindfolded – but more on that in due course.

In terms of the duties of the ruler, it would be his duty, in light of this principle of *Tolerance*, to act against even the 'True Church' and, conversely, to prosecute innovators or individuals who established religious views contrary to those of tolerance.

In this line of thought, the *moral* becomes what, for an *individual*, is called to be done, in contrast to the duties of the ruler who needs even to disregard specific moral acts in favour of encouraging tolerance for the general wellbeing of *all members of the State*. In some ways, a little like a benevolent father who allows his children to take steps that are in themselves erroneous, though by these engagement deeper learning and appreciation becomes possible as they mature.

This line of thought I present from Bayle (something very similar to Locke's, by the way) is not something that has generally been adopted, nor is it reflected in modern (or contemporary at the time) political view. For the Emperor that even accepts such a view, the inherent problem is that *as individual* he would be called to moral acts that are compelling, yet undoubtedly in conflict (at least at times) with the call for tolerance.

Church and State

In what we have considered, we see the political differences between Church and State – yet the two are not necessarily separated. The three different models that arise following this period are still extant and quite different: if we consider the formal separation of state and church in the USA, it has quite a different sense to the *secularism* (or *laïcism*) of

France, or indeed to England, where the head of state is simultaneously the head of the Church.

Nonetheless, here we have the image of an Emperor that, whether he faces, in the card sequence, towards the Pope or away from him, makes a statement by his very direction.

Reflecting on the above, place the Emperor and Pope adjacent each other, enter the scene and, imagining being the Emperor, consider what may need to be done to increase *tolerance* in the context of various religious pronouncements that may have local consequences. How would the Emperor take the first step?

Emperor as Charles V

One of the suggestions I made in the chapter on the Empress was that the card may very well have been considered to have been Isabella of Portugal. In part the suggestion was due to both herself and Charles V appearing to be the most likely candidates as being depicted on all TdMs. This, to be sure, only if specific individuals, rather than stations, were in any manner intended.

Charles V was elected to the imperial crown in Frankfurt in 1519, and would certainly still have been thought of as Emperor by the time Noblet carved his deck. Furthermore, given the relative impotence of the reigning Emperor in 1650, Charles V is likely to have been considered something akin to what an Emperor should in fact be like. Additionally, Charles V, in part because of his territories in the 'new world', was considered the Ruler of the World, over whose dominions the Sun ever shines.

Rubens's painting of the Allegory of Charles V as ruler of the world certainly also sheds light on his crown.

What is also interesting here is that the golden cloth across his lap may be an emblem of the Order of the Golden Fleece (the standard emblem for which he here wears as pendant), and the globe shows the extent of his dominions.

Neither the Noblet nor the Dodal show a pendant hanging from what does appear to be a golden chain around his neck, though the Conver does. If it was intended to be depicting the Golden Fleece, the pendant would look like the one here depicted: a golden ram suspended from a golden chain, the latter often rather thick or broad.

Numerous images are extant of Charles V, each instructive as to what may be expected to be included for Emperor.

In each case, it is significant that he is shown in armour, as it is in such

that, admittedly somewhat ambiguously, he appears on most decks. On the Noblet, interestingly, he is also wearing ermine (shown by the 'pate-d'oix' on his sleeve), something that neither the Dodal nor Conver depict.

Let us return to heraldry for a minute, and again look at the shield.

Eagle

Mention of the shield was made in chapter five with regards to III the Empress. Here again we are faced with an irregularity: the eagle faces *sinister* (left), rather than the expected *dexter*. On other TdMs, this is not the case, as already shown a couple of pages back.

Whereas the Hapsburg eagle of Charles V, as common for Emperors of the period, was a double-headed eagle, the single-headed eagle was also used. Given that the Visconti-Sforza decks also depict the single eagle, it is possible that a combination of lines of influence, as well as the dual usage of the single Eagle, can still apply to Charles V.

For example, the earlier Emperor Sigismund (1411-1437 – only two generations earlier than Charles V), is shown on one depiction with two different versions of the arms, perhaps one more specifically applying to a regional crown.

Incidentally, this last mentioned and earlier Emperor (Sigismund), though another potential candidate as the individual depicted on the card, seems to lack many of the attributes that would have called him to mind to Noblet's contemporaries – only Charles V seems to evoke the charisma and universality that Charlemagne had some 700 years earlier.

In the above image depicting Sigismund, we can also clearly distinguish the Imperial raised crown above the double-headed eagle, as opposed to the non-imperial crown above the single-headed eagle shown, importantly, *dexter* –another indication that the image is likely reversed on the Noblet.

Globe

Finally, the held globe, surmounted by the cross, has the standard tripartite division of the world into Europe, Africa and Asia – with Jerusalem at the very centre. These globes, though by the time of even Charles V totally outdated in terms of *representation*, were nonetheless continued in emblematical and symbolic fashion. Perhaps one of the best I have seen, amongst the hundreds in existence, dates from a prayer book from the 13th century (though the map is at 180° relative the globe):

As to his throne... details have yet to be clarified.

V - Le Pape

Spiritual direction

Unlike our previous cards, the Pope is depicted with two other individuals: "where two or three meet in my name, I am there among them" (Matthew 18:20).

Here is the work of the Spirit undertaken in *community*.

The Pope

Let us first compare the Noblet version of the card to others of the period and to some later TdMs. It is sometimes by contrast that details emerge that may not otherwise be as apparent or obvious. Below are the cards from the Vieville, the anonymous Parisian, the Dodal, and the Conver. The Noblet fits in the centre between the two on the left and two on the right. In terms of period and region, the Vieville and anonymous Parisian date from the same time and place as the Noblet, and in terms of design, the Noblet is a TdM as are the Dodal and Conver.

It has often been claimed that the Pope is sitting. This is not, however, evident at all from any of these images. Rather, he appears to be *standing* on or within a raised platform or podium. Even the Parisian deck (second card on the left) can be seen as standing if we consider what may be taking place in all these cards: the Pope in the act of both *blessing* and *guiding*, counselling or preaching.

This aspect of spiritual counselling or directing is one that, I would suggest, is often overlooked or perhaps looked all too briefly, yet forms one of the most important functions of the religious life lived in community.

Spiritual direction serves different purposes, each of which can be seen to be an aspect of this card. Amongst the various aspects, we'll focus on those that are more visually reflected hereon.

The director or counsellor's task is to guide and instruct by drawing from the depth and wealth of a tradition, as well as by being able to tune in to the moment and speak words pertinent to both the ever shifting present and the specific individuals to whom guidance is being given. This places the individual having such a role with a responsibility of total honesty and a needed sensitivity, for the recipient or recipients of such guidance is or are also asked to have implicit trust in the advice given.

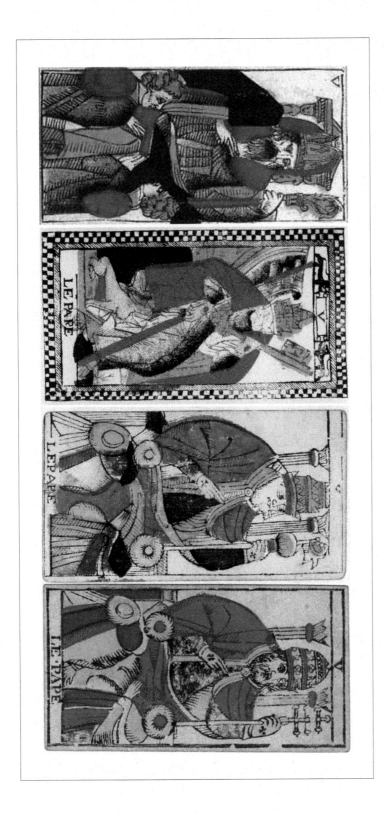

This trust requires neither blind acceptance nor lack of questioning. On the contrary, the questioning forms part and parcel of a deepening towards understanding. It is rather a trust that the spiritual direction will be provided by a person who is in position of guide very much because of his or her own inner work and familiarity with the works of others who have come before, *within* the tradition expected from the position.

It is from these considerations of spiritual direction and the explicit trust that the very modern view of the Pope's infallibility, and the long tradition of *obedience*, derives. It is the same 'obedience' that is expected when one seeks advice from experts from any other field – whether in medicine, architecture, psychology, 'life coach', or sport: in those fields we generally expect that the depth of understanding and experience will instruct us to appropriate actions.

Obedience

The 'obedience', of course, is not a blind obedience, but rather one that is balanced and instructed both by one's own past experience with previous guidance, as well as by an ongoing reflection as one's own understanding develops in the context of the specific steps one takes.

Such guidance can here be seen not only as spiritual, but also psychological. In the context of historical development, the two are not as distinct as contemporary attitudes suggest. In terms of spiritual direction and counselling, it would generally be expected that due attention be paid to the overall health of the person in one's charge, including having the person attending to their physical and emotional needs.

In the context of spiritual direction, obedience has a long established tradition, yet one that has not only been seriously questioned throughout its history, but more seriously during the Reformation and the times during which the Noblet emerged. In our post-WWII world with its attendant atrocities, and in light of some experiments undertaken during the 1960s (such as especially the Milgram experiment at Yale) the very concept of obedience as something somehow considered a virtue has taken, to say the least, a heavy battering. Whilst acutely aware of its negative value when taken to extremes, much of our social and cultural makeup nonetheless reflects a need for cohesion through obedience.

Obedience is here depicted or, rather, *implied*, on the card image not so much as obedience to rules and regulations around which a society coheres, but rather to the Pope or one's spiritual director (ie, to another *individual*) and ultimately to the precise direction and guidance the Pope gives in the context of spiritual counselling. Guidance that may, nonetheless, have various other consequences, such as abstaining from certain foods or activities, or, alternatively, *participating* in various activities and *consuming* certain foods.

The New Advent Encyclopedia makes in part the following entry under religious obedience:

> Religious obedience is that general submission [...] in order to be directed by them [one's superiors] in the ways of perfection according to the purpose and constitutions of their order. It consists [...] in a man's allowing himself to be governed throughout his life by another for the sake of God. It is composed of three elements: the sacrifice offered to God of his own independence in the generality of his actions, at least of such as are exterior; the motive, namely, personal perfection, and, as a rule, also the performance of spiritual or corporal works of mercy and charity; the express or implied contract with an order (formerly also with a person), which accepts the obligation to lead him to the end for which he accepts its laws and direction.

> Religious obedience, therefore, does not involve that extinction of all individuality, so often alleged against convents and the Church; nor is it unlimited, for it is not possible either physically or morally that a man should give himself up absolutely to the guidance of another. The choice of a superior, the object of obedience, the authority of the hierarchical Church, all exclude the idea of arbitrary rule.

It continues:

> By Divine law, religious persons are subject to the hierarchy of the Church; first to the pope [...]

Not for obedience's sake

Though I have focussed on obedience, it should be clear that this obedience is not for obedience's sake, but rather for the trust one has to place in the guidance of a knowledgeable guide on the perilous spiritual journey. Obedience, in such a case, is equivalent to being in a state of blindness and having to implicitly trust the direction one is given walking a narrow ledge above a precipice. It is not the obedience for the sake of obedience that is important, but the direction of the journey and its destination.

In the case of the spiritual guidance, the destination is towards deification, along the way acquiring knowledge of the important common landmarks one will encounter in order that not only the goal be reached, but that the journey may in turn be communicated to others seeking to similarly travel those paths.

Tradition marks these spiritual highways with consistent signposts, with obedience a guide towards these in one's travels, and the spiritual goal ever drawing us to our spiritual home – three parts ever present.

Pulpit or throne?

I must admit that over the years I have increasingly seen the various card depictions of the Pope not only as standing, but standing on a pulpit from which his oration, or his call to a crusade, or his instruction to a deepening sense for the Spirit, or his simple message of hope, forgiveness and salvation, may be given.

In all of the major churches and cathedrals I have visited in France (literally hundreds – and I must admit that I do not recall if this was also the same for *all* the Italian and English ones also visited), about half-way within what would be the centre of a congregation if the space was filled, a raised pulpit was present.

These are often quite elaborate with carvings and, of importance in understanding our image, are raised against a large pillar, with curving stairs to reach the platform, as shown here.

These images of either gilded or stone pulpits can be supplemented by literally hundreds of others of similar worth. Yet my purpose is here more to consider the card image as *possibly* presenting the Pope as standing, even with, perhaps, a cardinal and bishop or with one upholding the Gospels for the Pope from which he may read.

It is worth recalling that it is from such a place that the weekly instructions and guidance took place – even as bishops complained that, even in the 17th century at the time of the Noblet, the churches of France remained relatively empty.

Being there

Let's take one of the earlier exercises we used and take the time to vividly bring to imagination the setting of a large cathedral with numerous people, permeated by utter silence except for the graced wisdom of an oration that seems to reach each person in different ways.

How does he speak?

What are his mannerisms? Is his attention in the present, or does it seem to be in the invisible sphere? Does his blessing come from himself, or does he seem more the vehicle for a power beyond his personal capabilities?

Does he *care* for his flock as sheep, or as individual spiritual beings temporarily incarnated? Does life appear to be considered of intrinsic worth, or worthy of being deepened with living abundance *via* the grace of the spirit?

Should he be concerned with *tolerance*, or with seeking to lead others into the spiritual realms? What are *his* responsibilities?!?

Papal representation as God

Many of the images as they occur in tarot – especially forms of the Marseille – have their counterpart in other depictions. This we have already seen with other cards. Some of these strike one as bringing with them different nuances or a sense previously perhaps thought through or described, but without the full effect until seen independently. This was certainly the case for myself when I came across the following image[1] from a '*Book of Hours*: God by a Master of Morgan':

---

1   reproduced on page 27 of *The Origin of Wisdom: Mysticism*

Here we see the triple-crowned representation of God, symbolically giving, with one hand, the dispensation of the Old Testament or, rather, specifically the Tablets and hence the Torah, and with the other hand the new dispensation of Christ himself and hence the New Testament.

Note also the long strains on either side of his head, reminiscent of the Orthodox Jewish payot, with which God would have been represented if following classical sources.

This *payot*, though not as long as above, is also usually represented on TdM-type decks, including the ones shown on the page opening this chapter, on the Noblet, and even on the Cary Sheet, if we are to take the surviving partial image as being that of the Pope:

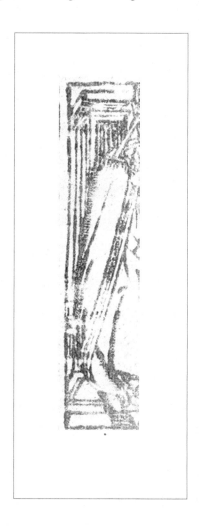

In both the image of God from the *Book of Hours* and in the Cary Sheet, he is of course seen as *seated*, though other triple-crowned representations of God can be found with neither pulpit nor throne. If for no other consideration, and if we recall that very early decks remained without titles, a triple-crowned bearded individual would certainly be reminiscent not only of the Pope, but also, and importantly, of what he signifies within the orthodox Catholic community: God's representative on earth.

As such, the Pope's authority, when properly exercised, is as what his title 'Papa' indicates: benevolent *paternal* direction and guidance.

It may again be worth considering the social dimension of the Christian context here and, perhaps, specifically given the card representation, three aspects. There is, first, the statement from Matthew (quoted on the first page) about the divine presence when two or three meet in his name; then there is the way to the Father that is by way of the Son (*Cf* John 14:6 – well illustrated in the image below); and finally the call of the two greatest 'commandments' – to *LOVE*, on the one hand, God with all one's heart, soul and mind and, on the other, one's neighbour (Matthew 22:36-40). These would, I would suggest, not only be important aspects or living impulses of any sermons ideally delivered in the name of Christianity, but also each illustrated in economy of presentation in the card at hand, and particularly well in the Noblet.

Freedom

If it can be argued that the Pope blesses and points to that which is beyond the veil of appearances, it raises our own understanding by way of faith and achieves one of the claims at times made on behalf of religion: 'religion will set you free'[2] – a statement at odds and quite contrary to the opposite claims resounding not only from the voice of Marx, but also from much of our daily experience *via* the eyes and ears of television.

At this stage, the concepts of Love, Obedience and Freedom all seem to intertwine in apparent paradox, a paradox that may perhaps be examined and unveiled by way of contrast.

So let us here place side by side the Pope and the Devil cards, and allow the concepts of Love, of Freedom, and of Obedience to play themselves out in each of these cards, each taking on differing tones and shades as the image either exemplifies, and is in turn exemplified by each of these concepts, or instead is seen to subvert, rigidify or *codify* these.

Suit of Cups, Swords and Coins

Taking the ten pip cards from the suit of Cups, and *looking specifically at the arabesque* (the floral arrangements), similarly reflect on what is taking place with Love, Freedom and Obedience.

Harkening back over some of the concepts we also looked at over the past few weeks, let us also take the pips from the suit of Coins and Swords. With the *arabesque* on the suit of Coins, how is *loyalty* playing out? and finally, with *overall design* of the pips from the Swords suit, how is *tolerance* affected or reflected in each card?

Although the above is but two short paragraphs, I would suggest taking the time to carefully look and reflect... and *note*.

Once some brief notes have been made for each of those thirty cards, let's undertake a three card setting and develop a narrative *using those*

---

2   A modification from Christ saying (John 8:32) 'Then you will know the truth, and the truth will set you free' – with the implication, in the modified version, that *religion* presents truth.

notes as an initial basis. Only from those thirty cards (ie, the pips from the suits of Cups, Coins and Swords), randomly select three cards (face down). Turning one at a time, *speak* your notes as though you were speaking to an actual person sitting adjacent or opposite you. As you begin to reach the last words of the narrative for the first card, turn the second over and *continue* the narrative without a break, as though the movement of your hand turning the card was not connected to your speaking. Similarly, as the end of the narrative for the second card is approached, turn the third card and continue the spoken narrative from your notes.

This exercise is not so much to allow the numerous nuances from the many aspects of the cards to emerge, but to simply allow those notes and reflections to begin to speak a little, and aspects directly connected with the arabesque to also appear as the narrative is spoken.

Here, the *spoken* word remains an important consideration, and with that, we return to the Pope.

Which Pope?!

We cannot for each card ask if a specific individual was intended by the depiction. What is curious, however, is that the Pope is generally depicted with beard on Marseille-type decks – something that since the 13th century had not been the case for Popes apart for few rare exceptions. In fact, the beard was something that distinguished East from West even before the great schism of the 15th century.

Certainly by the time of the Noblet, Popes had been wearing a beard as initially a sign of mourning following the sacking of Rome in the early parts of the 16th century by none other than Charles V. Yet the practice was earlier instituted, again as a temporary sign of mourning, by Pope Julius II. So which Pope? Perhaps Julius II, Clement VII, or even St Gregory (shown below).

His triple crown we have already commented on. His throne or pulpit, likewise. That there are two individuals at his feet can be seen in different ways according to whether we consider he be sitting or standing on a raised platform.

Certainly, these seem to be mildly differently represented on various decks, with the Noblet having only *one* with what is likely to be either a cardinal's hat or, alternatively, a pilgrim's hat. The other individual, on the Noblet and TdMs in general, appears with no hat.

The Pope's crosier or staff is undoubtedly one of the most changeable aspects of the card, yet the triple cross was in use long before the time of Noblet. In fact, if we look at various early cards (such as on the first page of this chapter), what is perhaps surprising is the *lack* of consistency – and to assume that the triple staff was not common even in the *16th* century is simply not the case. For example, the following panel, from the 15th or 16th century, depicts St Gregory with both triple crown and triple staff (*Cf* below).

Finally, on the Noblet and other TdMs, his hands bear crosses. Or, more precisely, his *gloves* bear crosses, these not so much as stigmata but rather, I would suggest, in emblematical *similicra* of the hands of Christ upon the hands of what is regarded as his current representative on Earth in the person of the Pope.

If there are any items that are 'missing' from the deciption, or that we may expect to have been represented but have not in fact been, they are the keys of St Peter and the Fisherman's Ring. These, however, are perhaps not only unnecessary, but their omission inadvertently serves to move the image from Pope as the see of St Peter in Rome, to Pope with broader connotations.

So, instead, we have in the Noblet a relative simplicity of design that appears to suggest an obvious reference without the need for details.

Sacraments

With the Pope we move away from individual, to relations with others clearly depicted. Also, with the Pope, we have implicitly the seven sacraments: baptism; the eucharistic service or mass; penance; confirmation; marriage; holy orders; and the anointing of the ill – each of these having significant demands and responsibilities and none could, according to views of the period, be undertaken without the implicit approval of the Church, at whose head stands the Pope.

Looking and patterns

Taking the Noblet Pape in isolation from other cards, observe what each of the three persons depicted is looking at, allowing this to become a *motion* of observation, as though a projected point follows the gaze of the first figure in the lower right of the card, to the left-hand one, to the Pope, and outwards from the card.

And finally, for some lighter (and perhaps irreverent) reflection: could the two smaller figures simply be applauding a great speech they just heard!?

This aspect of joviality can, importantly, be used to consider details that may at first be unclear, allowing for possibilities that instruct us to card details as well as more serious considerations within the card, whether or not intended.

NUMBER

Number and Tarot

There are a variety of ways in which number is directly pertinent to tarot. In the first instance, tarot used as a game has scoring value that nonetheless varies from one locality to another. With this we shall not be significantly concerned. Mention should be made, however, that the cards with the highest scoring value are the Kings, the Bateleur, the World, and the Fou – each of which is worth 4.5 (counted as 5 with a pip or other trump). Those three trumps just mentioned also determine the total score a person needs to have in order to win the game: having none of them requires quite high scoring, having the three reduces the number of total points needed.

In the game these three are termed (in French) the 'oudlers' – something akin to 'outers' or outliers – an interesting reflection as these are the three that are on the 'outer': the first, the last, and the un-numbered.

Another obvious number connection is that most cards have a number included in the depiction. Needless to say, this does not mean that very early decks had any numbering. On the contrary, the earliest extant decks lacked such. With the pips, numerals are of course redundant, and with the trumps, they are various ways by which to overcome an increase in value, one of these by simply regarding the last trump played as 'covering' and hence trumping all cards placed literally below.

What nonetheless emerges is a clear ordering that with the Marseille certainly becomes standardised – though variations do exist outside the Marseille sequence. The Noblet is amongst the earliest TdM showing this clarity of sequence or value.

Since ancient Greek times at least, numbers have acquired a range of qualities in addition to their quantitative value. At times, this may be due to simple similarities in pronunciation – an obvious and well known example from Chinese (as also in Japanese and Korean) is the number four that sounds similar to the word for 'death'. At other times, the qualities may be by association due to the particular letter used to also represent the number. Here it should perhaps be remembered that both Hebrew and Greek used letters to also depict value: Alpha (and *Alef*) also standing for 1, Beta (and *Bet*) for 2, etc.. If a particular letter ('i') or its name ('Iota' and 'Yod') also acquired meaning, then the number would inevitably come to similarly have that connotation.

Again, with this, it is not that letters were 'allocated' or *attributed* a number, but that the shape was both a letter and number – something that our modern European (or Asian, for that matter) mind finds at times difficult to consider. For example, the number '32' is *written* as 'LB' (or, rather, as 'ΛB' in Greek, and 'לב' in Hebrew), without needing to 'decipher' it, anymore than we 'decipher' it when written as '32' – or perhaps the inverse is more appropriate: in each case we need to learn to read and decipher its meaning, after which we 'read' the words or numbers as though entirely natural.

In this example, not only may a number actually form a word – in the example above, 'heart' in Hebrew – but a particular number may be written in a particular manner in order to reflect a preferred intimation.

Only three years after the imprint of the Noblet, A. Kircher publishes *Oedipi Aegyptiaci* (vol II), in which he adopts and adapts from the Greek and *allocates* numerical value to the Latin alphabet.

I note this more for a brief background as to the various uses of number in use at the time as, of course, only Roman numbering is used on the Noblet and TdMs in general (some exceptions do exist over time). This does not mean that numbering was either generally avoided or not used. For example, the designs of many cards, especially the pips, display precise geometrical pattern that the card designer would have used in order to depict the image with precision – to this we shall return in a short while.

Roman numerals

All trumps, with the exception of the Fool, incorporate a number by Roman numeral. The form used is the earlier *additive* form, whereby only addition is used: so 'XIIIVL' would be read (even if not presented in the manner normally expected) as 68. Four can only, in the additive form, be represented as 'IIII', as 'IV' is 'one-&-five', ie, six.

Using the additive form certainly also prevents any accidental errors in carving – though I personally do not think that this would have been the consideration, but that, rather, the additive form, still in use at the time, was simply the style adopted.

Visually, this also 'breaks' the trump sequence into definite parts: I-IIII; V-VIIII; etc.

Pips and Roman numerals

Perhaps surprisingly, a number of *pip cards* also show a Roman numeral numbering the items depicted – and do this clearly in the additive form[1].

Separating the pips that include Roman numerals from those that do not, note how many are in fact so numbered for each suit. Note especially the six and eight cups and its numbering in terms of the additive form.

Seeing Unintended Roman numerals

Due to the design of the Sword and Batons suits, it is also possible to see therein a variety of Roman numerals. I am of course not claiming that this was the intended depiction. Rather, the stylisation that results from the depiction allows us to see these as such. In the context of reading or reflection, such may at times be another useful adjunct.

To see this aspect, allow the attention to shift from foreground to background and the focus to 'read' the number. For example, taking the top right-hand part of the four swords (here rotated slightly), allow the focus to shift between representations of 'I' and 'II':

Though this may be a useful exercise in allowing the mind to see into imagery by allowing ambiguity and optical illusions to play a role, it may also become a temptation to assign to the image far more meaning than either intended or depicted: we may falsely attribute to dolphins or whales attributes of a fish, rather than mammal, due to apparent similarity. Though such may help understand similarities, a stepping back to what the image actually depicts is also called for.

---

1   I say 'surprisingly' as there seems to be no need to write what is already clearly presented.

Seven Liberal Arts and Sciences

The mediæval curriculum generally consisted of three and four studies: the *trivium* and the *quadrivium*. The latter included arithmetic, geometry, music and astronomy, each of which relates to number theory in some way or other. For example, music to proportion; astronomy to measure across time and space; and arithmetic and geometry being more obviously directly understood as branches of mathematics.

For the visual artist, aspects of geometry would not only have been used, but in the education of the artisan would have formed an important part of his or her training, with undoubted reference to neo-pythagorean thought and other now far more obscure references.

Much of what follows in relation to numbers will take as its basis *geometrical* considerations, with only a brief mention of the Pythagorean number 'meanings'.

In reflecting on the early development of the Marseille, we should perhaps also call to mind that a transition was similarly occurring in the world of both the sciences and philosophy (the sciences being, in any case, considered part of 'natural' philosophy at the time). One of these changes was how mathematics was to gain importance in those worlds. Descartes's works were still contemporary, and Newton was but a boy as the first of Noblet's decks from this woodcut emerged. Girard's *New Invention in Algebra* had appeared around the same time as Descartes's early works.

A little earlier, and of relevance to us, is the 1525 work of Dürer: *Instruction in measurement with compasses and straight edge*. Here is a master woodcutter instructing others in the craft, and referencing the Roman architect Vitruvius who talks about the proportions of the human body in the latter's *De Architectura* (Bk *III*).

Even if only considering the above, we are lead into questions about the influence of authors and craftspeople who reference their own skills back to a tradition that links across disciplines and into allegory and classical culture. For example, is the stance of Temperance so depicted so as to reflect, in addition to its more 'literal' and allegorical meaning, some previously unconsidered proportion?

Numbers and their relation

Number 'meanings' do not arise in a vacuum. I have already alluded to the semantic and homophonic connections that some numbers have to some words. In terms of homophony (or near homophony), each language will of course bear striking differences. For example, much is made (locally) of the New Zealander pronunciation of 'six' as something more akin to the Australian pronunciation of 'sex'. Similarly, I have on occasions when travelling misheard 'ten' and 'tin' or 'ton'. In French, the word for nine sounds the same as one of the words for new: each 'neuf' (though the latter written as 'nœuf' in old French).

With the modern increased usage of numbers also being used as abbreviations or sms-code for words, I also wonder what subliminal impact this may have as a resonance into how a specific number may be 'understood'. For example, '2' standing for 'too' (ie, 'as well'); '4' for 'for'; and have even seen street or house numbers with '3' with small decorations above the upper curve to make it look like the Sanskrit '*om*'.

Many other number words have, in English (in the following examples, but the same can be presented in other languages), similarities to other words that the meanings of the homophones may be brought to mind all the more easily to the poetic soul:

> 'one' and 'won'
> 'two' and 'too'
> 'three' and 'tree'
> 'four' and 'for'
> 'five' and 'fire'
> 'six' and 'sex'
> 'seven' and 'sever'
> 'eight' and 'ate'
> 'nine' and 'mine'
> 'ten' and 'ton'.

There are of course many other possibilities, as indeed suggested by nursery rhymes ('seven' and 'heaven', for example). These may play into how we even begin to see numbers and their relation, at times unconsciously, having long forgotten our own childhood linkages. For myself, for example, it took some reflection to recall that I once 'heard' and saw in imaginative thought a connection between the number four and buses, and the number five and cars – based on a vague linguistic similarity (in French) between 'four' (quattre) and 'bus' (car), and that cars, having a *higher* speed than buses, have a correspondingly higher number value – a strange logical sequence of thought that resulted in inexplicable number associations in my young mind. All this from the time I was about four or five years old and probably playfully manipulating similarities in sounds and order.

Based on this, it may also have been that *five* seems *lighter* and *faster* than the heaviness of *four*. Should I also have had either particular like or fear of either car or bus, such may have penetrated into my sense for the number without having had any correspondingly conscious awareness of this ever taking place (fortunately for myself, this was not the case – but we can imagine how this may be the consequence for each of us given a specific set of developing events and circumstances).

For those who are multilingual, further cross-references may also have played into number-sensitivity. For example, 'four' as meaning either *4* or *oven* depending on the language.

In addition to all this, reflection on symbolic significance may also arise as we allegorically reflect on pure numbers in various geometrical ways.

Let's do this first in the context of a sphere, and then with 2-dimensional and more familiar shapes.

Sphere and number-points

This exercise allows us also to alter our perception of many pips from simple representation to quite rich and geometrically vibrant relations. Also, and importantly, we begin to question and allow to emerge various qualitative statements about numbers in ways that make ancient statements about the same far more meaningful.

Let us begin by imagining a plasma-like or glass-like hollow sphere hovering in space. In other words, all there is is the translucent and transparent surface of a sphere upon which various points of illuminations will be added.

For this exercise, I would also strongly recommend notes and diagrammes be made. For some, the imaginative exercise may at first be somewhat difficult. If, however, imagining a rabbit and hound upon a small spherical asteroid is more comfortable than points upon a sphere, then my all means do that first – the only problem with this latter is that the nature of the animals and their specific relation may get in the way of considerations of the geometry of position-relation.

One more consideration: each point of light we'll add is to move as far away as possible from any other points already thereon. In other words, each point has mutually repelling forces to every other point.

Let's begin, and reflect on the nature of each number:

1: with a single point, it may simply move about the surface.

2: adding a second point, these quickly move in diametrically opposed positions. The movement of one point results in the corresponding movement of the other, a little like two children around a table, one moving to try and catch the other, whilst the other correspondingly compensating to maintain maximum distance. Their relative position is that of polar opposites – and we can also imagine that their position forms a polar line upon which the sphere may also rotate.

3: with a third point appearing, the former two have to re-orient themselves upon an equatorial (or longitudinal) band, arranging themselves as the points in an equilateral triangle.

With these three already, what are some of the *qualitative* differences that appear to result in their respective interactions?

4: when a fourth point is added, the equilateral triangle is pushed away from the fourth until these four points arrange themselves into the vertices ('points' or corners) of a tetrahedron. This is also, incidently, the first 3-dimensional shape that results from this exercise, and the simplest of the Platonic solids.

Again, reflecting on each one, particular relations arise that begin to acquire qualitative differences, as well as greater solidity or fixity. But let's see what now happens as we move on.

5: with five points, no stable equidistant location upon the surface is found, and so perpetual motion occurs. The stabilities of the former four suddenly gives way to motion-forces that with each jostling for equidistance gives rise to, instead, unequal relations.

6: when introducing a sixth point, however, the relative motion of the previous number can again find harmonious relation, resulting in the second of the Platonic solids, the octahedron (a four-sided pyramid under which is its reflection). Here, we have two 'polar' points on our sphere, and four points arranged as a square upon its equatorial belt.

In a sense, the polar relation of 2, the equatorial relation of 3, and the pyramidal relation of 4 are incorporated and in a new way reconciled in 6.

7 and 8 in some manner repeat the active and stabilising five and six pair:

7: with a seventh point, the form of the six is again broken to everlasting motion. Yet, with the eighth, the stability of the cube is formed.

Both 9 and 10 again result in perpetual motion, and it will not be until 12 is reached, and then 20, that stable forms again emerge.

In terms of the numbers one through ten, there is a wealth here that begins to reflect in possible *meanings* as to number theory.

Pythagorean number qualities

For the sake of considering what emerges for Pythagorean views, other considerations would also be brought to bear. One of these, and a very important one, is whether the division of a string into 2, 3, 4, 5, etc results in either harmonious or discordant sound.

One of the key references used was *via* Iamblichus's *Theology of Numbers*. Nichomacus was another source.

In any case, the qualities of the number are not narrowly fixed, any more than 'keywords' to describe a house would be. They arise out of deep considerations and reflections on the properties and relations between numbers in the context of theological and metaphysical views of reality. For example, even the numbers one and two have quite different connotations to the monotheist and the dualist-gnostic.

The *linguistic* sense played into number meaning even for the Pythagoreans: 'one' is related to Apollo in that the very similar word 'a-pollon' means 'non-multitude'. As a consequence, of course, this also resulted in the Sun, light, truth, life and a host of other of the God Apollo's qualities being reflected in considerations of the number one.

Some Pythagorean qualities for the subsequent numbers follow:

    2 - birth
    3 - knowledge
    4 - righteousness
    5 - immortality
    6 - marriage
    7 - due measure
    8 - harmonious
    9 - assimilation
    10 - memory

Obviously I have selectively chosen only one amongst many qualities each number is seen to carry by Pythagoreans. Conversely, 'marriage' is seen to be reflected in *various* numbers, not solely six.

Trumps in pips

After using tarot for some time, some numbers may become closely 'tied' to the *trump* which bears the number.

Here it should perhaps be useful to distinguish between cardinal and ordinal numbers: one *vs* first; five *vs* fifth; etc.. In the sequence of atouts, it seems that it is the *ordinal* value that is of significance, whereas with the pips, it is the cardinal.

In that sense, the Chariot is the seventh card, whereas the seven cups *has* seven cups.

Still, with habitual use, 'seven' can come to be closely seen as 'chariot-like', and these qualities applied to pips of that number. This appears to be a method of attribution that is increasing in popularity. The question that needs to be carefully considered is whether attributions that, arising from the trumps, reflect relative order, have their meaning properly reflecting cardinal attributes – whether based on geometry only, or other mathematical reflection.

In other words, if we consider the trumps as twenty-two images that have, over time, acquired an *order* and hence their respective *ordinal* number, it does not mean that their '*number*' reflections, or number attribute, are to be conversely applied to the pips. Having said this, a couple of specific trump numbers do arise as significant: Justice which, from supposedly ancient times was seen to be connected to the number Eight; and Death, having various cross-references to the number thirteen.

Geometry

A similar exercise to our earlier spherical one can be made within a two-dimensional circle. In this case, of course, the 'divisions' are on the circumference, and the points linked to make (once the third is reached), a triangle; square; pentagon and pentagramme; hexagon and six-pointed Star of David; a heptagon and two different heptagrammes; an octagon, interlaced squares and unicursal octagramme; nonagon, triple triangles, and stellar nanogrammes; and finally the decagon and its various options.

Drawing these, we begin to sense into some of the differences that manifests, and the distinctions and differences between the unicursal (for example the pentagramme), dual (for example the double-square), and different stellar forms (for example the nine- and ten-pointed stars).

Let's briefly – and only briefly – again take time with these and see what occurs in reflection.

In the above, apart from each successive point, I have only joined together every second point to generate the forms. Joining every third point or, where possible, every fourth, generates alternate shapes. For example the unicursal octagramme on the eighth circle, and the double pentagramme on the tenth.

Each of these do lead to different kinds of reflections that in turn instructs the imagination with qualitative features of numbers, which in turn affects one's understanding as to a number's attributes. It is these that may also lead to particular considerations with regards pip cards.

With these, there are two groupings that suggest themselves: on the one hand cups and coins, and on the other batons and swords. Let's look at these.

Cups and Coins

Both cups and coins are depicted as discrete implements. In other words, both of these have individual items that do not overlap in any manner.

It could be expected that their respective arrangement is duplicated, yet this is for most of the cards not the case: cups and coins are not represented in geometrically similar ways.

Of course, for the two it may simply be an easier method by which to display each pair. From the six onwards, however, quite distinct patterns emerge.

The six cups are more obviously seen as two 'pillars', whereas the six coins suggest either one of two depictions: on the one hand an upward pointing triangular pattern below which is its mirror image; on the other a central rectangular form above and below which stands single coins. In this latter form, it also calls to mind the octahedron (four-sided pyramid over an upside down one), the 'stable' shape following the perpetual motion of the five points in the sphere exercise.

With the sevens, compare how these are not only to each other, but then also to the respective fives in those suits.

The eights now 'reverse' the sense we saw in the two suits, with this time the coins being more pillar-like, and the cups showing a different kind of vibrancy. In this case, cover the top corner cups, and *see* the remaining six cups arranged in a triangular fashion – a little as for ten-pin bowling, save that in this case there are six.

The nines are each quite rich in the manner in which joining imaginary lines transforms the relative flat depiction in various perspectives, and, again, comparing each of these to earlier cards in their respective suit brings to light different geometrical aspects.

With the tens, something that may be quite unexpected occurs. By this stage we are already familiar with the ten cups. It remains, however, geometrically quite different to others in the deck. The only comparison – from this more unexpected geometrical dimension – is what occurs with the ten swords.

So let's now move to the batons and swords.

Batons and Swords

Being longish implements, both batons and swords respectively cross (except for their aces). Yet this need not be so, as other early decks reflect. In some of those decks, *smaller* figures display, respectively, batons and swords (these latter straight rather than curved) as sequences of vertically arranged images that do not intersect.

The sequence of batons in the Noblet and other TdMs shows a simple and clear progression. In fact, one only needs to look at *one corner* of the card and quickly 'at a glance' determine whether the corner has one, two, three or four batons. This is then simply doubled (because crossed with the batons coming diagonally from the other side), and add a single one if a vertical baton is also depicted – unless two vertical ones show, in which case the ten baton is represented. At most, one has to be able to *see* only four: a number well within the normal acceptable psychological visual range.

The sequence of swords is similar, save for the curvatures rather than straights. From a geometrical perspective, what is interesting is that each (curved) sword is made from a semi-circle, with the inner swords therefore *smaller* than the outer ones: *concentric* circles have formed the suit.

We had already noted their circular aspects when placing cards adjacent each other in chapter three. Here, the question that is also worth considering includes what geometry is implied by this concentricity. Though mentioned in the booklet accompanying the deck, let's also call to mind that only the ace through to five of the original Noblet deck are still in existence. The six through to ten Jean-Claude Flornoy has recreated using standard Marseille depictions consistent with the rest of the extant Noblet – for which I remain extremely grateful. It should be noted, however, that the ten-swords card *may* have been, though this would be unexpected, rather differently represented, as it is, for example, on the Bologna, with a vertically and, interestingly, horizontally but only *partially* depicted ninth and tenth swords.

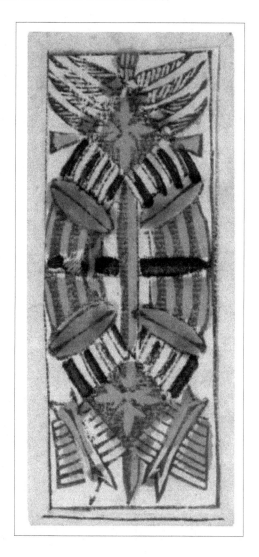

Let's have a look at another aspect of the suit of swords, for not only do circles get generated by placing cards adjacent one another, but each card is itself (again, apart from the ace), a series of circles as though 'cut' in half and pushed across until the image is formed. Below is the 'circle' from the two swords 'expanded' out.

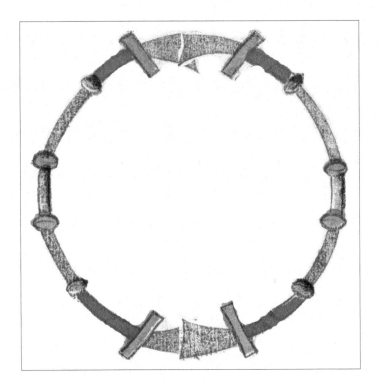

These two swords, incidentally, have not been retouched in order to make them more circular: the circle is actually there on the two-swords card, all I have done is to take the images of the two swords and place them adjacent one the other, rather than overlapping. For the above purpose, I used the image from the original Noblet.

Taking in imagination each the eight, nine and ten swords, and allowing the curved depictions to move outwards until circles are formed, note the distinctions that arise for each card... and what of it?!

Comparing now the crisscrossing sections on batons and swords, of note is that despite the same number of implements, the swords, due to their curvature, *doubles* the number of crossing for the same number depicted in the suit of batons. At least this is the case for the even-numbered cards with the exception of the ten, but *not quite* doubled for the odd-numbered implements!

The geometry between them is also distinct if we consider how the batons have a central point with an intense and abundant imagery, whereas the swords, by contrast, have *space* within their centre. Each of these considerations plays into how the one, as compared to the other, may become meaningful in a developing narrative, as can be discovered by re-visiting earlier imaginative exercises.

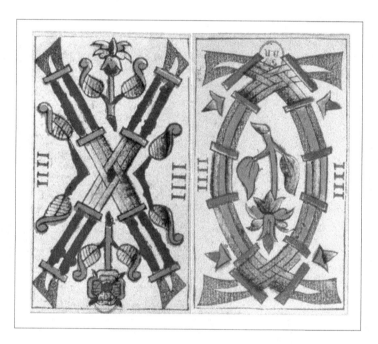

VI - L'Amoureux

L'Amoureux

It is one of the characteristics of the Marseille that, unlike a number of other decks both before and after, it unequivocally displays three persons and a winged figure with bow and arrow.

There are, however, *two* cards in the deck that display this general structure of three humans and an angelic (of whatever hierarchy) 'cherub'.

Taking both L'Amoureux and the Judgement cards, how does the interrelationship between the *people* appear to be presented? And how about between each human being and spiritual (or winged) figure?

Divine and Human Love

If the previous card in any way pointed to the transcendent, with this card we appear to be led firmly back to the earthly realm. Even if Love is divine, it seems it is not the divine love that is here depicted, but rather to focus far more on the love of lovers.

Though there are differences, as mentioned, in early card depictions, the dominant constants are twofold: the arrowed cherub or angelic being or, more simply, Cupid, on the one hand; and on the other the linking in various ways the arms or hands of a couple depicted.

What is also pretty consistent is the direction of the arrow towards what appears to be the 'younger' of the two 'women' (if they are both indeed women) who also appears to be of a similar age to the central young man.

If *Agape* (usually rendered in Latin as *Caritas*) can at times be said to be the preferred word for Love Divine, these then seem to depict its complement: *Eros*.

Let's consider briefly these two different senses of Love amongst the dominant *three* forms found not only in ancient Greek, but also used in the New Testament – and consider these three forms in light of not only the Noblet card, but also other early representations. The reason I wish to here compare the Noblet to these other forms is to highlight how, though I have just focussed our preliminary considerations on *Eros*, the image allows for multivariate reflection.

First a few brief further words on the central three concepts of Love found not only in Plato, but as central terms that have played out in European Philosophy in general and as a consequence have also very much affected our own contemporary views of Love.

Philia (φιλία), Eros (ἔρως), and Agape (αγάπη)

Let's consider for a moment the relevance of the Cupid and the arrow in relation to these three concepts of Love.

Philia and *Eros* are the two main concepts found with the ancient Greeks. The first is, essentially, friendship. It is a love for the other that has all the essential characteristics of affection as virtue, described as that felt towards an equal. In contrast, *Eros* is passion-filled and 'fierce and wild' (Cf Plato's *Phædrus*).

By the time of the Gospels and their dominance in western culture, it is no longer *Philia* and *Eros* that are contrasted, but *Agape* and *Eros*. Though *Philia* is also used in the New Testament in relation to the love between Jesus and his disciples, it finds little use therein. And, in contra-distinction to the relative paucity of the use of *Agape* in ancient Greek texts, this concept now becomes dominant.

We can see how *Agape* becomes dominant by analogy with the Sun: it sheds its benign rays upon the whole Earth. This is the same sense in which *Caritas* – later rendered as 'Charity' – derives its unconditional loving aspect.

It may be worth pointing out that both *Agape* and *Eros* can have a certain 'passion' associated therewith. *Philia*, by contrast, appears to occur without the equivalent depth of passion but rather arising as a rational quality.

Pre-empting some of the points that will arise, it is worth considering two different but in so many ways related aspects. Firstly, how can each human figure be made to represent these three concepts of love? In other words, *which* of the three figures is more a semblance of *Philia*, which of *Agape*, and which of *Eros*? Secondly, in human relations there can often occur a transition from *philos* towards *eros* and thence towards *agape*. The *eros* element here has both the potential to sexual relation as well as also to uncritical infatuation and the 'honeymoon' phase. The actual tendency into the sexual realm of course very much dependent on both one's sexual inclination as well as one's existing personal intimate relationships.

Passion struck

Looking at the cards, let's consider how and whether there is a sense for

each of those three concepts in the image as given.

Above, in order, are the Charles VI, Cary-Yale, the Visconti-Sforza, the Dodal, the anonymous Parisian, and the Conver.

If nothing else, the obviousness of the *touching* between the figures depicted should be apparent in all these images and, with this, the passion aspect.

Even when restrained – as in the Cary-Yale and the Visconti but certainly *not* the anonymous Parisian deck! – there is a sense that passion lies within the image, and is not simply *Caritas*.

Even the partial depiction of the Cary Sheet seems to display something akin to the central characters of the Charles VI image, and we can easily imagine that would the whole be found, we could reasonably expect the arrowed winged Cherub or Cupid:

Who is being struck?

Except for the first two depictions (i.e., except for the Charles VI and the Cary-Yale, in that the former's arrows appear to not be precisely aimed, and the latter's cupid has *two* arrows, one above each of the two heads), the other cards can be seen with the winged being or cupid – perhaps depicted with more precise aim than may at first glance be anticipated – with an arrow aimed towards the central person which, in the TdM depictions, we will initially assume to be the sole *masculine* figure.

If this is the case, it also says something very specific about the card and its acquired title: it is *he* that is struck with the passion of the flesh wound of the arrow.

Conjugal Love

One of the consequences that can be expected from considering the amorous relation depicted is marriage.

If the Cary Sheet (the partial image earlier shown) and the Charles VI (the first image on the previous page) can perhaps be seen as reflecting courtly Love, the Cary-Yale and Visconti-Sforza seem to already have moved to, more simply, their wedding.

In a wedding, however, there are, by social convention, at least *three* individuals depicted: the couple and the celebrant.

Below are a number of early images depicting similar aspects to those on the previous cards, although generally also depicting something more (or something different) than what is actually implied by our card imagery.

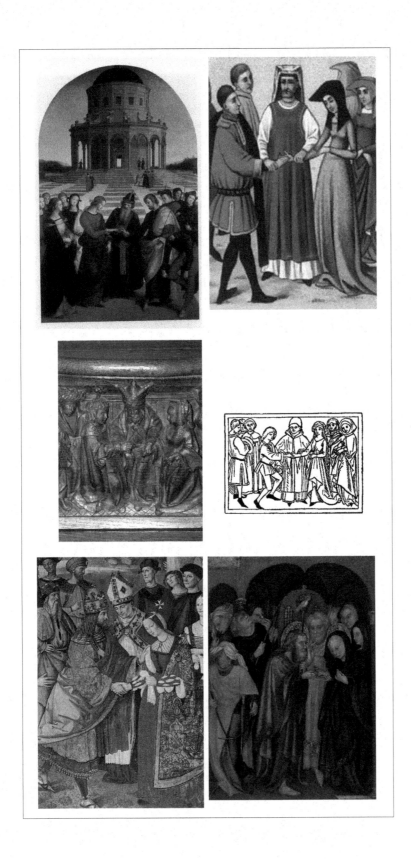

It is this sense of wedding, also thereby allowing what first emerges as perhaps only *Philia* to be transformed, with *Eros* and by the social grace of *Agape*, that seems to render the concepts of Love and the depictions we are considering with a plenitude that is worth much reflection.

Comparing our tarot card to the two images above, could it be that the figure on the *left* of the Noblet image is celebrant (or even the groom)?

Certainly, in all these (and many other) depictions, what seems standard is that the celebrant is depicted in centre, and the couple on either side, hands in the act of being joined. Yet, what is also distinct is that Cupid (on the Noblet and other tarot, rather than these images) aims his arrow towards the right of the card, where both younger ones appear to be shown.

In some ways, and to pick up the points earlier raised as questions, these aspects of 'friendship' or the love of equals (*Philia*), followed by passion (*Eros*), followed by a more universal benign love (*Agape*) can be seen as reflected, from right to left, in the three figures on the TdM. Writing this, I am not, however, suggesting that such was the *intended* depiction!

Act of marriage

Marriage, within both protestant and Catholic orthodoxy, is (and was) considered a sacred act and one of the sacraments.

Presumably, then, we also need to reconcile the passion from the arrow's piercing to the union as sacrament. The very act of union as consecration suggests that passion is the very substance that brings people in closeness together, and that the very burning desire comes not as expression of selfish abandonment, but as an overall over-shadowing that consumes with an over-riding *care* the recipient or object of our passion.

Such, then, transforms, legitimises, and continues to legitimise Love as *Eros* – which is here thereby shown as legitimate and placed accordingly. *Eros* also hints at burning desire for the transcendent, for we perhaps should also recall that the card is placed not between or adjacent Empress and Emperor or, perhaps, where it could also be expected adjacent the Bateleur, but rather following the Pope.

Cupid

Take the time to compare the various decpicted cupids – perhaps not only as shown on the previous pages, but also of the hundreds of representations across time.

One of the inevitable reflections will be of Cupid and Psyche. And here we again bridge the celestial with the Earthly realm.

Wherever we turn, *Love* brings with it a sense for the transcendent; the 'other'; desire; passion. It is accompanied by yet an ardor that, though dolorous and pointed, melts all other worldly considerations. It consumes, yet consumes not but feeds its own furnace with a spiral of the irrational that is at the same time deeply rational.

Most of the cupids depicted on the cards shown are blindfolded. Perhaps we can consider this as an indication that cupid, being blinded, will randomly strike.

Alternatively, the blindness can be considered as further evidence that the arrow is loosened not with the aim of the eye, but with the precision of the heart. Cupid, in each case, seems intent on his aim.

Botticelli depicts this aspect well in his Primavera (top, next page).

And of course, Cupid is often equated with *Eros*. The latter being

considered the Greek equivalent to the former and the Roman god of Love.

L'amoureux

"L'Amoureux", then, is quite an apt title, and not one that can be rendered as either 'the Lover' nor as 'the Lovers'. If an English rendition is to be considered, something like 'the Love-struck' would perhaps better capture the sense of the word – yet something of the ambiguous *sounding* of the beginning of the word that is used as its title would also be lost.

Last week we considered that *some* words at times give rise to reflections due to homophony – in earlier times also called the 'language of the birds' – as they (ie, the birds) mimic sounds without supposedly intending meaning.

With "L'Amoureux", we have the complement of *Eros* as Cupid in that "L'Ame" denotes "Soul", and hence calls to mind *Psyche* (incidentally, 'lame' is also a term used for 'card' or 'trump').

Cupid, on the Noblet and TdM-*I* versions, still shows his full-grown or adult status. On TdM-*II*, this is already more ambiguous and coud instead be considered more 'child-' or 'cherub-' like. What is clear, however, is that the winged figure has a precise harkening to mythological status that is also rich in both literary reference and iconography.

Card as story of Eros and Psyche

Let's take the image as representing the story of Cupid and Psyche as an imaginative exercise.

As the story as we have it derives from Apuleius in the second century in his *Metamorphoses* (or *Golden Ass*) and is picked up numerous times especially from the Renaissance, it has various forms. The form below is taken (and further shortened) from a much condensed version from ancienthistory.about.com:

> Once upon a time there was a king with three daughters. They were all beautiful, but by far the most beautiful was the youngest, Psyche. She was so beautiful that people began to neglect the worship of Venus. Venus was very jealous, and asked her son Cupid to make Psyche fall in love with a monster. When he saw how beautiful she was, Cupid dropped the arrow meant for her and pricked himself, and fell in love with her.
>
> Despite her great beauty no-one wanted to marry Psyche. Her parents consulted an oracle, and were told that she was destined to marry a monster, and they were to take her to the top of a mountain and leave her there. The west wind took her and wafted her away to a palace, where she was waited on by invisible servants. When night came her new husband visited her, and told her that he would always visit her by night and she must never try to see him.
>
> Although her invisible husband was kind and gentle with her, and the invisible servants attended to her every desire, Psyche grew homesick. She persuaded her husband to allow her sisters to visit her. When they saw how she lived they became very jealous and talked Psyche into peeking at her husband, saying that he was a monster who was fattening her up to be eaten and that her only chance of safety was to kill him. Psyche took a lamp and a knife, but when she saw her beautiful husband, Cupid, she was so surprised she dripped some hot wax onto his shoulder, waking him. He took in the situation at a glance and immediately left Psyche, and the magnificent palace she had been living in disappeared.
>
> Psyche roamed about looking for her husband, and eventually in desperation approached his mother, Venus. Still angry, the goddess set various tasks for Psyche, all of which she passed, with a bit of help from ants and river gods. At last Cupid found out what was going on, and he persuaded Jupiter to order Venus to stop her persecution of Psyche. Then they were married and ever since Psyche was made a goddess.

For our purposes, let us metamorphosise the card to reflect the whole story: the three figures as sisters, and cupid, rather than releasing the arrow, self-wounding.

Though the words in the above version lack Apuleius's fullness and subtle notions, let us use the card as snapshot to a range of not only imagery, but passion-filled engagement. It is to these that I would suggest the centrality of the card rests.

Card as two alternatives

We have been considering the image as principally that of Cupid and the passion released by the arrow, resulting in the consummation that (at least officially) only occurred after marriage.

Yet one of the common claims is for this card to depict a choice between two 'sisters' – and I use the term in allusion to Petrarch's 'Triumph of Love', in which he says:

> Behold then Theseus, captive, though so famed,
> Led between sisters twain who both met death:
> One set her love on him, he loved the other.

Here we have a different rendition – not yet the 'choice' oft claimed, but rather the tragic chain of unfulfilled Love.

Nonetheless, we can begin to reconsider the image in terms of that central man between two women, perhaps not 'choosing' in the sense of equal option, but rather being both recipient and appreciator of ardour, passion, and unrequited love.

In this case, not marriage, but rather the unconsumated passion of youth.

But of course, there is the third alternative in the image itself: that of the two women representing the opposites of vice and virtue – pairs often depicted, but admittedly somewhat differently to this form.

In the context of the card itself, the vice and virtue may be considered as the distinctions on which we earlier reflected: *Eros*, and *Agape*. And who is which?

Personal relationship

In part due to the passion that is reflected by the piercing of the arrow, this may be a more difficult card by which to distance oneself and allow its nuances to emerge of their own accord. How and where do we individually sit with such passions? How often have we genuinely felt the depth of passion and loss of reason the arrow's piercing engenders?

How do we perceive others when we observe them in that state? Do we regard it as something to be relished and savoured, or 'worked through' in order to get back to 'sanity'?

Do we feel protective of those close to us who may be struck by Cupid's arrow? and are decisions made under such power rash? or do they reflect an inner wisdom of the heart that the head would never be able to undertake of its own accord?

Is there a sense of jealousy as expressed in the story – whether as Venus or as the sisters (the step-mother and ugly sisters come to mind as equivalent)?

What of the loved one who loves a third – as in Petrach's description of Theseus – is the sense of 'loss' in part due to the sense of 'right of possession'?

How do we listen to the loved one? by our own hearts? by our eyes? by our insightful reflections?

In *Philosophy of Freedom*, R. Steiner wrote:

> It is said that love makes us blind to the failings of the loved one. But this can be expressed the other way around, namely, that it is just for the good qualities that love opens the eyes. Many pass by these good qualities without noticing them. One, however, perceives them and just because he does, love awakens in their soul.

How does this sit with our own views of *being in love*? And what could it mean to *not* be in love!?

These are questions that all inform our own relation to the manner in which this card will be seen – and to be awake to its subtleties opens one's eyes to the workings of the heart.

Revisiting pairing exercise

In chapter one, I suggested pairing the cards in order to begin to see patterns and relations.

Let's again place the trumps in pairs, using the Roman numerals as a guide, and observe whether new reflections arise. We have already noted, two weeks ago, something akin in the depiction of the Pope and Devil cards.

Here, let's note, and expand, some of the similarities between *L'Amoureux* and the *Maison Dieu* (VI & XVI).

I will first make one final suggestion as to the depictions of the three depicted individuals: the figure to the left of the card as the mother, and that to the right as the lover of the central young man.

He is then faced with a choice which is inevitably fated and already hinted at by the direction of the arrow hovering above them: to choose to remain as child with his mother, or to choose his lover and leave the maternal nest.

With the arrow of Cupid, the established maternal home (the 'tower') is blasted, the maternal crown toppled, and the arrow of love felt like a destructive thunderbolt, with the couple seemingly ejected from the former established house.

Allegory

Who or what may be considered as married? certainly the young couple. Allegorically, however, it can also represent the union of especially important arts and sciences. In the mediæval world, one such work was Martianus Capella's *The Marriage of Philology and Mercury*. There is certainly nothing within the image to indicate this specific work. This point I raise here is more that not only marriage, choice, the pangs of love, and even the consequence of the pointed arrow striking at a particular time when facing a particular direction leads to allegorical and symbolic considerations. The 'marriage' or union of any two disparate fields, disciplines or ideas may thus be allegorically depicted by an image such as this card presents.

Whilst on the one hand it is useful to maintain careful attention to the specific imagery presented on the cards, it is also noteworthy that we are increasingly moving to rich concepts and ideas that head in realms beyond the purely human.

With that in mind, let's revisit our pips and court cards in a short but expanded spread with L'Amoureux.

Five cards

Keeping *L'Amoureux* separate and already on a table-top, randomly select four cards from the pips and courts mixed together.

Allow those five cards (arranged in any manner) to begin to speak a quick narrative.

Once the narrative is spoken – the trick here is to not dwell, but speak – allow the whole separate card of *L'Amoureux* to inform and re-build the narrative.

Coloration

I would suggest that coloured paints, crayons, pencils or other colouring implements be used to render this card, presented in outline on the next page, in a manner similar to that presented in the deck.

Though tempting to seek alternate colour combinations, I would suggest that at least one copy be completed copying Jean-Claude Flornoy's own colours, these taken from the only known remaining Noblet.

With this chapter ended, we are one third of the way through this course.

Chapter 10

VIRTUE

Virtue

We have already considered quite a number of virtues over the past weeks yet, to be sure, those that have long been termed the cardinal and theological virtues have yet to be explicitly enumerated.

In the previous chapter, in connection to VI – L'Amoureux, we also had occasion to consider the various concepts of *love* in both Ancient Greek and as the 'chief' of those three virtues mentioned by St Paul: *viz.* Faith, Hope and Charity.

What is also absolutely clear with the Marseille decks is that none of these three virtues are so named. This does not mean that virtues, such as *agape* (or *caritas* or *love*) cannot be exegeted from the image given. Rather, as we peruse through the sequence of cards, unless we are already either familiar with typical representations of virtues by similar imagery or 'impose' such on the images, only three virtues are specifically named.

These are, of course, Justice, Fortitude, and Temperance. Indeed, these form not only part of the four cardinal virtues on which discourses exist since Ancient Greek times, but are the three that form what are also specifically termed the *Moral Virtues*. We'll come back to this concept in a short while.

To my reflections, I should perhaps mention that by precisely and exclusively not only showing, but *naming*, those three specific virtues, what is reflected is a very clear Christian Aristotelian world view. No matter how I may be tempted to see therein other influences, the exclusivity of the naming points in that direction.

As earlier mentioned and something that will again be mentioned, this does not mean that other virtues cannot be seen reflected in the course of tarot's imagery. Indeed, not only can such be clearly seen, but these are also consistent with especially neo-platonic views of the world with which the period was immersed. Rather, that in this game used (whether or not designed) for gambling, the specifically *moral* virtues are presented and named.

But what is a 'virtue'?

In light of considerations from St Thomas Aquinas, a virtue may be characterised as an inclination, or at least an *aptitude* and *habit*, that leads one *to act or to react* in a *consistent* and expected manner towards what is considered *good*. 'Vice' being characterised in the same manner, substituting the last word with 'evil'.

This does not help us much at first reading, yet here is a whole view of the world and human nature characterised by both a psychological viewpoint, views of underlying ethics, and even, dare I suggest, epistemological and metaphysical views – these last of which we shall return in a much later chapter.

Let's again consider that view in light of the cards.

Aptitude

Firstly, virtue reflects an aptitude.

Picking any three trump cards, what aptitude or ability is characterised? What is the image showing that I may have the capacity and ability to DO? Never mind for now whether this ability is also considered something 'good' or not – simply reflecting on what ability (or capability) is where I suggest focus be initially placed.

For example, looking at a couple of cards we have already considered, the Bateleur may be considered to have dexterous ability; and the Papesse to have the ability to focus on a portion of text and allow an intuitive insight to be reflected (*Lectio Divina*) – other aspects also come to mind, but here I simply mention considerations that have already characterised former chapters focussing on those cards.

Aptitude, appropriately applied, reflects the *character* of the person, and also whether he or she reflects well the person she or he *seeks to be*. Whether or not this is desirable will be dependent on the nature – or what are deemed the essential characteristics – of the being in question.

For example, a 'virtuous' race-horse is one that gallops well and fast. By contrast, a 'virtuous' sheep-dog has other characteristics, such as protecting and rounding sheep. Each of these reflects characteristics that we understand as 'essential' to what a race-horse or a sheepdog *is*. We could now ask what the characteristics are that are essentially human, thereby arriving at human virtues.

We may, however, also question what is virtuous for a specific individual in the context of a specific situation. For example, different 'virtues' would characterise a three-year old, compared to a twenty-one year-old, compared to a seventy-two year-old.

Similarly, one's worldly position may require that different virtues be characteristic of the *position* one occupies. And here again reflecting even on the differences between the cards we have already considered may bring to light not only differing aptitudes, but how what may be quite apt and virtuous for one character, may, by contrast, be *unvirtuous* in a different person: one would not expect the virtue of prestidigitator dexterity to be a skill used by the Pope in his capacity as Pope – though I am sure we may well imagine contrived situations in which such would be useful.

But let's consider a more general virtue and allow it to reflect a few court cards:

Take the concept of courage as an example: how would courageousness manifest in the Valet of Cups; as contrasted to the Queen of Swords; as contrasted to the Cavalier of Coins; as contrasted to the King of Batons?

The Golden Mean

By distinguishing the differences between what may be differently appropriate for different individuals, we are lead, in refletion, to similar conclusions to that of Aristotle's notion of the *mean between extremes*, and consider this as characterising virtue.

A courageous person is neither rash nor cowardly, and similar statements can be made between extremes for any characteristic that can be described of a person, or indeed animal or even of a tool.

Each virtue, within this Aristotelian understanding, has two adjacent extremes that renders the virtue unvirtuous.

This aspect is generally quite at odds with 20th century thought, itself reflecting views developed principally in English and German philosophy: we still live very much in a world permeated by Utilitarian and Kantian deontological views. Ours is a world permeated by considering the 'good' as either that which leads to the greatest amount of good (or happiness) for the greatest number; or, alternatively, by the even more pervasive Kantian view of the universalisation of ethical concepts – something is 'good' if I can imagine it applicable for all in every possible situation. Both of which lead to considerations that ethical considerations can be 'codified'[1].

---

1   a couple of years after writing the above, I discovered that Charles Taylor, in his *A Secular Age* (p707) also writes something similar, and from a perspective with which I entirely concur: 'the "code fetishism", or nomolatry, of modern liberal society is potentially very damaging. It tends to forget the

There have been recent moves in the philosophical world to re-embrace virtues (in both ethics and epistemology). What is perhaps important here is that neither the Kantian nor the Utilitarian views formed part of the worldview during which tarot arose – though it could be mentioned that the foundation of Utilitarianism occurs in Paris with the publication of Helvétius's *De l'esprit* (*Of the Spirit*) in 1759 – a year prior to Conver (working in distant Marseille on his deck), and Kant's views appearing only just over twenty years later.

Still, these things are about a century later than the Noblet, and form new thoughts and ideas that were to later radically alter Europe and its intellectual landscape, which neither the Noblet, nor for that matter the Marseille-types, nor even tarot in general, come to reflect, as the imagery is grounded in a worldview that generally reflects neo-platonic and Christian aristotelian views.

Let's focus a little more on the Golden Mean as such in terms of virtues.

Firstly, it should be perhaps considered that this does not mean the *centre* between two 'nasty' extremes. The extremes are certainly considered vices, but the virtue has room to manoeuvre within the extremities – a movement as appropriate response to the specific situation in which the individual finds him or herself. It is precisely this ability to consider appropriately the situation and move accordingly that also permits the development of the virtue *as characteristic habit* within an individual.

Each situation is unique, albeit with traits having more or less similar nuances to other situations. It is recognising the traits as appropriately similar that certainly aids in the development of the virtue. It is as much, however, recognising the *dissimilarities* between one situation and the next that tempers the virtues.

Cardinal Virtues

Let's again have a brief mention of the cardinal virtues: they consist of Justice, Fortitude, Temperance and Wisdom – in Greek (for these words do on occasions arise in tarot literature) the Areté ('virtue' or excellence) are: dike (justice), andreia (courage), sophrosyne (temperance), and

---

background which makes sense of codes: the variety of goods with which the rules and norms are meant to be realize, and it tends to make us insensitive, even blind, to the vertical dimension. It also encourages a "one size fits all" approach: a rule is a rule. One might say that modern nomolatry dumbs us down, morally and spiritually'.

sophia *and* phronesis (theoretical wisdom & practical prudence – distinguished in Aristotle's works).

It is interesting that this last is considered in some ways to not be a virtue of the same type as the others – and even Aristotle makes this claim in his *Nichomachean Ethics* (which is the better known of his ethical works – though it should be noted that, unlike Plato's works, Aristotle's are derived from his students' notebooks, in this case from Nichomachos).

Even St Thomas Aquinas talks of Prudence in a manner that suggests that, though a virtue, it is one that stands somewhat outside the other three cardinal virtues, and rather underpins or, in a sense, penetrates, infuses and imbues the other aptitudes and dispositions *as* virtues.

We shall later again pick up this virtue of Prudence when considering the Chariot, for reasons that will become apparent at the time.

In some ways, then, it may be appropriate to have this over-riding virtue remain un-named in the Marseille – though we should not thereby consider that it is not present.

In fact, if part of wisdom – or rather *phronesis* or Prudence – is directly and specifically concerned with how to best act in any specific situation, the whole *game* of tarot, as game of both chance and skill, becomes symbolic of this important metaphor for life.

But the same can also be said using a sequence of cards to allow a narrative to emerge. In other words, the *reading* becomes itself an exercise of *phronesis.*

To speak what is appropriate at the time and in the circumstance; to be circumspect; to be honest and imaginative; astute and equitable; thoughtful, insightful and empathetic.

When we reflect on precisely the act of reading, it becomes an important development for a whole list of virtues that have at some stage or other been enumerated by various people through the ages. This also implies, consequentially, that due *care* be exercised.

With regards to the other three cardinal virtues, we shall explicitly meet them in ensuing chapers as we reflect on Justice, Fortitude and Temperance.

How they came to be called 'cardinal' stems from consideration these are the 'hinges' (*cardo*[2] in Latin) on which other virtues connect.

Five Card Narrative

a) Let's develop a one page outline for a story using five cards, with a specific background scenario in mind.

A couple (let's say they are at least fifteen years either younger or older than yourself – but decide before going ahead) has recently moved into rented accommodation in a city some distance from their family, both having obtained professional work there. The accommodation is relatively small, but manageable.

Each card drawn will form the basis of a chapter – in this instance consisting of notes of only a paragraph long. For the purpose of the exercise, I would suggest allowing even the personalities of the couple to emerge as cards are drawn, pausing after each card, allowing a whole episode to arise and be noted prior to the ensuing card being drawn.

I would here recommend that the above be completed before even reading further this chapter and the second part of the exercise, so as to really allow for the *narrative*, the *story*, to set the tone.

b) *After* the five cards have been drawn and notes made, also note what particular characteristics have emerged for each individual. What *virtues* do they seem to reflect? is one more considerate than the other? what about loyal? or honest and truthful? is one more sceptically oriented? religious? do they seem to share much in common? and what they do share in common, is it apparent? is it merely superficially similar?

Again, I would suggest making notes.

What seems to drive or motivate each of them in their responses to the outer world?

What do they individually enjoy doing without their partner? what do they individually enjoy doing *with* their partner? And of their partner, what small thing does each find so appealing and likeable – and what so frustratingly infuriating?

Again, I would suggest not only making notes, but completing this prior to continuing to move to the third part of this exercise.

c) Now for the reflective part.

---

2   *cardo*'s similar beginning to *cor* (heart), and to *cordo* (rope) should also be noted, especially in reflections on virtues.

Going over your notes in reverse order (with, I would suggest, either a different coloured pencil or, if using electronic text, selecting the text and altering its colour or underlining it), pick out each small element that reflects your own past or present personal situation. I would suggest doing this twice.

With a different colour (or italicise), again select each element that this time reflects either relatives' perceived lives, or your own parental home when growing up, or friends' or neighbours' perceived relations.

With a third colour (or making it bold), select passages that seem to reflect dreams, hopes, aspirations, concerns or fears you may have had in fantasy about possible relationships.

d) If the five cards have been put away, I would suggest to place them sequentially, and re-reading the story outline and looking at them a second time, to retell the story outline afresh, allowing those additional insights to cast their influence.

How has the story been altered in any way? has their personality and characteristics become either more or less caricatured? or, if not caricatured, accentuated or attenuated? do they now seem more living as separate fictional characters? or less so and more as very much part of one's own immediate personal life?

It is perfectly acceptable to make use of one's personal life experience be part of the exercise. After all, this is what forms the basis for much of our personal understanding – whether by having lived it, or by empathy and vicariously experiencing what it 'may be like'. There are, in any case, numerous situations that we may only experience during this life by empathy, imagination, and reflection.

These form part of the practical and personal repertoire of lived life from which we may draw.

The exercise may also highlight the importance of personal situations that may emerge in the context of a reading: to recognise one's own personal situation, and allow it to be worked through (at times, and for some, this may also require the assistance of others expert in this field as professionals), makes for important self-knowing. As inscribed at the temple of Apollo, *Gnothi Seauton* – know thyself.

Gnothi Seauton and Virtue (areté)

In fact, the very concept of virtue implies an awareness of one's peculiar skills and being. Jaeger, in *Paideia: The Ideals of Greek Culture*, writes:

> The Greeks felt that areté was, above everything else, a power, an ability to do something. Strength and health are the areté of the body; cleverness and insight the areté of the mind.

If there is one key characteristic about virtue, it may be that it focuses our attention on not only what is possible, but what is *appropriate* for a given situation (located in time and place for a particular social situation) involving a specific individual in relation to others.

In that sense, by reflecting on each specific situation, its own virtue – the mean between excess and deficiency – may be discovered.

Reflecting on the story written in the last exercise, excesses, deficiencies or omissions may perhaps be perceived. These reflections enable a better sense as to what the story that has its own virtue may become with virtuous applications.

I have at times wondered if Robert Southey's story of the Three Bears (later retold as 'Goldilocks and the three bears') did not have an Aristotelean influence. In any case, it is this 'middle' concept that reflects virtue: neither too hard nor too soft, neither too large nor too small, neither too hot nor too cold, neither too high nor too low.

We can well imagine each trump presenting excesses (or overdoing it) as well as deficiencies (or simply not doing it sufficiently). In the context of a reading, it is not simply whether a particular card emerges, but also its further interpretation: it being read as either presenting a situation in which what is depicted is in excess, deficient, or 'just right' – in this last instance considered, therefore, virtuous.

The 'just right' will of course depend on the situation and context.

Golden Mean - and cards

Below is a red line. The task is to place a mark thereon that divides it into two harmonious parts, the only 'constraint' is that the mark made is not to be in the centre (nor appear to be in the centre).

I would suggest to take a separate (and blank) piece of paper and draw thereon a line ten units long (whatever unit you prefer, whether it be in

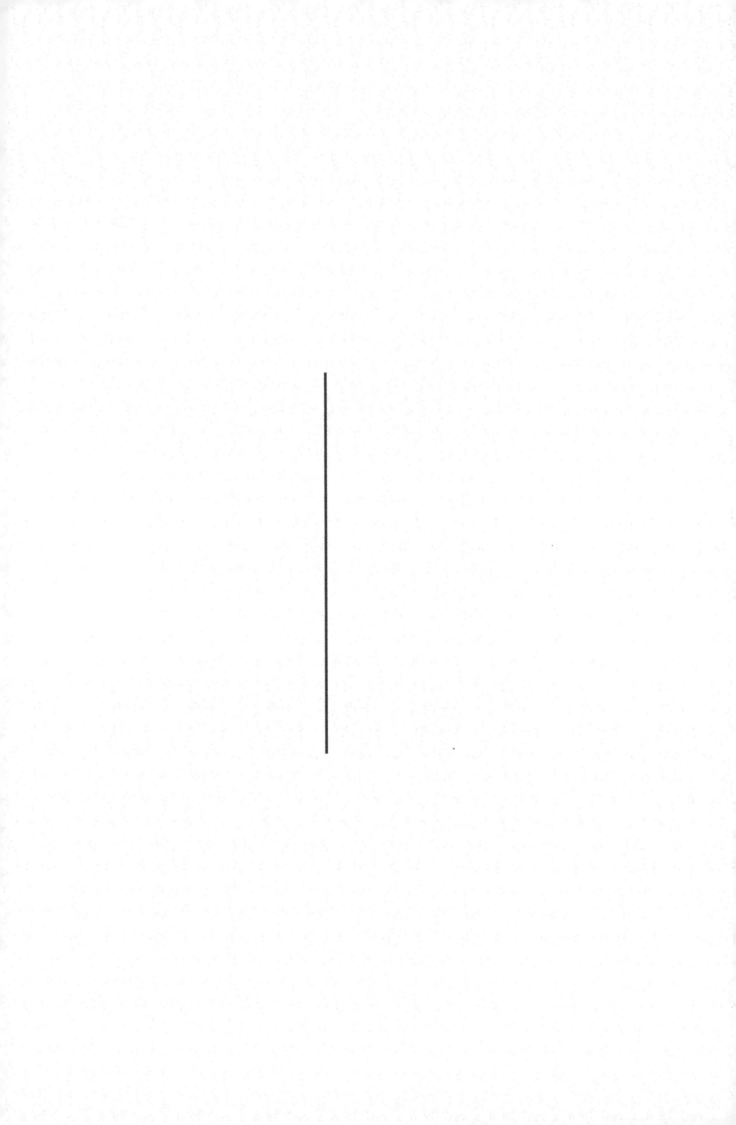

centimetres or inches). Hovering the point of a pencil back and forth until the location seems right, mark the line.

As I will shortly make a comment about whereabouts on the line each person is likely to have marked it, I would suggest doing it prior to reading any further.

This division of the line into two harmonious parts is the mathematical (or geometrical, to be precise) golden mean. It divides the line in such a way that the relation between the smallest to the largest part is the same proportion as the largest to the whole undivided line.

For most of us, even if we have not done this before, the mark made on the line will be between six and seven units, more likely closer to the six. The approximate value of the golden mean of the ten unit line will be just before the 6.2 measure (again, whether in centimetres or inches).

For the master craftsmen who worked on the cards, the golden mean, and how to obtain it easily with ruler and compasses, would have been known, as would its approximate value – also approximated in the relationship between adjacent numbers in the Fibonacci sequence, and hence in the *numbers* found in that sequence, including 1, 2, 3, 5, 8, 13, and 21. Given the total number of trumps, its 'golden mean', ascending, would be card XIII or Death, and *descending* it would be card VIII or Justice.

Pips and the Golden Mean

But let's consider the golden mean – of neither too little, nor too much, but just the right and sufficient amount – in the pips.

Firstly, if we place the pips, one suit at a time, sequentially, we can observe that near the lower end there possibly isn't much (or many implements) depicted, whereas at the other extreme is (or appears) overabundance.

It may be, in some context, that either of those is in fact the appropriate and virtuous quantity. Simply looking at the cards, however, we can also grasp a kind of harmonious or virtuous amount a little over the half-way point. For myself, I tend to see this in the six and the seven – precisely those numbers that cleave to the golden mean.

This can provide another aspect of seeing the pips (in terms of their number): there is an optimal quantity that, when reached, provides an optimal quality. Less, there is felt deficiency; more, the overabundance

can become burdensome.

In terms of the value of the number of the golden mean (ie, between six and seven as mentioned above), I personally find it highly interesting that the two cards that in some manner reflect the 'highest' of the virtues held by Christian and Greek thought – namely Love (the theological virtue discussed in the previous chapter, *agape* or *caritas*) and Wisdom (the chief cardinal Greek virtue, *sophia*), are also numbered around this golden mean.

As to how and why wisdom is here mentioned as reflected in the ensuing card of the Chariot will become apparent in the next chapter.

Areté and eudaemonia

What does it mean to live the good life?

First and foremost it would require the practice of virtue.

For the card player, this would mean not cheating; playing prudentially; acknowledging, in all this, the effects of providence; and trusting that similar character traits would be held by others.

In fact, the very game of tarot seems to also reflect much of worth of Aristotelian ethical and political views: one never plays by oneself, but in communion with others; the dealt hand shows the operation of fate; the virtuous play reflects bravery, temperance, and just play, all under the impulse of prudence; and the whole has meritorious qualities of social contact.

Areté (virtue) does not have to be explicitly mentioned in the trumps, for it is reflected therein by the mere balanced resolve of those cards we have already considered, and all others.

Even if, in this early part of the 21st century, we are still very much under the (fortunately diminishing) influence of Kantian and Utilitarian ethical thought, the view that we possess virtues, and that they may be developed by exercising each of them, was common enough at the time of the Noblet.

Perhaps a question could be: which card or cards *do not reflect virtue(s)*? If any, how is their character distinct to what a virtue depicts?

Coming up

Thus far, we have approached our study by weaving back and forth from trump to other considerations reflected, such as the pips, court cards, or even this one on virtue. Over the next six chapters, we shall focuss through the trump sequence from VII the Chariot until we reach XII Le Pendu.

One of the consequences is that perseverance will likely be required as normal mid-section apathy can also sneak in. At the very beginning of the course, I suggested that a regular study period be adopted. I am confident that those who have so adopted such a rhythm have already found it of benefit – this is likely to become even more pronounced over the next ten weeks.

In preparation for the next chapter, I would suggest obtaining a few sheets of tracing paper or, failing that, some sandwich-wrapping paper (or similar partially see-through paper).

VII - Le Chariot

The Chariot

Let's begin by having a careful look at the chariot:

The above image is a copy of the card with which Jean-Claude Flornoy had to work, from which he created the deck we now have in our hands.

But I'll repeat my opening statement: let's have a look at the *chariot*. Not the horses, not the charioteer, simply the chariot.

It has often been claimed that such a chariot would not be able to move due to its wheels. I beg to differ on this: if drawing a chariot front-on, then it is pretty much how the wheels will appear unless the artist is able to render perspective accurately – something that the history of art describes as only coming to be developed in Europe around the same time that tarot develops. We should not therefore expect clarity of perspective in a context in which such is still developing and also, importantly, when such details are generally not significant.

This is perhaps a good time to consider each card from a sense of perspective-drawing, for none appear to display this skill: in fact, in these cards perspective is usually achieved by one means alone – that of overlap. In the context of this card, as an example, the horses are presented as closer to the viewer in that they hide the lower portion of the chariot, which itself hides the lower portion of the charioteer. Artistic techniques such as the perspective point-of-horizon (also called the *vanishing point*), as well as that of relative size, both seem to be absent.

Imagine the chariot (without horses or charioteer) facing you as in the card image. What would be apparent includes its frontal section – and part of its side wheels. On the next page (to avoid the image being noticed prior to the above considerations) I have included an image of an etruscan chariot nearly front-on, and a replica of a Roman (non-war) chariot more side-on.

With *only part of its wheels* being visible, the drawing is artistically correct – though clearly not in perspective.

The total lack of perspective is also presented by the relative size of charioteer and horses: the torso and head of the former is the same size as that of each horse from hoof to head. Even the most midget of horses stands taller – yet we generally appear to accept this as appropriate representation for the card. It is, again, the symbolic representation that seems of greater note, rather than its accurate artistic rendition[1].

In a similar vein, the surface of the Bateleur's table is represented as tilted, and from which the items thereon are certain to slip, yet, we

---

1   the other manner in which to view the relative size is, of course, as if the chariot carried a giant figure, such as, for example, Pallas Athena – to which we shall return.

can also see this as a reflection of poor artistic rendition, re-focussing our perception to its symbolic or intended image.

This aspect of both carefully looking at the image as presented, as well as seeing it as indicative of the artistic style, bears important consequence. Firstly, the apparent depiction of its impossibility of movement (an aspect of the first part: looking at the image as presented) is mitigated by its explication in light of what a frontal view of a two-wheeled chariot would actually look like. Similarly, we should not infer from the relative size of horses and person that the latter is somehow from the race of giants – whether as Gigantes or Titans (nor, for that matter, the horses from the realm of miniatures).

So to what could the card have possibly referred?

Chariots

The ancient world is of course filled with chariots of various types depicting, amongst other things, two types of representations.

One type of chariot represents the means by which to travel into the spiritual realms.

Here, though the visions of Ezekiel and the 'fiery chariot' come to mind, the image is quite distant from our trump depiction. A more appropriate similarity would be the vision of St Francis rising in a Chariot as seen by some of his followers (below).

What is at the very least consistent in this image are the two horses, the type of chariot, and the apparent absence of reigns.

Even here, however, there are distinct and significant differences. For one, *our* charioteer appears to be armoured, crowned, and bearing a staff (or equivalent).

This is far more consistent with the *second type* of chariot: renditions of triumphal representation as depicted, for example, on coinage (and other places, such as the platter depicted below), indicating rulership of some kind.

Here also, incidently, the horses are proportionately much smaller than warranted, and in this and many other cases, shown in opposite directions (without implying tension).

This immediately calls to mind the *third* form of representation, closely connected, in any case, with the second: that of *procession*,

whether from a successful campaign, or, alternatively, of the processional floats of various carnivals.

There is in our card image something that is reminiscent of aspects of a representation of Minerva, which is none other than Pallas Athena (Παλλάς Αθηνά) – goddess of war as well as of wisdom, borne armoured and represented with a spear. She is also, interestingly, connected to the horse (and chariot) as Athena Hippeia (Αθηνά Ἱππεία).

A number of relevant images here come to mind and a quick online search for further information may be appropriate. Below is, amongst others, Francesco del Cossa's (15th century) Triumph of Minerva/March[2], with Minerva with spear seated atop the chariot. What is also of interest here is the relative size of the horses to not only the figure, but also the surrounding people: clearly they are not to proportion!

---

2   from Ferrara. Other Triumphs, such as that of Apollo, do not correspond as well to the image of the tarot Chariot – though we could also consider this card image to stand for representations of Triumphal procession in general.

The 'Missing' Canopy

What is of course also clearly different in the above imagery is that none of the ones I have shown have a canopy. In fact, canopies are relatively rare in chariot representations in Europe – though relatively common in Assyrian, Hindu and Chinese depictions (though in these there other details that remain distinct from our trump image). All this shows, I would suggest, that the common usage of chariots will inevitably also lead to its frequent representation in art and symbolic imagery.

The fully canopied chariot seems to lead us to consider it more as of a full-blown carriage – yet the standing charioteer retains his status as princely and triumphant warrior.

There are two dominant considerations that would have been brought to mind and well-known. These still have their frequent usage in, on the one hand, the work of the Catholic Church; and, on the other, works referencing Plato.

Both of these touch on distinct aspects: the first to the virtue of wisdom (in its various guises); the second to the tripartite division of the human being.

Wisdom

Following its earlier description from its 1755 edition, the recent edition[3] of the *Catechism of the Catholic Church* describes (section 1806) the cardinal virtue of Wisdom as the *auriga virtutum*: the charioteer of the virtues:

> Prudence is "right reason in action," writes St Thomas Aquinas, following Aristotle. It is not to be confused with timidity or fear, nor with duplicity or dissimulation. It is called *auriga virtutum* (the charioteer of the virtues); it guides the other other virtues by setting rule and measure. It is prudence that immediately guides the judgment of conscience. [...] With the help of this virtue we apply moral principles to particular cases without error and overcome doubts about the good to achieve and the evil to avoid.

It is in large part the appelation of wisdom as the 'charioteer of the virtues', as well as the above description (or similar ones) that leads some amongst us to see in this card the otherwise unreferenced cardinal virtue of wisdom.

This is in part further 'supported' by considerations of wisdom as incorporating *providentia* (or considerations of what is coming from the future); *memoria* (or considerations as to what is pushing from the past); and *intelligentia* (or an understanding of the principles at work in the present).

There is, in this, a striking resemblance to what Cicero (Bk II:53) also mentions – though without any reference to chariot imagery:

> Prudence is the knowledge of things which are good, or bad, or neither good nor bad. Its parts are memory, intelligence, and foresight. Memory is that faculty by which the mind recovers the knowledge of things which have been. Intelligence is that by which it perceives what exists at present. Foresight is that by which anything is seen to be about to happen, before it does happen.

There is, in this tripartite discussion of wisdom (though the term is single as *sapientia* for Cicero – standing for both *sofia* and *phronesis* – something distinguished in the Greek, but that the Latin renders with the single term), already consideration that perhaps other than simple horses and charioteer are represented.

If wisdom is the charioteer of the virtues, then it stands to reason

---

3   2nd edition, DoubleDay, 1995

that the horses (and the chariot itself, perhaps) in some way can be seen to represent those virtues. And yet they don't, for they are separately represented. So in this case, the threefold aspect (charioteer and horses) stands for its own tripartite aspect with, perhaps, *intelligentia* as charioteer and the past and the future the two driving forces.

And here we are lead straight into Plato's distinct, but now increasingly related (and trust this will be apparent with a little reflection), considerations of the tripartite human being.

Chariot imagery in the Phaedrus

There are a few passages from various of Plato's texts with which, I would suggest, someone interested in tarot should probably be acquainted. The Phaedrus is one of these (my emphasis):

> Of the nature of the soul, though her true form be ever a theme of large and more than mortal discourse, let me speak briefly, and in a figure. And let the figure be composite – a pair of winged horses and a charioteer. Now the winged horses and the charioteers of the gods are all of them noble and of noble descent, but those of other races are mixed; the human charioteer drives his in a pair; and one of them is noble and of noble breed, and the other is ignoble and of ignoble breed; and the driving of them of necessity gives a great deal of trouble to him. I will endeavour to explain to you in what way the mortal differs from the immortal creature. The soul in her totality has the care of inanimate being everywhere, and traverses the whole heaven in divers forms appearing – when perfect and fully winged she soars upward, and orders the whole world; whereas the imperfect soul, losing her wings and drooping in her flight at last settles on the solid ground-there, finding a home, she receives an earthly frame which appears to be self-moved, but is really moved by her power; and this composition of soul and body is called a living and mortal creature. [...]

> As I said at the beginning of this tale, I divided each soul into three – *two horses and a charioteer*; and one of the horses was good and the other bad: the division may remain, but I have not yet explained in what the goodness or badness of either consists, and to that I will proceed. *The right-hand horse is upright and cleanly made*; he has a lofty neck and an aquiline nose; *his colour is white*, and his eyes dark; he is a lover of honour and modesty and temperance, and the follower of true glory; he needs no touch of the whip, but is guided by word and admonition

only. *The other is a crooked lumbering animal,* put together anyhow; he has a short thick neck; he is *flat-faced and of a dark colour,* with grey eyes and blood-red complexion; the mate of insolence and pride, shag-eared and deaf, hardly yielding to whip and spur.

Here we have one of the clearest written images of the chariot card. It may be worthwhile, before further comments, to re-read the last paragraph quoted and specifically look at the Noblet depictions. I use the plural, in that we can see that though Flornoy clarifies the image, the precision of his usage of colour appears to inverse the dark and light horses. In the original, the one on the charioteer's *right-hand*

side (ie, to the left of the card) faces the direction of movement and is depicted as *lighter* in colour, whereas the darker one's body (and therefore legs) is to the charioteer's *left*, with the horse's body facing the 'opposite' direction to the common gaze of all three figures. The result, though, again, accurate in terms of colours applied, inverses the apparent light and dark horse locations on the card.

Plato's *Republic*

Plato also discusses the tripartite aspect of the soul with perhaps even greater clarity - but without the imagery of the chariot – in the *Republic* (Book IV). Therein, and unlike the Phaedrus in which the distinctions are between the *logos* (or intellect) driving – or being driven! – by *thumos* (or emotions) and *eros*, he distinguishes between the intellect (*nous*), the passions (*thumos*), and the appetitive (*epithumia*).

In any case, as reflecting a three-fold aspect of the human being, we are lead to considerations as to how our thinking relates to our emotions and our will – to put it in more modern terms.

Precisely using Plato's imagery and looking at the Chariot card, we may begin to also consider how our own passions and appetites drive us.

We may also consider how the horses are moved by not only what lives in them by habit but also by what comes from the future.

In all this, the charioteer seems very much at their mercy. Yet a charioteer who controls not his horses seems unlikely to be able to stand, or to stand with ease, as he does.

The Future

This may be a useful place to pause for a while and consider an overall tension between various types of tarot readings.

I have already mentioned the reading as narrative – or story – that may guide and inform to bring insights into a situation. A direct consideration between 'knowing' and 'doing' needs to perhaps also be considered.

For some, it will be deemed impossible to actually foretell the future due to it not being as yet formed. Others will see in the future something akin to the past. This does not mitigate against human freedom, but can rather be seen as an observation as to what (for the past) has occurred or (for the future) will take place.

The 'difficulty' with the relation between foresight into the future and freedom becomes only too apparent, however, if someone was in fact able to clearly see a specific situation that they also had the direct power to affect.

If a situation is accurately 'seen', then there is another aspect that becomes of importance: the knower is faced with utterly relinquishing genuine hope to alter the future as perceived to be occurring.

The alternative view is often described such that the future 'perceived' is the *likely* development given current impetus and inertia, and that this may be altered by either active engagement by any number of people or by other factors (such as, for example, a natural event like unexpected rain).

These two views related to perceptions of the future are relatively commonly held.

There is perhaps another (or third) consideration that can be seen to reflect aspects of both of these. In part, there is a 'pull' by the future (similar in part to the Aristotelean *final* cause), working as equivalent force to the 'push' from the past (similar to the Aristotelean *effective* cause).

In the image of the Chariot, the concept of these causes can perhaps be seen as the two motivations to movement: the horse that sees the homestead may be moved by its 'pull'; the other by the 'push' of the whip.

In a reading situation, the motivation may be to – amongst other considerations – either try to know how the future is panning out or, alternatively, to see how to best shape it. These may be regarded as two and distinct motives. Both seek to *understand*: the one, by seeing, becomes better 'prepared'; whilst the other, by shaping, becomes willing co-creator.

Perhaps two characteristic terms may be applied to distinguish the one from the other: the first engages by thought; the second by action. And yet, both are supplementary: one answering 'what is going (or is likely) to occur?'; the other 'what am I to do?'. These are questions we all face as well as reflect upon with the assistance of various tools and skills – from keeping informed about local or international daily matters by means of various media, through to meditative practice and an ever keener sense for both the needs of others and our own.

Drawing the card by tracing

Before doing what I consider one of the most important exercise with this card – *being* or *becoming* the charioteer, let's pay absolute careful attention to the card's details and also face what Jean-Claude Flornoy faced as he recreated the deck we now have.

Firstly, observe the number of colours used on the original image. Then, using the tracing paper and the image of the Noblet I presented on the first page of this chapter, trace only the black lines – the woodblock 'outline', in other words. I'll call this 'sheet 1'.

Now for the 'stencils'.

Using a separate piece of tracing paper for each colour, place the sheet over your sheet 1, decide which section will be of that colour (be guided by the original and the Flornoy version), and re-draw the outlines that will contain the colour. Repeat for each colour.

At the end, you will have a page of pencilled outlines (sheet 1), and pages that only outline sections that will take specific colours.

The Flornoys have used this method to create the hand-finished atouts-only version of the deck, and the stencilling method can also, in part, be seen in the ATS Newsletter from December 2006: newsletter.tarotstudies.org.

To complete the task, either colour each separate transparency with the specific colour in the relevant place (at the end all sheets can be super-imposed and looked at with bright light behind) or, if more daring, cutting out the sections that require colour will prepare these as stencils.

Sheet 1 can be blackened on the reverse, then placed on a sheet of paper. Carefully going over the line-work will reproduce the outline thereon. The stencils can then be overlaid one at a time, using a paint-brush to paint their colour to the card being created by this process (ensure each layer is dry before proceeding to the next).

Completing this should give a sense for not only the details of this card, but also the process by which cardmakers worked. The stencils also give an indication that, after various applications, the overall sense of the image is to a fair extent 'lost' to whoever has this task.

Being the Charioteer

Have another careful and full look at the card and then, in active imagination *become* a charioteer, and observe, through your own eyes, what is seen. Both the horses and yourself are looking in the same direction – at what?

In that position, what is the relation between the horses and yourself? How do they 'decide' to move – and at what cadence?

Observe the canopy – what is happening to the cloth on its sides? Observe the floor of the chariot, and the inside of the front.

Look at each horse – what appears to be characteristic differences? Is one more temperamental than the other? are they both calm and responsive? do they seem young or aged? at this time, tired or full of energy needing to be spent and released?

Similarly, with the state of the chariot itself, does it appear to be in a good state and have all the merits of strength and flexibility of something new, or could it do with a service and some repairs?

How about yourself as charioteer at this time: have you travelled far? or are you in a procession or carnival? how do others look upon you?

Does the position you hold reflect awe and/or severity? where are you going?

And why the crown?

How does being in the chariot compare to being a cavalier in each of the four other suits?

The Shield

At the front of the chariot is a 'shield' in which are the initials 'I.N': i.e., Jean Noblet (remembering that 'I' and 'J' were indistinct until recently).

This is generally one of three cards used to identify the *atelier* or workshop in which the deck is made – the other two cards being the Two Coins (or Deniers) and the Two Cups. In more recent times, identification details on the Two Cups card has been dropped, but the other two cards remain as useful identifiers – sometimes in distinct ways. For example, the 20th century Grimaud deck has the publisher (Grimaud) on the Two Deniers, and the person taking responsibility for its design (Paul, or perhaps Saul, Marteau) on the Chariot (as 'SM'). This aspect is seen in most, but not all, TdMs.

Though undoubtedly significance can be made within the instance and context of a specific reading, at other times it is probably better understood as simply signifying the designer's initials.

Despite this, some tarot books present the initials as though standing for far more than the history of card design warrants, namely: simply a small and faint recognition and acknowledgement of individualistic trademark.

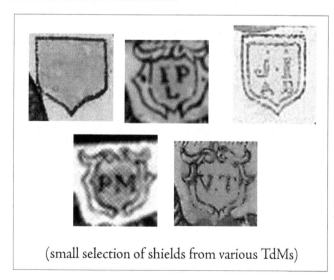

(small selection of shields from various TdMs)

But whence the design?

Despite all I have said, there is much about the basic design of this card that remains incomplete. The overall pattern can certainly be seen to echo the works of Petrach or Fracastorius – but never adequately. If the overall design is considered, I am left to wonder how close to some common source are much later decks such as the Piedmontese and Milanese Dotti. And the staff... is it staff, spear, or sceptre?

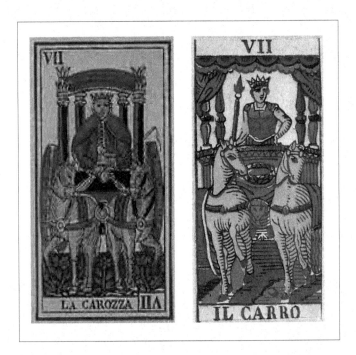

VIII - JUSTICE

Justice

There is a severity to Justice, and perhaps one that is more poignant than may at first appear. Perhaps a quote from a modern author will suffice to bring to mind an aspect we tend to overlook:

> Once again, the legal code and its practices provide a window into broader movements of culture. Think of the horrifying description of the torture and execution of a man who had attempted regicide in mid-eighteenth-century France, which opens Michel Foucault's *Surveiller et punir*. It's not that comparable horrors don't occur in the twentieth-century West. But they are now seen as shocking aberrations, which have to be hidden. [...] It's with shudder that we learn that parents used to bring small children to witness such events when they were offered as public spectacles in earlier times.

Charles Taylor Sources of the Self, 1989, p.13

Am I, however, even justified in invoking such atrocity with Justice in front of us? Am I not here confounding legal codes (or Law) with the concept of Justice which, since ancient times, has been considered one of the key virtues?

Legal codes or laws are drawn-up, however, to supposedly clarify what is just and enable its application to all citizens. Yet the question also remains for each and any legal code or law enacted (whether enacted by decree, act of parliament, or other means): Is it *just*?

For the question to make any sense whatsoever implies that no matter how closely a particular law may appear to be just, its very *justness* rests outside its codification, and instead on something for which we may develop specific sensitivity.

To be sure, this neither precludes nor excludes legal aspects or the law in general. Rather, these are ideally reflective of the concept of justice... and when they are not, there are (or perhaps, I should say, there *should be*) calls to have the law amended to reflect a more just position leading, hopefully, towards a more just society.

Key symbols

There are two principal symbolic or, perhaps more appropriatey, *emblemetical* representations of Justice which have formed part of her allegory since early times, and a third that has become significant as a consequence of a change that occurred somewhat around the time tarot emerged.

The two common symbolic emblems are the sword and the scales – or, to be more precise, the Sword of Justice and the Scales of Justice, yet neither of these were generally present with either *Themis* or *Dike*, nor with the Roman *Justitia* emerging from those former Greek allegories. There are some representations of *Dike* with the scales, and *Justitia* ascends to become the asterism of Virgo, but sword and scales as standardised representation appears to emerge around the same time tarot develops.

The Sword is generally considered not only representative and symbolic of power, but also, very specifically and especially when considering its forms in earlier times, of *punishment* – in this case the punishment of 'evil doers'.

The scales generally call to mind *equality*, and here the implication is that justice will compensate (or equalise a loss or reward) in equal measure to what has transpired. The 'equality', of course, interpreted in vastly differently valued forms. For example, the breaking of a king's finger would have been considered of vastly superior value to the breaking of a peasant's.

Hence, and in part, Justice is not hoodwinked or blindfolded. Though the blindfold emerges a little earlier than the Noblet (around the 1500s), it is rather its opposite dimension that is important: Justice needs to be able to really see the situation in order to respond with appropriate effect and justness. I have at times wondered if the blinding of Justice may have been introduced with the opposite intent to the manner in which we now consider it – a kind of jest that was quickly transformed.

One of the earliest blindfolded Justice I have seen comes from the *Ship of Fools* produced in Basle in the late 15th century (below).

Personally, I vastly prefer, in any case, the image of Justice as we have it on the Noblet and tarot in general: she has open eyes and able to ascertain what is to be seen and perceive the circumstances in its individualised context.

Admittedly, and as mentioned earlier, the blinded figure was also becoming relatively common at the time of Noblet's creation. Within a decade of the deck, Louis XIV had issued a bronze medallion that depicts on one side his own portrait, but significantly on the other Justice with blindfold.

Although I have stated my preference for *Justitia* to be without blindfold, there is a case to be made for its opposite. It could be argued that Justice ought to consider the merits of the situation without looking as to whom it pertains, and hence, her blindfold focuses the attention without regard to social status or personal favour – a common occurence that would be far more apparent in former times than these days. In the development of the blinded Justice, I do not want to give the impression that the change was capricious. For example, in *On Isis and Osiris*, Plutarch writes 'in Thebes there were dedicated statues of Judges wanting[1] the hands: whilst that of the chief-judge had also the eyes closed, showing that Justice is above bribes, and not to be moved by prayer'.

Seeing into the situation

When we looked at Ⅲ the Empress (chapter five), we observed that both herself and Justice look directly ahead. In the case of Justice, she appears to tower over us (or at least we seem to be looking up a little at her face).

Let's consider three examples.

Firstly, imagine the case of a young child coming home to state that he or she has lost a favourite toy to another child living a few houses away. How would the blind-folded *Justitia* handle the situation in contradistinction to the seeing one?

Next, imagine the situation where a person snatches the purse or wallet of another. Again, how would blind-folded *Justitia* come to consider and deliberate on the situation in contradistinction to *Justitia* without a blind-fold?

Let's take another exercise, with careful attention to her face. Looking at the card, observe how she looks as she considers the situation of the fifth time a nineteen year-old lad is caught shoplifting from a large supermarket just prior to hopping on his bicycle (take the time to reflect and *look* at the card before reading the rest of this paragraph); and now observe how she appears as she considers the situation of the fifth time a fifty-five year-old woman is caught shoplifting from the same supermarket just prior to her getting into her late model top-of-the-range Mercedes.

---

1   *On Isis and Osiris* § X. The term 'wanting' = 'without' hands, and the passage reflects Diodorus Siculus Bk 1 Ch 48.

The concept of Justice

The very concept of Justice has seen some changes over time. For Plato – and hence an influential view until recent times – Justice was seen as reflecting the Good. The *Just* social-state reflected *just* individuals who harmoniously contributed to its healthy function.

This is quite at odds with the views of Justice held by Hobbes, which is more akin to being whatever societal laws dictate. In his sense, the 'just' is an application of the law – inversing common-sense notions

We can – and do – question whether specific laws are *just*, and so it may seem that Hobbes's notion is somewhat inaccurate. The problem can be reconsidered by asking if by 'just' we are actually dealing with *moral* or with *legal* concepts.

We should also consider, as we did in a previous chapter, Cicero's consideration in *De Inventione*:

> Justice is a habit of the mind which attributes its proper dignity to everything, preserving a due regard to the general welfare. Its first principles proceed from nature. Subsequently some practices became established by universal custom, from a consideration of their utility; afterwards the fear of the laws and religion sanctioned proceedings which originated in nature, and had been approved of by custom.

Despite such lofty ideals and reflections, in practice, then as now, Justice is equated with the law, seeing it as somehow providing for an orderly, effective and equitable society.

It is in considering the notion of the 'equitable' that we return to the scales.

An eye for an eye

There is no doubt to my mind that early codifications of 'justice' have this notion of 'an eye for an eye, tooth for tooth, hand for hand, foot for foot' (*Exodus* 21:24) of what is deemed *equitable* at the forefront. For example, skipping the later 'similar' formulations in the *Tanakh* or *Old Testament* (which is of course far better known and is in itself more relevant to the development of tarot), the Code of Hammurabi states that:

> [196] If a man put out the eye of another man, his eye shall be put out.

> [197] If he break another man's bone, his bone shall be broken.

Reading these as well as many other legal codifications shows how various societies, including our own, have struggled with the very notion of what is *equitable*. In fact, if one reads in full Hammurabi's code and many other former laws, what can at first be astounding are the number of offences that are deemed to warrant death.

Related to equitable is that of due *compensation*. In part this notion will also reflect not only the socially determined values, but also the political and economic structures. For example, an extreme capitalist notion guiding a particular society will differ significantly from an extreme communist one, and its attendant views on the 'welfare state' and who is ultimately responsible to alleviate the needs of the indigent. These are examples where people in those respective societies are (more often than not) quite at odds with those in the other[2].

The aspect of compensation or distribution of wealth in an *equitable* manner need not imply an *equality*: it would not have been considered neither 'just' nor equitable for a bonded servant to receive equal reward for, for example, coming to the rescue of a merchant attacked by brigands, as if a nobleman did the same.

In contemporary times, Rawls has brought to the fore considerations in his highly influential political philosophical works. He basically argues for justice as 'fairness', this having a two-pronged principle: on the one hand that each person has equal basic liberties; whilst on the other that, subject to fair equality of opportunity, there may (or rather: *will*) arise social and economic *inequalities* resulting from the unequal actual participation of individuals[3].

Another aspect of the Scales

The scales are actually used frequently in three quite distinct types of imagery during late Mediæval and Renaissance times, and perhaps these three need to be kept separate one from the other.

The first is of course with Justice herself, and as such possibly has the longest tradition. I say only 'possibly', as this will depend in part on how the third of these is seen.

---

2   *Cf* H. De Soto's *Mystery of Capital* for a modern assessment of extra-legal situations and the concept of the 'justice' in relation to this.

3   *Cf* especially his *A Theory of Justice*, 1971, and his *Justice as Fairness: A Restatement*, 2001. These cannot be under-rated in their influence on late 20th and 21st century political thought and our developing concept of Justice.

The second is attached to St Michael (or the Archangel Michael). With Michael, we have another similarity in that both he and *Justice* hold swords.

The third is with the weighing of souls at the time of the (Catholic conception of the) Last Judgement. This last is somewhat reminiscent in iconography to the Ancient Egyptian depiction of Maat being weighed as a feather against the heart of the newly dead: in each case, the weighing 'assesses' what is an equitable consequence to one's life.

In both the first (Justice) and the third (Last Judgement) case, what is apparent is a notion of Justice using the implement of the scales to formulate what is equitable.

With the second case, the Archangel Michael is more likely to have acquired the scales as emblematic of his seasonal celebration: with the two St John's at the solstices, St Michael is celebrated at (or rather, very near) the Autumnal equinox – with the solar entry into Libra (using a tropical or common zodiac), the representation of which is of course the scales.

Another clear distinction between Michael and Justice is that whereas the former bears armour, Justice does not. And, in addition, Michael is usually (along with St George) defeating the dragon.

With Justice and the Last Judgement there is a closer connection. Yet, what we usually have in the latter is a *winged* angel and *no sword*, with the imagery including not only people emerging from graves but also, importantly, the scales holding individuals.

With Justice, the scales are empty, to be used for weighing and balancing, but not depicted as actually weighing anything as yet: it is the *allegory* of Justice, not the depiction of any event (whether actual or mythical) such as that of the Last Judgement.

On the subject of wings, I have wondered from whence those depictions behind her on the Noblet derived. The forms do appear a little like 'petrified' wings, and could, instead and more likely, be draped material resting on the back of her chair.

Sword as power and punishment

In one of the earlier chapters, I already quoted Suger from the 12th century:

> The archbishop of Sens, Daimbert, [...] on the day of the discovery of the

holy protomartyr Stephen [third of August, 1108], he anointed Louis with the most holy oil of the unction. After celebrating masses of thanksgiving, he removed the secular sword and girded him with the ecclesiastical sword for the punishment of evil-doers, crowned him with the royal diadem and bestowed on him most devoutly the sceptre and the wand [...]

Here we have not only the concept of the ecclesiastical sword differently considered to the secular one, but also its use clearly mentioned: "for the punishment of evil-doers".

In the image to the left we have Justice, on the one hand compensating (or recompensating) with the scales, and on the other the sword being used for punishment. The image forms part of a far broader one depicting an Aristotelean 'Allegory of the Good Government' (from a fresco attributed to Lorenzatti in Sienna, early 14th century).

Again, considering the primary function of the sword as a weapon designed, like the pistol, for its use at relative close range of person upon person, its adoption on the image of Justice is rather significant.

Let's consider the implications of the sword in a similar manner to what we did for the blindfold. Firstly, in a more general manner, what would be the consequences of Justice *not* having a sword (as she generally didn't in former times)?

Secondly, in the situation of the two aforementioned shoplifters, what would be the difference in Justice *not* having a sword?

How is the sword the object of retribution, and how is this distinct to its function as power?

Considering that the sword is also an emblem of nobility – in that only the aristocracy were permitted to carry one – there are other considerations that relate inevitably to the political spectrum at play.

The Social Order and Justice

The sense of justice seems to very much depend on a number of factors, including the accepted social order as well as, importantly, concepts of the *self within that social order*. For example, a dominant belief that self is a reflection of the social group in which one happens to be born (the 'caste' or equivalent system) will lead to quite a different view as to what is just than if holding a view of the self advocating individualism expressing itself even against the current mores of the day.

In the forst of these social setting, 'justice' may see its expression in

– for example and to use an extreme case – the slave being well looked after by his or her master, and in turn the slave forbearing in his or her tasks. Irrespective of our own particular views on the matter, there were, during periods in which slavery was deemed acceptable, both slaves and slave-owners who were considered 'just', 'fair', and 'equitable' in social conditions that were themselves considered to reflect justice and an equitable social order, at least by those who accepted the then *status quo*.

Lest this be taken in any manner suggesting that I agree with any form of slavery, let it be clear that I do not in any manner or form – I have too much of a streak of individualism and desire for personal liberty, and this to the extant that I *intrinsically* value this aspect that has also come to characterise Western society in general.

The *self* is in Western culture seen as somehow needing to be liberated from the chains of 'accident' of birth and circumstance, and Justice will be, in such social setting, considered effective when it provides the means by which an individual may 'liberate' him or herself from such social 'accident'.

By contrast, this may be considered as sorely unjust (and at times described as 'uncaring') by those who accept social settings where acquiescence and participation within familial and 'caste' settings brings about the greatest social cohesion and considered to maximise the potential for self-actualisation.

Judicial means which encourage social acceptance and cohesion would in this latter circumstance be viewed as more 'just' than one that encourages people to break these social molds. These distinctions are periodically brought to consciousness as societies oscillate from one to the other along a pendulum (the pendulum nonetheless constrained within its own social setting).

Human Rights

It has become increasingly common for bills and declarations of human rights to have been adapted by various levels of government. In fact, in some countries or regions, such is, or is becoming, the norm rather than the exception.

The USA's model is relatively well known, but numerous others exist that have ramifications for its citizens. These remain, however, either often un-examined by its citizens, at times unknown, and certainly its relationship to the prevailing concept of whether it serves or reflects

Justice something that merits another reflective step.

Numerous societies do *not* subscribe to such 'rights', perhaps for reasons that are difficult to even begin to delineate. I would suggest that first and foremost the very concept of inalienable rights reflects a modernist individualism, and that a move against individualism towards communalism – or inherited social distinctions and values – would, on the whole, mitigate against such adoption.

When the Noblet was designed in 1650, the concept of 'rights' was at best in embryonic form. By the time that Conver made his deck in 1760, its fruits were beginning to appear, and not much later we have the principal works that provide the foundation of 'Human Rights': Thomas Paine's 1776 'Common Sense', its influence on the USA's Declaration of Independence (that same year), and its preamble (adapted from Paine) of 'unalienable Rights' of 'Life, Liberty and the pursuit of Happiness'; the *Déclaration des droits de l'Homme et du citoyen* of the French revolution (1789); Thomas Spence's 1775 pamphlet, which was reprinted twenty years later as 'Rights of Man'; and Thomas Paine's massively influential 1791 *Rights of Man*.

In recent times, these have given way to the United Nations 'Universal Declaration of Human Rights' (1948) and in Europe, the recently adopted 'Charter of Fundamental Rights'[4].

The sense of 'Justice' has certainly undergone some fundamental changes since the time of Noblet, and possibly none so pervasive as this change to a communal understanding of 'fundamental' and 'inalienable' rights.

The question remains, in terms of the card, as to whether these maintain both the sense displayed by the balance – the sense of equitability – and the sense of power displayed in part by the sword, and in part by her crown (which I do not discuss here).

Also, where goes the concept of 'punishment of evil doers' when Rights is taken to be a reflection of Justice?

---

4   Australia does not have a Bill of Rights, but over the past decade moves have been afoot to introduce these. Cf, on this, one astute view from Bob Carr, former political leader in the State of New South Wales, and Leeser & Haddrick (eds)'s *Don't Leave Us with the Bill: the case against and Australian Bill of Rights*. I mention these as they are a rarity in today's world that takes for granted the supposed positive value of 'Bills of Rights'.

Swords: punishment & protection

With the sword being considered as instrument of punishment, we can also re-consider the whole suit of swords as possibly reflecting this aspect in certain specific instances.

Let's consider four sword cards in particular to begin this exercise: the three, four, eight, and ten swords. Which appear to depict more a protective sense, and which punishment?

In the context of 'Rights' (and irrespective as to whether or not we may agree with the Declaration), how is article 5 of the UN's *Declaration* reflected in those cards: "No one shall be subjected to torture or to cruel, inhuman or degrading treatment or punishment"?

Using the image (shown earlier) of the 'Allegory of Good Government', consider what is being presented, and then reflect on and place those four pips where they seems to best fit.

Coins: fairness

There is similarly an aspect of the suit of Coins that reflects an aspect of Justice – or what is fair and equitable.

Roman coins generally depicted, in point of case, a representation of *Justitia* on the obverse of the coin. Though this was more to depict the ruler (depicted on the other side) as just, there remains something of note in what is 'fair and just' both in terms of trade, but also in terms of compensation.

This is not new, and, to again quote from the 18th century BCE Code of Hammurabi, monetary payment was instituted as a reflection of what was then considered 'fair' compensation, though we would hardly agree with the example in our own time. Here are some selections from §198-204:

> If he put out the eye of a man's slave, or break the bone of a man's slave, he shall pay one-half of its value.
>
> If a free-born man strike the body of another free-born man or equal rank, he shall pay one gold mina.
>
> If a freed man strike the body of another freed man, he shall pay ten shekels in money.

In fact, we often have little else by which to provide a sense of due compensation, and the scales of justice appear here to attempt and weigh how to best manage a situation that appears to be without equitable redress especially if an 'inalienable right' is wronged.

Justice and Truth

There is one final consideration to which we should touch: the important concept of Truth in relation to Justice. In his *Summa Theologica* (Q.109), St Thomas Aquinas argues not only with Aristotle that truth is a virtue, but more importantly (in our context) that "truth is a part of justice".

There is an important element that comes to the fore in consideration of this card, in that Justice becomes only manifest if, and only if, truth (*Aletheia*) is there also. It is in part this aspect that can be seen in Michael's destruction of the dragon as lies and deceit, here depicted next to Justice herself.

Considerations of the card of Justice, then, evoke considerations of the concept of truth and the various means in which the social order can be both equitable and meaningfully reflect considerations of the self in light of social norms.

VIIII - L'Ermite

The Hermit

We have so far considered either individuals (I–V) or ideals and virtues (VI–VIII) that stand very much within society. With the Hermit, we once again move not only to an actual human being, but also one that suggests a removal from normal social interactions – although he too has social consequences and interactions.

Considerations of the Hermit inevitably lead to those who exemplify its life. In the life of the Saints and Desert Fathers, the single individual that appears to come to dominance in terms of the eremitic[1] life is St Anthony (sometimes also shown with St Paul of Thebes, whom he buried).

In contradistinction to the other individuals we have met, the Hermit has a *calling*, a *vocation*. The Bateleur certainly had an engagement and engaged in his trade. The Empress and Emperor were so by social declaration. Similarly, the Pope was elected as such by his peers (often having entered the Church as familial piety dictated, rather than personal calling). Only the Papesse shows something similar to the Hermit, yet she too reflects very much, as woman of a convent, also the refuge sought and to be found within cloistered doors.

By contrast, the Hermit, as hermit, is called to leave the world as he knows it. St Anthony, amongst others who later heard similar words, did just this when once he heard a preacher read Matthew 19:21:

> Jesus said, 'If you wish to be perfect, go and sell your possessions and give the money to the poor, and you will have treasure in heaven; then come, follow me.'

The story of St Anthony's life – *via* the work of Athanasius - was not only well known throughout mediaeval and Renaissance times, but also his central influence on both the eremitic as well as the monastic life.

To *call* a card 'Hermit' is nearly a short-hand to calling it 'St Anthony'.

Yet, the card itself displays little of the central iconographic tradition for St Anthony. Specifically, the lamp (if that is what it is) is not usual for St Anthony.

There are many other figures from the annals of the Saints that are also called to mind, some in part due to their influence, others, such as St Francis of Assisi, in part because of that same call to 'sell, give to the

---

1   from the Greek *erēmos* – a deserted place

poor, and follow me'.

It is perhaps noteworthy that those who have been recorded as doing just that have come from the ranks of those who have, in fact, significant wealth and things to sell: both St Anthony and St Francis came from wealthy backgrounds, and followed a call that not only reduced them to poverty, but also at various times brought them close to death.

The eremitic life, despite our over-populated world, continues for the few who are so-called. I recall the Dalai Lama commenting on his meeting of an anchorite monk who had been reclused in the Spanish Pyrenées for many years. Similarly, there are within larger communities individuals who separate themselves specifically in order to focus on the spiritual life. Even within convents and monasteries, some are called to so live a life as to be celled in relative seclusion.

In each of these cases, however, it perhaps should also be called to mind that no matter on the seclusion, there is also usually a sense of connection to the world around them. It is also obvious, at least once brought to consciousnesss, that those of whom we speak are individuals who have eventually had cause to enter into dialogue with the social world around them.

Let's consider for a moment that step taken by St Anthony and others – whether from the Christian tradition, or in the example of Gautama Buddha, from the far Eastern one.

'Sell and give your possessions'

As I look around me, I am ever so grateful with the blessings of material possessions to which I have access. Yet I can imagine being able to give away all 'my' possessions, taking the steps so required and come to a fearful trust.

So let's take a moment to *imagine* the radical giving away of all one's possessions (including those credit cards and bank accounts!), and finding an isolated place, whether it be within the desert (if such is within reach) or remote stony outcrop or mountain.

It is this 'fearful trust' that, for me, takes the shape of the radical trust implicit in the requirements of the eremitic life: trust for not only one's own personal physical safety and the provision of food (and water); but also the trust that one's *spiritual* and *psychological* safety will be such as to able to overcome the maddening assault of visions that inevitably accompany such exclusion from normal social human contact. In addition, there is the further implicit trust of oneself that the calling will be exercised with rigour, and that inner spiritual guidance will open one to radiant light.

Those who may have called to mind St Anthony when considering this card would also have called to mind images from his life story. Mentioning the psychological and spiritual terrors he faced, some of the most gruesome of paintings have been made from his life – as many such scenes were also described in, to be sure, the hagiography by Athanasius.

Yet it is by overcoming these and other difficulties that he presents himself as a wisdom-filled saint. It is as if, despite all the cases of dangers and difficulties he faced, his faith, his trust, remained unshaken and provided him an anchor by which to seek the light of truth.

This seeking for truth – for *Aletheia* – undoubtedly characterises one of the key aspects of the eremitic life and, though the lamp is not a common iconic representation with St Anthony, is entirely apt as reflecting that which is sought.

There are three other similar representations that come from times earlier than the Noblet that make use of the lamp. So let's, for a moment, consider these.

Lamp of the World

The first of these is Christ being described as the 'Light of the World'. The Saint, infused with this light[2], is then also described as a (or the) 'light of the world' or as 'lamp of the world' – for example, when St Francis died:

> O what a glorious saint he is! His disciple saw his soul ascending into heaven:

> Beautiful as the moon, Bright as the sun, glowing brilliantly as if ascending upon a white cloud!

> O true lamp of the world, shining more brilliantly than the sun in the Church of Christ! Now, you have withdrawn the rays of your light, as you withdraw into that luminous homeland. You have exchanged our poor company for that of the angels and saints!

Here, the reference is undoubtedly from a couple of Biblical passages. Specifically, Matthew 5:14-16 reminds me, at least, of the very depiction of our Hermit:

> You are light for the world. A city built on a hill-top cannot be hidden. No one lights a lamp to put it under a tub; they put it on the lamp-stand where it shines for everyone in the house. In the same way your light must shine in people's sight, so that, seeing your good works, they may give praise to your Father in heaven.

Also Mark 4:21-23, where Jesus said, in relation to receiving and handing on his teaching:

> Is a lamp brought in to be put under a tub or under the bed? Surely to be put on the lamp-stand? For there is nothing hidden, but it must be disclosed, nothing kept secret except to be brought to light. Anyone who has ears for listening should listen.

The Saint, monk, or hermit, called to such vocation, is then the lamp-holder.

It is not through theology, however, which is rather studied and learned, but through the life sought to be infused with that "light greater than the Sun's" – of Christ as *Light of the World* described, for example, in John 8:12:

---

2   *theosis*, a concept that has progressively been diminished in the 'Latin' (as opposed the the 'Greek East') West, is here an additional important consideration.

I am the light of the world; anyone who follows me will not be walking in the dark but will have the light of life.

These – and Old Testament correlated references – would undoubtedly have played much in understanding the lamp held by a figure titled 'Hermit', and calling to mind, appropriately, St Anthony and others.

A number of images of St Christopher also show him with lamp. Below, he is not only shown carrying over the stream the 'light and weight of the world', but also depicted near the entrance to his cell with lamp:

Seeker of Truth

There are other images that come to light that bear on similar iconography, especially in relation to seeking truth by the mere and relatively poor light of one's consciousness.

Various alchemical works come to mind. Of note is one from the

Atalanta Fugiens by Michael Maier (1618). Plate 42 (above) depicts the alchemist (or really, the natural philosopher or, in modern language, the scientist) seeking to find – and thus unveil and understand – nature by following her footprints by the dim light he carries: a struggle to ever perceive another small aspect of her traces, and follow the directions she leaves, wherever they may lead.

What is similar with the previous imagery is that in each case there is a sense that truth can be in some manner unveiled, and that we have the freedom to so pursue such calling.

Diogenes the Cynic

In the history of Philosophy, and in popular remembrance, there is also that other important figure to consider – if for no other reason than upholding the lamp in broad daylight calls Diogenes the Cynic to mind.

The central text comes from another individual bearing his same given name: Diogenes Laertius. This latter lived around the 2nd century CE and authors the important and popular *Lives of Eminent Philosophers*.

The Cynic's numerous sarcasms and witty comments would undoubtedly have appealed much to the French mind of the Noblet period, a period where tongue lashings appears to have been served as part of an illustrious sport.

Amongst a few of his comments are the following (numerous documents and sites present his various responses, the following come from millionsofmouths.com/diogenes.html):

> The question was put to Diogenes, what hope is; and his answer was, "The dream of a waking man."

> Chided as an old man who ought to rest, he replied, "What, if I were running in the stadium, ought I to slacken my pace when approaching the goal? Ought I not rather put on speed?"

> Once, while Diogenes was sunning himself, Alexander The Great came up to him and offered to grant him any request. Diogenes told him to "Stand less between the sun and me."

> As he was leaving the public baths, somebody inquired if many men were bathing. He said, "No." But to another who asked if there was a great crowd of bathers, he said, "Yes."

This very much reflects his view that not many men were *truly* men:

> One day Diogenes shouted out for men, and when people collected, hit out at them with his stick, saying, "It was men I called for, not scoundrels."

It is from such view that his famous walk through the streets of Athens stems, and for which he appears most remembered in later European art (see over):

> He lit a lamp in broad daylight and said, as he went about, "I am looking for a man."

In Diogenes, there is a sense of seeking after truth and knowledge, simplicity, and what we would now call *authenticity*, that marks all these three types of images that harken to our Hermit.

Such radical simplicity as a reflection of authenticity is also found when:

> Seeing a child drinking from his hands, Diogenes threw away his cup and remarked, 'A child has beaten me in plainness of living'.

It is in part this radical striving for the removal of ornamentation that brings together the three types of images I have here brought together: that of the eremitic life, with its obvious sense of simplicity and inner search for the light of truth; that of the natural philosopher, ever in search for *Aletheia* or Truth as revealed *via* Nature; and that of the cynic philosopher.

Authenticity, Truth and Freedom

The *Internet Encyclopedia of Philosophy* has this to add to an aspect of our concerns:

> Freedom is advocated [by the cynics] in three related forms: eleutheria, freedom or liberty, autarkeia, self-sufficiency, and parrhēsia, freedom of speech or frankness. [...] the notion of autonomy which derives from the imperative that reason rule over the passions is found in the ethics of multiple Classical and Hellenistic thinkers. A specifically Cynic sense of freedom, though, is evident in parrhēsia.
>
> An element of parrhēsia, which can be overlooked when it is defined as free or frank speech, is the risk that accompanies speaking so freely and frankly.

We shall again meet an aspect of this radical frankness in the Fool (and also have cause to briefly again touch upon Diogenes). What is of greater import here is that the path followed by each of our representatives shares at least the last of those three concepts of freedom: that of free expression, even often at the risk of death, and all in the name of Truth.

In terms of the modern sense of authenticity, it appears to arise a little later than the Noblet, in the works of Rousseau (with the sense of 'being true to oneself'). There is, in this very concept, a sense that one needs to assert a type of radical freedom which may be at odds with normal social convention. Again, this is also a fair description of the Hermit who forsakes his social standing – even his very livelihood and possessions – to enable such to begin to be possible.

Perhaps it is little wonder that the hermit and fool can be so closely connected in imagination.

But let us return to the image for a while, and also focus a little on aspects of the depiction that are vastly at odds with what I have thus far described – for the hermit, as bloke isolating himself on the outskirts of towns, was not always considered honest nor meriting trust.

La Fontaine's 'L'Ermite'

Jean de La Fontaine, in French national culture, stands somewhat on a par (though quite different in style) to the way in which Shakespeare stands as epitomising British literary representation, Goethe the equivalent German, Cervantes the Spanish, and Dante the Italian.

La Fontaine's works began to appear not long after the Noblet, and would certainly have been read, recited, and talked about during the same time the deck would have been actively used.

La Fontaine's "L'ermite" is too long to here quote at length, but here is a relevant taste:

> When Venus and Hypocrisy combine,
> Oft pranks are played that show a deep design;
> Men are but men, and friars full as weak:
> I'm not by Envy moved these truths to speak.
> Have you a sister, daughter, pretty wife?
> Beware the monks as you would guard your life; [...]
> To show that monks are knaves in Virtue's mask;
> Pray read my tale:--no other proof I ask.

> A hermit, full of youth, was thought around,
> A saint, and worthy of the legend found.
> The holy man a knotted cincture wore;
> But, beneath his garb:--heart-rotten to the core.
> A chaplet from his twisted girdle hung,
> Of size extreme, and regularly strung, [...]

> Not far from where the hermit's cell was placed,
> Within a village dwelled a widow chaste;
> Her residence was at the further end
> And all her store--a daughter as a friend,
> Who candor, youth, and charms supreme possessed;
> And still a virgin lived, however distressed.

> Though if the real truth perhaps we name,
> 'Twas more simplicity than virtuous aim; [...]

> Our anchorite, in begging through the place;
> This girl beheld,--but not with eyes of grace.
> Said he, she'll do, and, if you manage right,
> Lucius, at times, with her to pass the night.

> No time he lost, his wishes to secure:
> The means, we may suppose, not over pure.

[...] One charming night--no, I mistake 'tis plain,
Our hermit, favored much by wind and rain,
Pierced in the boarding, where by time 'twas worn;
A hole through which he introduced a horn;
And loudly bawled:--attend to what I say,
You women, my commands at once obey.
This voice spread terror through the little cot;
Both hid their heads and trembled for their lot;
But still our monk his horn would sound aloud
Awake! cried he; your favor God has vowed;
My faithful servant, Lucius, haste to seek;
At early dawn go find this hermit meek
To no one say a word: 'tis Heaven ordains;
Fear nothing, Lucius ever blessed remains;

I'll show the way myself: your daughter place,
Good widow, with this holy man of grace;
And from their intercourse a pope shall spring,

Who back to virtue Christendom will bring. [...]
Or it is decreed that you shall quickly die.
Now, mother, said the girl, I told you well;
Come, let us hasten to the hermit's cell;
So much I dread your death, I'll nothing shun;
And if 'tis requisite, I'll even run.
Away then, cried the mother, let us go; [...]

Our monk was on the watch you may suppose;
A hole he made that would a glimpse disclose; [...]

Our tale to shorten, Lucius kind appeared
To rigid rules no longer he adhered.
The mother with him let her girl remain,
And hastened to her humble roof again.
The belle complying looked:--he took her arm,
And soon familiar grew with every charm.

O hypocrites! how oft your wily art
Deceives the world and causes poignant smart. [...]

The fair at length her apron-string perceived
Grew daily shorter, which her bosom grieved; [...]
When home returned, the girl, each day and night,
Amused her mind with prospects of delight;
By fancy's aid she saw the future pope,
And all prepared to greet her fondest hope;
But what arrived the whole at once overthrew

[...] - a little female came!

Self Deceit and Temptation

Self-deceit can be seen as the opposite of authenticity, and is forever a temptation for the hermit and for the scientist, both of whom, in search of the light of truth, may not only have significant oversights, but be tempted to see only that which accords with their established view of what may be favourable to their own selves, rather than serving that which is claimed.

This 'self-favouring' as both temptation and deceit is also amply illustrated with the life of St Anthony, but is something to which, in seeking to shine forth our own inner-found light, we are undoutbedly each at times prone.

Iconography

In the making of icons (in the Eastern Orthodox Church traditions),

> the rules governing the making of icons are more specifically defined than those of paintings in other traditions. The "grammar" of the icon is in fact so closely controlled as to make iconography more truly a language to be "written" than mere painting would ever entail.

If we are to take tarot imagery as somewhat closer to iconic than to symbolic, then its 'grammar' will be dependant not only on focussing upon and understanding its parts in the context of its historical setting and development, but also in paying precise attention to these and, where possible, avoiding overlays – overlays that become ever so tempting in our search to interpret rather than to understand.

Noblet's 'LERMITE'

And so with all these considerations, let us look again at our Noblet and consider some implications:

We have an older man, with walking stick (in the past used for protection as much as assistance), holding aloft a lamp, set in a background that appears flat and desert-like;

His cloak calls to mind that here is likely also his sole possession and sleeping blanket;

He lifts his light high, perhaps to see better... or perhaps to light the way for others;

As *hermit*, he has undoubtedly spent many months is relative solitude, seeking what we would likely now call the *authentic*, *Aletheia* or Truth unveiled *via* the inner light glowing from heart and mind, awake to his actions being as much beacons as are his words;

Yet, deceptions are forever tempters.

Father Time

A brief mention should also be made of earlier depictions from the Visconti cards of the Hermit representing time and old age. That aspect we shall briefly visit in chapter eighteen.

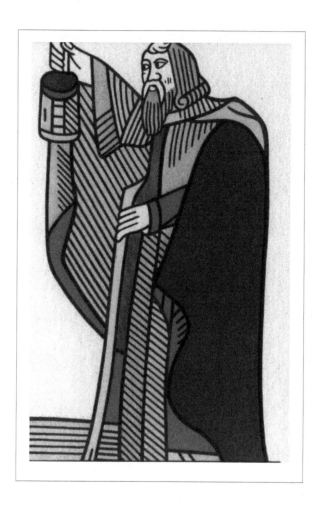

X - Roue de Fortune

The Wheel of Fortune

There are a few cards in the sequence that were *especially* influential in sending me scurrying through historical connections and developments. This is one of those, the other two being XVI and XXI. Not that other cards lack such aspect, of course.

This card has numerous details worthy of careful attention and reflection, not least of which are the beings depicted on its periphery.

With this card, also, my own first 21 years, in large part due to my father, are very much reflected. Before I briefly expose this personal biography, however, let's consider from whence the image derives and its context.

Boethius

We need go no further than Boethius's immensely influential early 6th century *Consolation of Philosophy*[1] to find the basis for the Mediaeval (and later) European pervasiveness of the image and allegory.

The whole text is image rich, and it is no wonder that it formed one of the most popular works in Mediaeval times and that it was translated in various vernacular languages (including English by both Chaucer and Elizabeth I, as well as in Old French and German). In Italy, it was highly influential in Dante's *Divine Comedy*. Llull, Boccaccio, Malory, as well as the works of Chaucer and of Shakespeare, and indeed the very imagery used on major *Lumière* ('Gothic') Cathedrals, all show direct evidence of his incredible importance and influence. Furthermore, the manner in which Aristotle came to be understood by the scholastics of subsequent years was in large part *via* Boethius – though in this case his other and earlier philosophical works.

The opening section of Book II of the *Consolation of Philosophia* is of principal import when it comes to Fortune herself:

> 'If I have diagnosed the cause and nature of your condition, you are wasting away in pining and longing for your former good fortune. [...] I know the many disguises of that monster, Fortune [...].
>
> If you are trying to stop her wheel from turning, you are of all men the most obtuse. For if it once begins to stop, it will no longer be the wheel of chance.

---

1   or, more aptly, 'Consolation of <u>Philosophia</u>', as Philosophy is therein allegorised.

'With domineering hand she moves the turning wheel,
Like currents in a treacherous bay swept to and fro:
Her ruthless will has just deposed once fearful kings
While trustless still, from low she lifts a conquered head;
No cries of misery she hears, no tears she heeds,
But steely hearted laughs at groans her deeds have wrung.
Such is the game she plays, and so she tests her strength;
Of mighty power she makes parade when one short hour
Sees happiness from utter desolation grow.'

Here Boethius listens to *Philosophia* (c. 1460):

Such is his influence in the world of philosophy and of ideas that I personally rank him as one of the most influential European thinkers of all time. And the work for which he is best known remains readily conceptually accessible to readers from a wide variety of background (unlike, I would suggest as an example, many of the works of Aristotle).

To be sure, the concept of *fortuna* antedates Boethius[2]. What he does, however, is raise her to a specific mental picture such that what becomes of great noteworthiness is not the figure of *Fortuna* herself, but of something he really brings afresh and anew: the wheel upon which we inevitably travel throughout our lives. In contrast, *Fortuna* was *Tyche* ('luck') in Ancient Greece, a concept at times overlaid with the workings of the three fates.

Looking at the image of the Wheel of Fortune adjacent which Boethius speaks (or listens) to *Philosophia* (on the previous page) shows well some of the various other aspects we have in the past considered: it draws us in to participate in the event, especially if we read his text at the same time. Also, the very words used, *viz*, "if it once begins to stop, it will no longer be the wheel of chance" (or, in the words of another and earlier translation: "if Fortune begin to stay still, she is no longer Fortune") brings our imagination to *active* participation. For it is *Fortuna* that is represented, and for that the wheel must move.

Yet, she is capricious and inconstant, unlike the 'eternal' movement of the stars which can be forecast by their constancy. Whereas the celestial realm moves and is constant, here below Fortune may play and move with erratic fickleness[3]. It is in combining these two concepts – that of the celestial and the earthly realms – that we arrive at some representations of the Wheel of Fortune, and indeed possible considerations of astrology, with the planetary movement providing clarity of direction, of season, of various cycles. The only 'cycle' that the Wheel provides is one where change must of necessity occur – echoing Heraclitus that everything is in a state of flux.

Inconstant and Capricious

This, for the Ancients, was very much one of the key factors in not being able to predict the future unless ordained by one of the gods.

---

2   Here I would, following the works of others, suggest that especially the neo-platonist Proclus and Plotinus are of influence, more so than Plato and Aristotle.

3   To be sure, even the heavens have apparent fluctuations when specifically considering the planets, for which epicycles were invoked as explanation by the Ancients. Still, these were meant to explain how apparent change was in fact due to the circular constancy of wheels within wheels.

Either it was ordained and hence able to be communicated by the sibyls (or equivalent), or it was left to the vicissitudes of *Fortuna*.

And it is in part this that continues to play in modern tarot readings as divination and 'fortune-telling': in what manner is the wheel's movement sensible – in both this word's meaning as '*reasonable*' and '*able to be sensed into*'?

Instead of seeking to answer the question directly, let's *sense* into the actions of movement.

Imagine yourself in the position of *Fortuna* (in the image below), and move the wheel as you wish. Whether clockwise or anti-clockwise, a little in one direction and then in the other... up to you.

Noblet

Compared to the other TdM's, Noblet shows some clarity of spokes that appears to have slowly eroded over time. Let's see what I mean: The cards are from a Visconti-type, the Noblet, a Dodal, and a Conver (next page).

If in the Visconti we still have the very traditional depiction of *Fortuna* actually included in the image (in her slightly less usual form as hoodwinked) and turning the wheel directly with her hands on the spokes, by the Noblet, not only has she disappeared, but there is now the

common wheel axle and handle and, instead of *four* figures around the wheel, only three remain.

These three figures also seem to lose detail over time. In the Noblet, they appear more like an ape or monkey-like figure descending, an ass-like figure ascending, and a human-like crowned figure atop. By the time of the Conver, the three are far more difficult to distinguish – yet still sufficiently clear if the symbolic meaning is known (to which we shall return shortly).

These animal-figurines are quite different to the more classical depictions showing, generally, all human beings in different parts of the wheel (though there are exceptions to which we shall also return).

The images I show above also have distinct differences of direction of rotation: the TdMs move counterclockwise (as judged by the orientation of the side figures, presuming, to be sure, that the head leads movement). In contrast, the Visconti and the other two previous images have the figures move *clockwise* – though, again, there is no *universality* of represented direction even in very early imagery, something that can be seen from the image in the next column.

If we look at the centre of each wheel, what is striking in the TdMs is that the 'hub' is depicted as a representation of the world – or, to be more precise, the Earth, divided in the mediaeval three-fold division we have already touched upon in a previous chapter (this is already beginning to be a detail that is lost in the Conver).

Of the three TdMs, only the Noblet shows the axle shafted to each supporting post: both the Dodal and the Conver seem to have forgotten the far side. Finally, the *base* on the Noblet has no 'cross-beams' connecting the two sides.

The 'obvious' meaning

If we consider for a while the more obvious allusion to *Fortuna*'s Wheel, it shows the ups and downs to which humanity is inevitably subjected whilst on Earth – and this see-sawing both individuals as well as social groups, or indeed even nation-states.

At a general level, it applies to life's ebbs and flows that may even have seasonal regularity (such as the enjoyment of fresh berries). Indeed, for the community aware of its reliance on land and its produce, the Wheel turns with both regularity, yet remains fickle in terms of its recolte.

For most of us, these 'ups and downs' are perhaps more reminders of the joys of festival and youthful rides on a ferris wheel – its origin intimately connected to *Fortuna*'s Wheel (here from the works of Bocaccio).

For some, the wheel has more extreme and lively reflections: on a personal note, as a child of a father who (at the time) made his living from professional gambling, the financial highs as well as the lows were vast, and were, to a child, an invisible cause of the various alterations in our access to everyday things. A week spent living in what could only be described as super-luxurious accommodation, being driven in a brand new limousine, would be followed by another in which we would resort to staying with grandparents out of apparent lack of alternative options. And his own life has continued to display this seeming fascination to experience the full rim of *Fortuna*'s wheel: from wealth beyond the reach of most; to poverty that (in his case) cannot reasonably be accounted for; and back again to wealth.

Whether it be wealth, or power, or health, or happiness, or social position, or whatever, there remains, of course, another aspect to the situation: ie, our own particular way of meeting the trials and tribulations that we are served – for whether at the top of wheel or anywhere else on its periphery, trials it brings, and ways of meeting these are various.

Here, then, another early consideration may be worth noting upon which reflections shed further insight, for whatever is served by the wheel's movement also demands of us ways in which to embrace life's unfoldment.

The Wheel's Rim and Centre

Upon a wheel, the greatest movement is at the outer edge of the wheel – along its rim. At its centre, there is a 'stillness'.

By analogy, by striving to move towards the centre of the wheel, we may not fall as low, but neither be raised as high.

In the movement of the wheel (as attached to a wagon, for example), it is also strange, once we carefully consider it, that its centre moves 'as far' as its rim. Such became part of an old paradox named "Aristotle's Wheel" (though it originates in a later text). Consider this: a wheel is rolled for one revolution along the ground (the blue lower 'a' line in the image below), therefore, the centre moves across the orange upper 'c' line, and the inner circle would also make one revolution along the green middle 'b' line. All three lines are therefore of equal lengths.

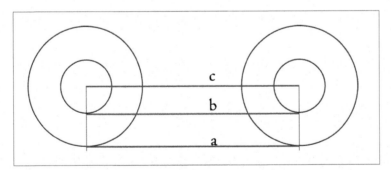

The paradox is that if the 'a' line (the larger rim unfurled once) is the same as the 'b' line (the smaller rim unfurled also only once), and again the same as the centre moving across, then the circumference of the smaller and larger rims are exactly the same – which we know not to be true.

In terms of the motions of a suspended wheel, as the one of Fortune, the paradox has similarities to considerations of the apparent conflict of the possibility of both foreknowledge and free-will, and thus similarly brings to mind this paradox that also occupied the thoughts of our forebears.

Astrological considerations

This consideration of the rotations of the inner and outer rims is also worth considering in light of the centre of the Wheel as depicting the Earth, and the outer the movement of the planetary bodies – that other great movement that, this time, as far greater stability, though, with the planets, also 'meander' across the otherwise apparently fixed stars[4].

Here, to be sure, it is not *Fortuna*, but an angelic being that turns the wheel – a wheel that nonetheless also has implications for the realms 'below' (cf image overleaf).

Again, the realm of the Earth is centrally depicted, and in this case, the seven traditional planets, with Mars on top, depict also the manner in which even in the heavens, rulership amongst the planets is not fixed, but moves.

The image shown on the next page is one of the early 'finds' that originally lead me to consider alternatives not usually considered. *Could the depictions be planetary?* As perhaps may by now be obvious, there is a polymorphous influx that plays itself into the images we are given.

Wheel of Life

Even without considering the vicissitudes of life, there is undoubtedly the inevitable movement of growth, peak, and demise that also accompanies one's life. This is also apparent in two other images on the theme as shown on the page after next.

The Wheel of Fortune also asks us to be aware of the inevitable change that accompanies the normal cyclical movement placed upon us by time itself. Not only is there growth, maturing, and eventual death, but within each of these there are smaller cycles of growth, coming to fruition, and decay or letting go.

Perhaps this aspect is worth considering especially when we struggle to face situations that are even beyond the hands of *Fortuna*, but rather

---

4   though here a reminder that these meanderings was, again, explained by the epicycles of circles within circles. See, for example, the Ptolemaïc view.

more in the hands of the Fates whose spindle not only spins the golden thread (or silver chord) of life, but also apportions lots and, inevitably, eventually cuts the thread of life at some point.

There are, then, three distinct aspects that we are lead to consider in the workings of the wheel: the weavings appointed in the personal and social fabric of our individual lives; the vicissitudes of life's random events; and the cyclical movement of the wheel's turning, season by season, day by day. And our own individual response to the way in which these permeate our heart, our thinking and our will-force or *acts*.

Personal response

Perhaps it is in part this last – *how we respond* to the events in which we are placed – that shows differences between the human figure atop the wheel; the over-ambitiousness of the ass (as depicted in all positions along the rim of the Wheel in the 1494 woodcut on *ambition* – on the next page) that strives and struggles to gain to a position above its abilities no matter what; and the monkey who without effort allows itself to be flung from the rim's inevitable movement.

Platform as stability

If we look again carefully at the card, there is something different about the position atop the Wheel: it appears to have a platform upon which the individual is seated.

If there is indeed a platform, it may be that this also stands, though located atop, as untouched by the Wheel's rim and its constant motion.

Such equipoise requires a sense of inner tranquillity, acceptance and

equanimity, together with a certain control of thoughts and action, perseverance, as well as tolerance to what may be heading one's way and impartiality to its provenance[5]. These, of course, also form part and parcel of some of the virtues to be cultivated by each of us as we meet destiny's onslaughts.

Readings

When faced with a reading more akin to what is generally referred to as 'Fortune telling', we are faced, then, with considerations that seem to go beyond even the simple consideration of the motion of Fortune's wheel. Even if the reading-at-hand reflects her vicissitudes and even violent motions, perhaps the cards also show the equivalent to what Boethius faced: not only Fortune's fate, but also, in his case, the consolations of *understanding* with deeper care and tenderness with (again in his situation) *Philosophia*.

The narrative, in such a case, seems to serve not only as a reflection of the motion of the wheel, the cyclic inevitability of larger forces and considerations of the golden thread being weaved, but also provides guidance and insight into how to *meet* destiny's gifts and baggage of surprises.

In that sense, the narrative also speaks of the character of the person

---

5   Steiner also talks of these six qualities, in a different context, in his early work *Knowledge of the Higher Worlds*.

for whom the reading is directed and the manner in which insights may further be gained into the situation at hand.

Reason and the senses

There are, finally, images reminiscent of the Wheel of Fortune that also bear animals and human. In some works, the senses (usually, but not always, described as five in number) have an animal allocated at the rim, and atop – though really reflecting the whole wheel via its centre – a crowned human being to which the senses' spokes return their findings.

For example, Thomas of Cantimpré's 13th century *Liber de natura rerum* relates animals to sensory organs and appears on various images from the period.

In this case, what may be useful to consider is that not only the various faculties, but also the manner in which we acquire information, needs to be integrated in order for *sensory* to become *sensible*, allowing understanding and insight to arise.

The Ass and the Monkey

Irrespective of the various animal representations considered above, there remains clarity and consistency that the two figures on the sides of the TdM Wheels are of Ass (or donkey) and of Monkey, with the former seeking to ascend, and the latter in the descending (or 'falling') position.

For many years I considered that such must have been of symbolic significance, yet no tarot book (nor other materials I had read) satisfactorily addressed this aspect. It is only in the re-writing of this course that the specific details emerged. I mention this as there are still numerous details to tarot that have yet to be unveiled which only careful attention to detail, familiarity with early decks, and an increased understanding of symbolic representations in use in late mediæval and renaissance imagery will bring to light.

For myself, it was not 'just' that these animals are consistent across various TdMs, but also that they are evident if one looks very closely at the 15th century Visconti decks: not the main image, but the gold-leaf bears lines that makes of the ascending figure an ass, and the descending one have a monkey's tail[6] (see the close-up on the next page).

So what of these?

I suspect that this is one of those 'transformations' of human-to-symbolic animal that was ever-so 'natural' to those of the times, and that the ascent as Ass and fall as monkey were far more commonly understood than they today are.

According to the mediæval *Physiologus*, the devil was 'simia Dei' (God's monkey), and the monkey was associated with humanity's fall and continued to represent human sin into the Middle Ages[7].

As for the Ass, it probably derives from a joke that confounds 'Bisodia' as the name at times used for Christ's Ass but also infers fantasy (or more properly speaking phantasm). The Ass can also therefore be seen to represent false aspirations (the *Ass* upon which Christ sat is not to be confused with the Christ).

So we have, on the one side, the striving ascent beyond the natural position of the person (ass) in question; and on the other the fall (as monkey) by his own disobedience to divine precept. Yet each can also find itself in a position inappropriate to it by the whims of Fortuna!

Half way reflection

---

6   to be sure, *other* similar details are also included on that card, such as ears also appearing on the crowned figure atop, and Fortuna being winged.

7   Cf, for example, Corbey's *Metaphysics of Apes*, p.66

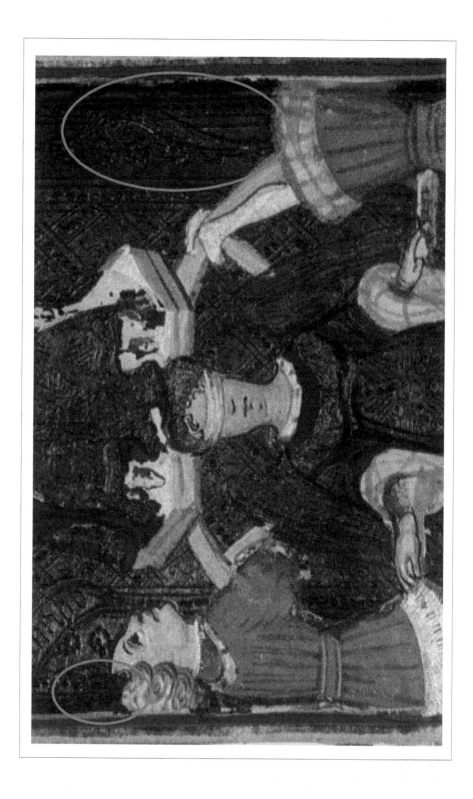

Completing this chapter, we are half-way through the series and suggest that some time be given to quiet reflection on the course thus far (without looking back through the chapters). A brief answer, in your own notebook, to the following question will prove beneficial in the ongoing work ahead:

'What has been of value over the past 15 weeks?'

XI - FORCE

La Force

Let's begin with the details depicted on the image itself and, for the sake of initially separating the differences that are all too often seen as one and the same, let's begin with the top section of the card.

Here we see that what she wears is hair netting surmounted by a crown, rather than a type of hat such as the one worn by the Bateleur:

Certainly they both have a lemniscatory quality – but that, I would suggest, was not the intent, especially given that the lemniscate did not become common until much later.

Her hair netting or *crespinette*[1] (also called a 'snood' or 'balzo') was a common fashion accessory over a reasonably long period of time amongst the more wealthy from late mediæval to renaissance times – though the hair-style itself changes significantly over the same period. In addition to being a common fashionable item, however, it has the

---

1   also commonly spelled 'crispinette'.

added dimension that her hair remains covered. In other words, she remains depicted as virtuous – which is appropriate, given that the card is one of the cardinal virtues.

Her forearms, similarly, show that she wears gauntlets. Here it may be more difficult to ascertain whether the intent was for only her forearms to be covered with gloveless gauntlets, or for the full gloved variety to be depicted – though certainly the colouration seems to suggest white gloves 'attached' to forearm gauntlets.

These forearm bands were generally used to protect the lower portions of the arms by both a variety of craftspeople as well as the armoured variety for warriors. In its fashionable aspect, however, it also became prominent around the same time as the crespinette, especially as elongated gloves.

As forearm (or fully gloved) gauntlets, they were also a common enough item of hunting clothing for the falconer.

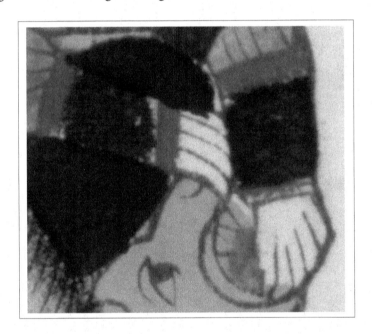

Holding the position

If you have a pet that is amenable and co-operative (or large soft-toy), gently open its mouth in the manner in which the card depicts it... but *first please note:*

There are only two ways in which this could take place: either by incredible brute force (a word to which we shall return) – in which case please don't persist; or by co-operation of the animal as trusting your intent, opening its mouth in *trust* and *submission*. Even when the mouth is opened by more a 'forced' engagement (for example, by animal-carers such as vets), it tends to signal that a *trust* is, in some cases very rapidly, established.

Looking carefully at the design, what is the lower hand doing?

Design and interpretation

Of course, here is where we need to again distinguish between the image 'intent' and the manner in which *our* seeing may bring to its interpretation more than intended. In the case of the card, it appears clear that the rough-cut of the lines gives an impression of the intent as the lion's mouth being held open by pulling and pushing with, respectively, the right and left hands.

In its detailed lines – detailed through our own perceptive sense – the left hand may be seen as freely inserted into (or upon) the lion's mouth, without effort and without necessarily holding it ajar.

Samson, Herakles, Allegory, or stellar depiction?

Of all cards, this one is amongst the ones to have been allocated the widest possible references. As symbolic representation, of course, it need not have a singular determinant. In fact, we can very well expect the opposite: *various* sources of influence made their way into the image as it stabilised into the pattern with which we are now familiar.

This was certainly not the case with earlier (and of course some later) representations, some of which more clearly alluded to one or another of the myriad figures of person-and-lion, whether as Daniel, Samson, or Hercules (Herakles).

In terms of general imagery, there would be little to distinguish a depiction of Samson from one of Herakles – unless contextually given by accompanying images (such as Herakles's other eleven labours, or Samson's other biblical tales). As to be expected, however, it is *Samson* that is commonly depicted by many stone carvings on cathedrals during the 12th and 13th centuries – carvings that are still not only easily seen today, but would have been far more prominent during the 17th century at the making of the Noblet (Daniel is also often depicted, but usually more atop pillars of Romanesque churches, and *not* as overcoming or

controlling a lion).

There is little doubt (apart from the Samson-Herakles ambiguity) as to whom the Cary-Yale 15th century card referred. Likewise, there is no doubt with regards to the gender and figure of the equivalent card in the Visconti-Sforza. Whereas the former is definitely masculine and either Samson or Herakles, the latter is definitely feminine and seemingly allegorical.

By contrast, on the Noblet we may well ask whether the figure is masculine or feminine and, additionally, whether the animal is leonine.

If the body-shape or vestments of the figure are a little ambiguous, her crespinette, I would suggest, marks her as clearly feminine. Similarly, and though Jean-Claude Flornoy in various places talks of the animal being more 'bear'-like, there are sufficient iconographic and historical precedents to affirm Noblet's intention as leonine. Apart from such other earlier decks like those shown above, the *lack of bear* representation associated with *fortitude* makes his suggestion rather tentative at best.

This does not preclude a high degree of likely influence from, especially, the story of Samson on the card's design – in particular his long hair. The other common depiction of Strength with a broken pillar lends credence that, at least in popular imagination, 'strength' and 'Samson' were somehow equated.

So let's have a brief look at Samson and consider the card in that light for a short while.

Samson

The story is found in the *Tanakh* or Old Testament at *Judges* 13 *ff*. Samson seems born with amazing strength and yet also appears to retain a child's innocence. Some of the key parts to the biographical narrative include his killing of a young lion (and later getting honey from its carcass in which bees had hived); his fight and killing of a thousand Philistines with his only weapon being the jaw-bone of a donkey; the source of his strength being his uncut hair; and his final destruction by the breaking of the supporting pillars of the building that crashed upon himself and more Philistines.

It is a story that is one amongst the most image-rich from the earlier parts of the *Tanakh*, along with the Expulsion from Eden; the Staff of Moses; the Parting of the Sea; the Ten Commandments; King Solomon's Temple; and the Judgement of Solomon. Not that other parts of the Bible were not as well known: to be sure, they were. It is rather that it would be hard to avoid Samson as one of the better known stories and source of imagery.

Below Samson extracts honey from the carcass of the lion he has previously killed:

Out of the eater came what is eaten,

and out of the strong came what is sweet.

Judges 14:14

In both imagery, story – or rather *stories* – and in the riddle (given above) that Samson sets the Philistines, there appears apparent contradictory elements that ask to be somehow resolved: where the apparently weak is strong; where the predator becomes progenitor of food; where power becomes subdued quality.

Yet in the story, each instance of his incredible strength is viewed and described as a supramundane gift. His strength, his power, his force, is not 'his', but provided by being overshadowed with divine presence. Yet this too would have been understood as part-and-parcel of the Samsonite story.

Other images depict Samson as prefiguring the coming of Christ, and his 'ripping' the mouth of the lion as corresponding to the effortless wrenching of the mouth of Hell by Christ in liberating those there trapped. For example, a 15th century *Biblia Pauperum* from the Netherlands not only shows this similarity, but also *describes* the scene thus:

'Samson signifies Christ who when he freed man from the power of the devil killed the lion (that is the devil)'

Honey and strength

In response to Samson's riddle, the answer is given as:

> What is sweeter than honey,
> and what stronger than a lion?

Judges 14:18

Here we can again pause and consider the image of the Noblet – or indeed any other TdM!

From the mightiest of beasts can be extracted the sweetest of nectar. In a reading situation, let's consider for a moment how this may apply.

A reading exercise

Putting aside card XI Force, consider two strong (political) candidates from the same side (or party), each bidding for leadership. They each have the might and power to perhaps force the decision their way. Let's draw four cards, two for each of these candidates, informing us a little about their relative merits and personal strength.

There is a choice that can be made as to whether to 'unleash' the might of the beast, or to extract, as Samson did, the honey from the carcass. What are the likely consequences of each, and how can, given the cards drawn, each be best undertaken?

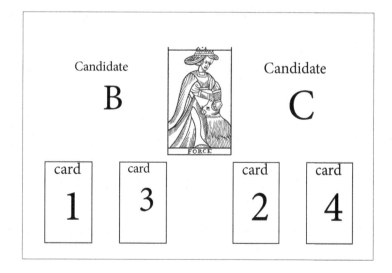

'La Force' as title

Even the common English translation of 'Strength' has a different sense to that in which 'La Force' would have been understood at the time of Noblet, and certainly earlier. Its meaning is a combination of three concepts: that of fortitude; that of strength, and that of force.

Even today, the two words that we use in English as 'Strength' and 'Force' tend to have the single form 'Force' in French. As for *Fortitude*, the word was introduced – or so it seems – as a latinised form of the French 'force' by Oresme when translating Aristotle for the 14th Century King of France Charles V (not to be confused with the *later* Roman Emperor mentioned with regards to the card IIII the Emperor, also called Charles V).

In this translation, the *Greek* concept translated is that of *Courage* – a term classically thought of in relation to the Lion's courageous heart and, in Plato, connected to the virtue required of the 'warrior' class (in the ideal city-state elaborated in his *Republic*). Interestingly, it is therein called *'andreía* (ie, the *feminine* form of ανδρείος) – *courage* (or 'manly' or even 'virile'), as opposed to the various Greek terms of 'power' or 'strength', the chief of which became the 'middle' three of the Dionysian hierarchy (*kyriotetes, dynamis*, and *exousia*). Part of the reason I mention this is that the last of these, *exousia* (εξουσία), is rendered in Hebrew with a term beginning as the open jaws of a lion with the eleventh letter of the alef-beit: כוח ('power' and 'force').

So here, we have the various concepts of courage (already mentioned in chapter eleven on the Virtues), fortitude, force, strength, and, by common Christian virtue association, *perseverance* (linked to courage) and *constancy* (linked to fortitude).

These two final concepts of perseverance and constancy, after all, present us with some key characteristics of courage and fortitude: without perseverance, one's engagement leads instead towards cowardice. Constancy similarly has some connotation of *holding on*, and in French, the same word form is used for both the act of releasing and to mean 'coward': 'lache' for the former, and 'lâche' the latter – again, by considerations of homophony (or its more picturesque appellation as the 'language of the birds'), a persistence in holding and maintaining one's position in the face of adversity can easily be seen as characteristic of the virtue of courage and fortitude.

In the annals of courageous acts, there are, then, overlaps and an interplay between these various concepts and ideas.

We could consider some of these through a wonderful tapestry of courageousness and fortitude dating from *circa* 1530 and produced in Brussels, Belgium – one from a series of seven tapestries now called the "The Triumph of the Seven Virtues": many famous and daring individuals are depicted for their famous acts – acts that often resulted in their own death, but for which the sacrifice was itself deemed of merit. Various places give explanations of many of the figures depicted on the image of the previous page. These do not, however, play a major significance to the point I make in this section.

Earlier, I mentioned *boldness* and should perhaps also mention that it is one of the more common renditions of the Latin 'Fortiter': to boldly go forth or boldly engage.

Achievement and boldness

What has ever been achieved without boldness? I am reminded of some of the outstanding speeches by various individuals. One of their common characteristics is the combined elements of daring, of boldness, of courage, and of fortitude: stuff of which inspiration can become contagious. To give an example, consider this by Winston Churchill during the middle of WWII (October 1941):

> Never give in - never, never, never, never, in nothing great or small, large or petty, never give in except to convictions of honour and good sense. Never yield to force; never yield to the apparently overwhelming might of the enemy.

"The apparently overwhelming might" – for such too is the image with which we are confronted in this card.

A sense of boldness, daring and courage can also manifest as exuberance and magnanimity – but not rashness. The rash, instead, would be viewed as without the virtue of fortitude. I once came across a description of Fortitude (or Force) as the complement or obverse of Temperance (to which we shall return in a few weeks): whereas the latter moderates the extremes of bodily pleasures, the former – the virtue with which we are concerned – is seen to moderate the extremes of the soul qualities of, at one extreme, fearfulness, and at the other, extreme rash recklessness.

Returning to the 16th century

Since chapter seven on the Emperor, I have been looking forward to adding a few additional notes on the period dominated by some of the most famous of Emperors (Charles V), French and English Kings (François *I* and Henry *VIII*), the Duchy of Milan with its Sforza rulers, the Medici Pope, and the important port of Marseille.

I take the opportunity here for two important reasons. The first is that (as mentioned in chapter seven) there was bitter rivalry between the Emperor Charles V and the loss of the French control of important tracts in what is now northern Italy – including Milan and Pavia. The second is the importance of the inter-relations occurring across this breadth of lands that also touch upon tarot's early development.

It was François *I*'s father who had ousted Sforza from Milan, but it was now under the dominion of Charles V.

Basically, in order to regain control, the French King François *I* (popularly known as "François Cœur de Lion" - ie, Lion Heart) sought to have his successor betrothed to the Medici Pope (Clement *VII*)'s cousin, thereby regaining the Milanese Duchy – even if this meant marrying well below the expected royal European households.

To seal the treaties and agreements, Pope and King met, not in Rome, Paris, Lyons, Milan or Avignon... but in Marseille – showing that travel even between France and the Roman part of Italy took the sea-route as an important alternative.

At the time, it was becoming increasingly common for important households (whether royal or otherwise) to have established exotic menageries or to be in possession of strange and wonderful creatures – for example, some kangaroos made it back to Paris a couple of centuries later.

Not only did a considerable portion of Marseille get razed to make room for parading entries by King and others, but, also:

> The French king took advantage of the occasion to rid himself of an un-welcome gift he had received from the Turkish corsair Barbarossa [...]. It was customary for great princes to exchange rare or exotic gifts, including animals such as elephants, monkeys, or sometimes deer, but the pirate had recently presented to François I a huge, tame Nubian lion with an insa-tiable appetite. With considerable relief, the French king passed this gift to Ippolito de' Medici, the pope's nephew and Catherine's dashing favorite cousin. Ippolito was delighted, and on his return to Rome, he commis-

sioned a portrait of himself posing with the lion.[2]

It was this same lion that was also said to at times occupy François *I* bed-chamber whilst the King slept.

Relative size of Lion and Figure

Let's have another look at the rendition of the Noblet and consider how a the size of a lion and a woman, drawn to realistic relative size, is likely to compare.

Of course, as for card V le Pape, a disproportion between figures can (and often was) used to indicate relative importance. In the case of La Force, a few earlier images from cathedral carvings show what was already relatively common and available to popular imagination. What is perhaps surprising is that their relative size, on both card and Cathedral petroglyph, is pretty much life-like.

2   HRH Princess Michael of Kent, *The Serpent and the Moon.* Some sections available online at: www.princessmichael.com/extract/index.html. Apart from other considerations, this should lay to rest the claim that lions were unknown in Paris around at that time.

It also appears significant that due to the common association of Samson with either Lion or Column, these *two* image forms became the norm to represent Force (*ie*, Fortitude): numerous images use either the lion or the column – and sometimes even both, as in the tapestry earlier shown.

From Lyon, France's 'second capital' and on the main road from Paris to the south, is a Cathedral quatrefoil (shown above).

This is undoubtedly a representation of Samson, amongst the hundreds that were formerly present – and even this one, as can be seen, is fast eroding (I took the photo in 2005).

Perhaps the more famous one is from Chartres Cathedral:

Observing a Lion

Some amongst us have the possibility of observing an actual lion, others will undoubtedly not have – or at least not for some time. If you are close to a Lion Park, or Zoological Garden, I would suggest spending an afternoon observing Lions – both at meal time and in mid-afternoon (during which they typically and sensibly enjoy a *siesta*).

These are, of course, neither animals in the wild, nor domesticated into pets. Their majesty, serenity, and amazing prowess is nonetheless certainly something to behold. The very deep growl they are also able to produce hints at their ferocious strength. Little wonder that in Ancient Egypt, Babylonia, and a host of other places, the Lion has had such a place in depictions associated with strength and regency.

Masculine and Feminine

There is one final point that seems obvious and yet on which we have not touched. We started by looking at the main figure and determining that she was feminine (even if ultimately derived from a masculine Samson). The *Lion*, however, is clearly lion, not lioness: its luxurious mane proclaims his virility and health. And yet, here it is subdued at the hands of a feminine figure that would without doubt have also been described as either virginal or asexual.

Other considerations

There are numerous other considerations that have similarity of design – especially with regards to the usage of the Lion in Alchemy, and with various ancient Greek (for example, Cybele), Egyptian, and Hindu figures. These, though worthy of further exploration, stand – in my view – outside the centrality of the depiction as found in TdMs in general, and outside the specifically Noblet imagery. With regards to Alchemy, we shall also return to the subject a little when discussing Temperance.

XII - Le Pendu

Le Pendu

This is a card that is often more *interpreted* than considered as presented. What I mean by this is that it is rarely seen for the brutality that it depicts – a brutality that admittedly appears to have been generally considered far more acceptable in former times than it now is (irrespective as to whether such brutality still *de facto* occurs).

Perhaps it is *because* of its brutality that so many among us make the psychological shift to considering it in myriad other forms: connecting to, or entering the card empathetically, is simply too difficult. Also, thankfully, few of us have actually experienced such or similar cruelty – whether upon our own person, nor even vicariously.

Yet, how many people, not only throughout history, but within our own respective lifetimes, have! Aspects of this chapter, in many ways, are not easy, but neither is the card if looked at in terms of its depiction. If nothing else, perhaps it may remind us that suffering, in its extreme and cruellest form, continues and that, from the perspective of the victim, it is a state that remains ever so singular and all-encompassing: there is no-one with whom to share one's pain.

With that opening, let's have a look at the image – leaving aside for the moment whether or not we may consider that his fate is deserved.

Despite all the instruments of torture that have been devised over time – and that seem to have been peculiarly acceptable during the late middle ages – the most common severe punishment was far simpler: a form of 'banishment' on the outskirts of the township, with the person often tied and left to the elements and to wild beasts both large and small.

Here we have in a very clear and simple representation a form of torture that was undoubtedly far more common than we would like to imagine. Similar 'banishments' and exposures also took the form of the victim being tied more-or-less spread out on the ground with feet and wrists pegged. Yet it seems that the reversed form of hanging, as depicted on the card, was also commonly practiced.

Frankly, this is an image that took some getting used to in seeing it *as it is actually depicted*. It is far easier, both psychologically and physically, to take it as metaphor.

What is the image?

Let's look at the card and compare it to other early cards and to similar representations from the period.

Starting from observing the image of our well-known Pendu, the very state depicted is more difficult to see *as is*. So also, let's begin by imagining being on the outskirts of a small late mediæval town and being faced with this character.

In imagination, observe how the other townsfolk look upon him. Perhaps the disdain of some, the sadness of another, the self-congratulatory stance of yet others. And the children, how do they look at him?

What may have he done to have been so punished? In the eyes of the local folks, is such punishment warranted?

Comparisons

One of the 'canonical' stabilisations of the TdM has been as represented by the Noblet: his left-ankle tied and his right leg dangling; two tree-posts and a top cross-beam; his arms (presumably) tied behind his back.

Below are the Dodal (a TdM-*I*) and the Conver (TdM-*II*). Though those general details mentioned as 'canonical' are there, observe especially that the arms are differently tied:

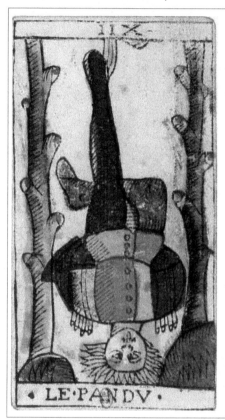 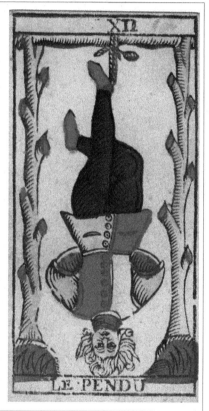

At times, such as on the Geoffroy (from *circa* 1557) and various Schaffhouse decks, the *two* ankles are tied (see the next page). Though both gibbet and tying are differently depicted, I frankly do not think that most early card users would have noted much of a difference: both forms were sufficiently common. Having said that, this detail plays an important part in considering the card 'as' the letter *Lamed*.

Another relatively early and common depiction is that, instead of the arms being tied behind his back, his wrists are weighed with two bags. Here, it has often been claimed that these are money bags – and that

 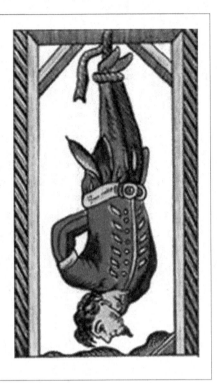

they may certainly have become, but sand, rocks or soil were the more common content: such prevented, as in the tying behind his back, the use of his hands; but also, furthermore, the additional agony of the weight against the ankle or ankles. An instance of this is also shown below.

For the 'dangling' bags, the clearest early deck, dating from about 150 years prior to the Noblet, in what has come to be (incorrectly) named the 'Charles VI' or 'Gringonneur' deck (adjacent page).

What is consistent across decks is that here is not a hanging by the throat as was to later become common as capital punishment, especially in Anglophonic areas (as the guillotine was for the French, and as burning on a pyre had earlier been especially for the Spanish); but rather a punishment that though often resulting in the death of the victim, may just as much *not* result in such.

In his series of essays on the development of the iconography of cards, Robert O'Neill especially talks of this depiction as 'shame hangings'.

Personally, given the widely dispersed prevalence of the practice, I would suggest that hangings used as 'temporary' shame punishments were its more 'benign' use.

'Common' imagery

Perhaps I should have titled this section 'imagery of commoners', rather than the 'shame' hangings of the wealthy and the landed aristocracy.

Despite the apparent prevalence of the practice, it is relatively difficult to find imagery from early days. This may be because of the vast volumes of images that have been reproduced and that are relatively easily accessible, the majority have been selected for specific purposes. Of the images of torture, the hanged man is not so grotesque when compared to numerous others that show humanity's culpability with regards to fellow human beings. When reversed hangings *are* reproduced, it is often in the context of demonstrating one or another instrument of torture, such as the "cat's paw" (depicted below – the images I had of this instrument being used on an *inverted* hanging being too damaged to recover), used to tear through the skin and flesh of the victim, or shown being brutally assaulted in order to break various bones – something to which we shall have to return (below also shown next to another person hanging with weighed bags or rocks).

It may also be mentioned that the inverted hanging was not the first (but likely the *final*) of punishments used, often *following* a series of interrogations (inevitably involving torture such as depicted here), his (or her – though the images generally depict men) flesh and bones mutilated, and his general health and strength significantly diminished.

With this as background, let's again have a look at the Noblet.

Arms and hands

Though it is easy to consider his hands as something other than hands as dangling from his shoulders, I personally think there is no doubt that both intent and depiction are of his hands.

There are only two ways that his arms can be so depicted behind his back – and I shall presume, in light of common and this specific

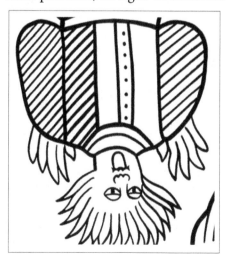

depiction, that they are tied approximately around the elbows: either he is extremely flexible (something that even if the case is unlikely to be what is presented); or, far more likely, either his elbows have been dislocated or his arms or forearms broken.

Reflection

Let's take some of these rather horrid considerations and reflect a little on how it may play into a reading-at-hand.

If depicting a specific person – and let's assume that the more literal torture does not apply – a whole wealth of inner torments may be what is depicted. The pre-hanging assaults felt at the hands of others; the isolation and feeling of neither being heard nor considered; the feeling of rejection and abandonment by one's community; the shame taken on as weight.

These can certainly be not only overburdening, but also, perhaps incredibly, lead to a death-wish to foreshorten the suffering.

Taken more metaphorically, there is a significant part that is played by the psychological disposition of the sufferer: what for some may be experienced as a transient difficult day will for others be experienced with the ferocity of the depicted hanged man.

In this, I am also reminded of a description from a sufferer of manic-depression that, during a particularly severe depressive phase, jumped in front of a passing truck. Fortunately (or should that be: 'fortunately') his injuries were only a few bruises and a couple of broken bones. Such pain, however, he described as insignificant when compared to the inner pain caused by the depression.

The hanged man, metaphorically, may accurately render the inner agony that many may suffer without any obvious external evidence.

Let's, then, take that aspect and consider the person so *internally* or psychologically tortured by the illness that besets them. The card may very well depict the condition of suffering, but it also, by the very depiction, offers a *partial* (perhaps even only minute) possible support: the isolation and abandonment may perhaps be bridged by under-standing and acceptance – a symbolic hand offered in untying the feet to the frame sitting outside the town, and permitting some form of redemption within the social body.

There are, of course, many other possible circumstances that may affect a person at a deep psychological and emotional level stemming from their experiences in and of the world, without these being 'illnesses'.

A reading

Shuffling the cards, consider any three of the following five individuals:

a) a young man from central Africa applying for asylum to either your own country (or a country of the 'first' world if the former is not an apt example);

b) a young woman from the Iranian/Pakistani/Afghan border-region finding herself in a South American country;

c) an 89 year old couple having lived all their life just outside of Berlin;

d) a local who lost a limb as consequence of a natural disaster (such as a cyclone or tornado, tidal wave or tsunami; asteroïd explosion or fire storm; or major earthquake or volcanic eruption);

e) a person who lives in your neighbourhood that you do not know, never having met them (perhaps there's a house in which you know not who lives).

On the reading surface, have three separate sections (to the left, top, and right, for example) upon which cards will be drawn and from which a narrative will be created. For example, persons A, B, and C may be given the following 'spaces':

Drawing one card at a time, place the first in section A and begin the narrative about the selected individual, then move to the second person, and begin his or her narrative, then to person C. Recommence and *add*

to the narrative of person A, B and C until the Hanged Man emerges – at which stage allow each narrative to be instructed by this card.

This becomes like the conversation between the three (or four) people, each taking turns in talking of aspects of their own personal biography, completed by revealing their own personal and unique experiences of suffering.

Now resume with an additional card (or couple of cards) for each, sequentially, to give an account as to how the suffering has been, is being, or will be resolved within the narrative.

Heresy and treason

There were, to be sure, many 'crimes' that would have been dealt with in the manner depicted. Some we may these days not even consider criminal – that of heresy of course easily comes to mind. Yet, we are reminded that even at the beginning of this 21st century, 'heresy' and religious apostasy are, in some places, punishable by cruel and brutal death.

The forms of torture and inverted hangings we have talked about were common enough as punishment for this very 'crime'. And particularly common victims (in Europe) were Jews.

Some of the clearest images of comparable depiction appear to come from the voluminous *Jews in Christian Art: an illustrated history* by Heinz Schreckenberg[1]. Here, we shall allow these images to bring us back to the many details of the card we have yet to consider.

The images to the right date from, respectively, 1477, 1553, 1642 and *circa* 1185, and cut across France, Switzerland, Austria and Germany. These, amongst others, perhaps better show that the practice was likely far wider across both time and place than has perhaps otherwise been considered. The dogs or flames shown in the first set also indicate that even on the scaffold, added suffering could be inflicted.

These depictions of what amounts to no more than intolerance of 'the other' can perhaps also be made the basis for metaphorical reflection: how our own respective norms 'hang' the person who holds 'heretical' views, even when not seeking to impose these upon others.

1   Though I had come across similar images elsewhere, I am specifically indebted to Stephen John Mangan for first mentioning this book with reference to the Hanged Man. Depictions are from pages 263, 360, 364 and plate 13 (between pp240 and 241), this last *not* depicting a Jew.

[the above depicts one of the torments of hell - unlike the other images specifically showing Jewish hangings.]

But let's return again to our Noblet image, for between the above depictions and the TdM are also some differences that may be of significance.

The Gibbet

Despite the gibbets shown above being similar to depictions in both the Geoffroy and Schaffhouse cards, the Noblet and other Marseille decks show these to be of far more crude rough-and-ready construction.

At its most basic, it seems to have been rather quickly and efficiently constructed: a couple of trees an appropriate distance apart have had their limbs sawn off, and a third tree-trunk (or large limb), also simply cleared of its excess branches, has been placed at an appropriate height, spanning the two trees that are still, apparently, firmly rooted in the ground (but see a quick additional note on the Gringonneur below).

We could very well imagine that once their immediate uses are over, the trees will continue to grow, those limbs sawn off simply looking as though pruned.

This is different to those depictions that show a 'professionally' constructed gibbets used, whether on the Geoffroy or the various woodcuts presented. The 'Charles VI' Gringonneur deck presents us with a mix of the two: the tree trunks or branches are relatively un-finished, but the verticals are nonetheless planted and spiked in the ground.

If my reading of the depiction of the Noblet and other TdMs is in some manner correct, then there is distinction between taking the gibbet to the place where the hanging will take place and, instead, taking the *person* where there are ready trees from which an impromptu frame can be quickly and easily made. This latter, inevitably, is outside the town's edge, perhaps at the very edge of woodlands where bears and wolves (and wild dogs and other beasts) may roam. This perhaps also implies that the victim may have been given little chance for a fuller and more formal legal trial (no matter how unjust we may deem those to have in any case been), but perhaps instead be at the mercy of a capricious group of townsfolk overshadowed by 'herd' mentality about the victim's presumed guilt: the victim may be even more innocent than *we* perhaps presumed.

Clothing

Similarly, we are presented, in each case of card depiction, with a clothed individual – though it should be noted that the Noblet seems to depict Le Pendu's penis, trousers and underwear (this last is not, in any case, common).

Here, one may have expected that this depiction be more common, whereby the victim is shown either naked, or with only a loincloth or minimal covering, as the following image of St Gregory from a partially (but severely) damaged church in Ani depicts[2].

Instead, on the Noblet and other TdMs, we are faced with what appears to be fully clothed individuals. This certainly does not seem, then, to indicate someone who has first undergone torture, but rather be the victim of a quick hanging. The only other general depiction of clothed individuals seem to be of those more 'global' (or communal) hangings of Jews or, alternatively, of nobles: again, then, usually a consequence of, in the first place, heresy, and in the second, treason.

Three other considerations

I have outlined what I personally consider are the central and most important considerations given the depiction shown. Nonetheless, with this and every card, other aspects may emerge or be considered. For this card, I shall mention three these, the first of which is in part based on

2   Ani is situated in what is now Turkey

the similarity of 'outline' of the central figure, the second is a reflection from or of the overall *image-form*.

The first of these is a similarity to the twelfth letter of the Hebrew alphabet. As I mentioned very early on, *if* there are any influences on the stabilisation of the TdM by a Hebrew alphabetic influence, it is neither clear nor obvious. *Alef* (the first letter) and *Lamed* (this twelfth letter) are the main two that bear resemblance to their respective trump order, and that as such can be viewed as perhaps meriting notice in terms of their *shape* (of course, a stronger influence would be by word-association, an example of which is mentioned for *XI La Force*, and also as presented by Mark Filipas in his *Alphabetic Masquerade*). With *Lamed*, the left 'leg' is as suspended above the normal writing line, and the right shows (in abstracted form) the right leg 'folded' at the knee.

The second consideration comes from the notebooks of cathedral builders (with some similar depictions used as astronomical tools). Here,

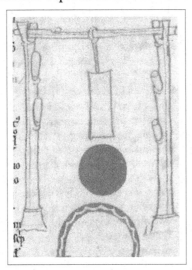

I shall leave the depiction of this pendulum to speak for itself as tool – but certainly one that opens avenues for quite varied and transformative considerations, including that of willing sacrifice and of initiation, both of which, of course, result more from interpretative reflection than from the image as given.

Finally, a brief mention needs to be made of the treason of Judas Iscariot and his 'numbering' as the *twelfth* disciple. This is evident from not only New Testament listings in all the synoptic Gospels (Matthew 10:2-4; Mark 3:13-19; Luke 6:12-17; as well as as John 13:29), but is also specifically mentioned as such by one of the highly influential Church Fathers, St Irenaeus, in his *Against Heresies* (Bk II 20:4):

> Judas, then, the twelfth in order of the disciples, was not a type of the suffering Æon, nor, again, was the passion of the Lord; for these two things have been shown to be in every respect mutually dissimilar and inharmonious. This is the case not only as respects the points which I have already mentioned, but with regard to the very number. For that Judas the traitor is the twelfth in order, is agreed upon by all, there being twelve apostles mentioned by name in the Gospel. [...]

Judas, to be sure, was considered as the archetypal traitor, whose treachery lead not only to the death of his own friend and lord, but to his own fall.

Brutality at door's edge

A final remark on the centrality of the image as depicted. Let us not delude ourselves into thinking that brutality is restricted to what only others are capable of. A friend, who has relatively recently passed away, once described to me a situation that occured in an Eastern European country around the time of WWII which she witnessed as an adolescent: a 'traitor' to the township was killed by literally having his arms and legs ripped from him by the townfolks whose rage surpassed their normal benign humanity.

What is, for each of us, our own limits to participate in acts we would normally consider beyond the pale of decency when placed in situations we can but hope to never face!?

About Readings, Eschatology & Metaphysics

Readings, Eschatology and Metaphysics

Of all the 'peripheral' topics, I feel a need to give a brief explanation as to why, especially, eschatology and metaphysics have been chosen.

Over the past seventeen chapters, I hope to have presented considerations that show not only the depth and breadth of the TdM's scope, but also that quite different worldviews can be considered or held by its users. Some of the considerations on which I shall focus this week include how the worldview one holds will not only have ramifications for the manner in which we are able to see into the images presented to us, but also, in the context of a reading, how either a fair compatibility of understanding between the reader and readee is required or, alternatively, the need to couch the narrative in a manner that can be more easily considered from world-views other than our own.

A reading example

To begin by giving a brief example of a reading, let's take three cards and allow *one* narrative description to emerge (remembering that in the context of a specific reading, other narratives, quite different, may be more apt). The three cards that follow were randomly selected at the time of writing the first notes that form the basis of this chapter:

Here I'm just going to allow my reactions and thoughts to emerge as I go along – in part to share the manner in which a reading arises for myself (which is not, however, unique), without in any way suggesting that this is the only manner by which either yourself or I may engage with the cards.

My first thought was one of 'surprise' (with tarot, it seems that one is simultaneously surprised, and not surprised at the surprise!) that the first card drawn was the very card we considered last week, and that the last card (Justice) can so easily be linked to it. I was also pleased that at least one pip emerged – statistically, of course, I could have expected two pips (or at least two non-trumps!).

As I look at the three cards together, the central one seems to hint at the reason or cause of the consequence manifesting in the hanged man. In other words, a suggestion that his inappropriate involvement and participation in an activity presented by the three swords has resulted in Justice using her active hand of punishment (even the orientation between the cards adds to this: the Hanged Man is on her *sword* side, not *scales* or compensatory side).

In this case, largely as a consequence of Justice appearing 'just' (upright, not reversed), I am lead to consider the Hanged Man as representing 'shamefully hanged', though to be understood in this situation (and in most actual worldly situations most of us are likely to face) in its metaphorical sense: he has been publicly shamed by the hand of justice for his involvement that, in this case, need *not be the law nor the legal system*.

Already all that I have typed (in my rather slow typing mode) has taken me far longer than the more flash-like weaving between the cards that has occurred within my imaginative narrative, which is far ahead of even these very words.

The very *processing* of the narrative as 'developed imaginative story' allows for ongoing insights into the interweaving between the cards to re-tune emerging insights into the situation-at-hand.

I have at this stage not yet talked about what it is that three swords may refer to – all I have suggested is that a person has acted inappropriately, and has had to face some 'just' humiliation as a consequence.

I may at different times have a more definite sense for the type of engagement to which the three swords refers (from financial, to sexual, to social). In *this* case, what seems of more import is not the specific, but that he has intruded in a situation in which it was not only *not* his prerogative, but not his place. The sense of 'intrusion' leads me in this case to consider some form of 'breaking and entry', and possibly being caught out before finding the materials or documents which he was in search of – represented to my imaginative reflection as the 'floral' emblems in the quarter sections but *outside* the curved swords.

So to briefly re-capitulate this overall reading: we have an individual who sought some items for which he intruded into an area that was not his domain, and, being caught out, was consequentially self-humiliated for so doing: he 'hangs his head in shame'.

The two curved swords here also suggests (in this instance) more the *vesica piscis*, and I am lead in imagination to something considered sacred, as though what the person did was to enter a sacred precinct to find items or remnants of holy relics or items considered sacrosanct.

Speaking the narrative

Let's take the above, then, as the imaginative scenario that instructs the developing narrative.

The description above gives no explanation as to why or how the person was found out – simply that he (as I have used the masculine pronoun thus far for the individual concerned) entered, was found out, and suffered shame.

I have neither provided the reading in terms of psychological or emotive terms nor spiritually-based ones. For example, the two brief statements that follow may have been spoken in light of the above by two different individuals 'seeing' in the reading the same as I have described:

> The person, having been found out seeking to steal those items, was overwhelmed with remorse at both his action and his public humiliation. He felt wounded and somewhat demoralised at the projected sense that his personal integrity was deemed to have suffered.

Contrasted to:

> The nearly instant karmic consequence of his being found out was perhaps a blessing from his spiritual carers, who saw that by suffering the humiliation he nonetheless had sufficient fortitude and that thus such action would not be left as seeds to be resolved in future lives.

I am certain that many amongst us would see that each of these ways of speaking (including my original description in the first instance) has its merits, and has its advocates. The point being that whereas the first 'speaking-in-the-act-of-interpreting' (at least in the manner in which I strove to present it) has the speaker's (ie, my) worldview invisible to the reader and also leaves such an embellishment *open* to the listener.

By contrast, the other two direct the listener towards, on the one hand, a psycho-physiological interpretation (and one that may of course be quite adequate), and on the other to considerations of trans-life spiritual realities (which of course may, again, be entirely apt). In the specific context of the reading-at-hand, the *person* for whom the reading is intended remains of paramount importance, as does also the integrity of the *reader*. As such, though each of these ways of reading may be adequate, apt, or entirely appropriate, each may also not be optimal.

Worldview

In *A Secular Age*[1], Charles Taylor describes well the worldview that permeated the mediæval and Renaissance mind-set. If we can for a moment realise that our current social situation is one in which *individual* difference of belief is regarded as more or less the norm (even if we too on the whole tend to a commonality of world-view); contrasted to this, in the non-pluralistic world-view permeating former times, even the relative 'free thought' accepted and in some places encouraged around the time of Noblet's creation was one entirely embedded within what was 'evidently' a spiritual worldview.

Certainly there were differences of views. Various religious and spiritual viewpoints certainly had their adherents – as shown by the larger religious movements, whether 'pagan' (to be contrasted to, and quite different from, the neo-pagan 20th century revival), Jewish, or the various Christian sects.

It was not for another century, following the creation of the Noblet, that some of the quite appalling 'proofs by demonstration' that animals were 'soul-less' – carried out in quite horrendous ways by Descartes and others – opened the way for more 'secular' *materialistic* and *physicalist* worldviews. Even for those involved in such 'research', of course, there was no question that at least *humans* were endowed with a spiritual substance or essence.

I mention this not only for the historical situation that can allow us to further understand the context in which tarot developed, but also to consider for a minute the potentially vast and contrasting mind-sets that we face in the context of a reading. At the very least, reflecting upon and even beholding three characteristic metaphysical views would greatly assist a reader in meeting with *understanding* those for whom they are reading.

1   Harvard Uni. Press, 2007

In that light, let's consider three dominant and contrasting worldviews and their metaphysical and eschatological views, for each has its own unique *gestalt*, or way of apprehending, which is far more than an ideology that may drive one to particular action. Rather, the permeation *of* and *by* such metaphysical and eschatological views *overshadows* and *underpins* both thought and narrative – including our own.

At the very least, a greater awareness of our own language-use that, either consciously or not, effectively reflects such *Weltanschauung*[2] is best brought to conscious attention.

Weltanschauung & Weltansicht

In our modern world, amongst the numerous ways the world is perceived, three appear as dominant and central exemplars. Variations, of course, cut across these.

We'll briefly consider here the following three to give more a *sense* for the manner in which vast *Weltansicht* orientations may emerge: the Judeo-Christian; the Hindo-Buddhist; and the Psycho-Physicalist.

Even simply stating the above world-views evokes in each of us different sympathies and antipathies. These speak not only of our own *Weltanschauung*, but also of the manner in which we are likely to couch our narrative.

Irrespective of our personal (and maybe even political or religious) rapport with each, let's consider these as exemplars.

The Judeo-Christian view posits a spiritual realm filled with myriad spiritual beings (whether these are considered as 'extensions' of a Supreme Being or as independent is not so important for this characterisation). In addition, there are two other characteristics that are essentially important: the concept of a *Messiah* (*Mashiach* or anointed); and that of the world (and its evolution) arising out of a creative *Fiat* from the spiritual realm.

With some similarities to the above, the Hindo-Buddhist view considers that the world is in essence something other than its appearance, and that we traverse it in limited consciousness until liberated by awakefulness.

---

2   This German terms, approximating 'worldview', 'world perception', or 'beholding of the world', is not adequately translatable. *Weltansicht*, though somewhat similar (literally: 'world sight') approximates more an *attitude* one exhibits in light of the *Weltanschauung*.

Again, we can notice similarities between these and the psycho-physical view, though this last's essential characteristics include the view that both world and ourselves are temporary manifestations within a spatial-temporal matrix of fluctuating forces.

These three *Weltanschauung* are not only quite distinct but, in their more extreme forms, seek to re-define or strive to understand the other worldviews as a small subset *within* their own general overview. This can be seen, for example, in attempts by physicalists to account for religious experience as particular and specific human (and perhaps animal) dispositions of the brain; or, alternatively, for the Judeo-Christian or Hindo-Buddhist to explain the physicalist position as an observation of a tiny fragment of manifestation in a world that is essentially spiritual in nature.

Specifically in terms of an eschatological view, the three exemplars call to mind vastly differing views: in the first (ie, the Judeo-Christian view), a clear and unequivocal ongoing existence of the person (not taking into consideration the dissolution within the divine godhead that some may posit, or the annihilation of the wicked postulated by others); in the second (Hindo-Buddhist), there is generally a sense of mindfulness that sees the individual as a drop within a vast ocean; and in the third (ie, the Psycho-Physicalist), the person is described as existing between the portals of birth and death (outside of which, the 'person' is not)[3].

In the context of the narrative, then, we are faced with not only our own *Weltansicht* and its concomitant *Gestalt*, but also the narrative's hearers may well be beholding the narrative within a structural understanding vastly at odds with the speaker's.

So what is perhaps *common* not only to each worldview, but the human condition itself?

The Quest for Meaning & Plenitude

What has at times been called the quest for *meaning* and *understanding* is inevitably *one* of the driving forces behind seeking a reading.

Here I suggest that we should differentiate this from another concept that may at first appear similar: that of *plenitude* or *fullness*, ie,

---

3   I am well aware that such overly succinct characterisation leaves much out of the picture, and that neither the variety within each *Weltanschauung* example, nor elements of commonality and overlap that may be found, is here presented.

experiencing a fulfilled life.

Let's distinguish the two concepts of *meaning* and *plenitude* as different driving forces.

The very first distinction that seems apparent is that of *time*: whereas the concepts of meaning and understanding seem to be reflective of the past, those of plenitude and fullness seem to be of the present and, when mixed with hope, of the future.

Meaning seems to address questions such as

'What is happening, and *why?*'

or

'What really happened, and why did such occur?

whereas *plenitude* suggest something like:

'What will my work/love/travel/situation be like, and why?'

We can already see here that the metaphysical views held will very much impact on how meaningfully the narrative is received. At the very least, the possibility of considering various ways of understanding the 'what' and 'why' drives much of not only our attempts at seeking to *understand* our world (physical, social and spiritual), but also to make it 'good', to give it plenitude.

I would suggest that the historical development of those three key worldviews (Judeo-Christian, Hindo-Buddhist, and Psycho-Physicalist) seek, in their own way, to balance notions that may pull us in different directions in, firstly, seeking to *understand* our situation; secondly, *fill* life with abundance; and *thirdly*, provide a means towards an impulse of integrity and absolute *authenticity*.

Authenticity

It is perhaps also this concept of *authenticity* that leads readings (and their attendant narratives) to take particular forms. To return to the example with which we opened the chapter, the first description has a 'sincerity' and authenticity as the reader (myself, in that scenario) strives to reach an *understanding* of the cards as presented. However, it may only be by the third example of the narrative I presented earlier, the one that begins by speaking of the 'karmic consequences', that the reading achieves not only meaning and authenticity, but also *plenitude* for a specific individual – something that for another person may instead *diminish* plenitude and even *lack* authenticity.

For the reader, *authenticity* requires being true to oneself, even whilst retaining sensitivity and empathy with the person for whom the narrative is intended.

Empowering

If I can for a moment also consider this term, frequently used in the world of tarot, I would suggest that first and foremost it encompasses those three previously touched upon: the increase of understanding or *insight*; the increase of fullness or *engagement*; and one's *self-truthfulness* or authenticity.

The reading or narrative as communicative act assists the intended hearer in any one or more of these, and in that sense, ideally leads to steps, in the healthy individual, to increased *light, love* and *life* – to use a well worn triplicity that could well be taken as keys with which to approach both tarot and the development of the narrative reading.

Three exercises

[1] – Let's pause for a moment and reflect on the Hermit – a card that in chapter fourteen I mentioned would be again considered when we reached this one.

He is certainly an individual who can be considered from his likely historical basis. Here we are more concerned with how he can be viewed cutting across time – as someone that has perennial value (as of course all cards have).

So firstly, how would the Hermit manifest as representative of those three characteristic worldviews presented earlier? What would be his distinct difference if representative of the Judeo-Christian, Hindo-Buddhist, and Psycho-Physicalist *Weltanschauung*? How would he respond to individuals with distinct *Weltansicht* to his own?

How is his lamp useful to even those who do not share his views or worldview – those who (literally) see the world differently, those for whom their *Gestalt* is radically at odds with his own?

How is the element of *time* and its passage reflected in the Hermit, and what can it tell us about *plenitude of life, insights*, and *authenticity*?

[2] – Consider something you have never before undertaken *and is possible for you to undertake* – for example, hot-air ballooning, or

underwater diving, or skiing (whether water, grass or snow), or taking a steam-train or helicopter ride, and draw *two cards* for how you would likely experience it.

Here, take the time before the reading to really reflect on what it may be like by fully immersing yourself in imaginative engagement in the act. Allow the narrative to develop, *note* it, and, if feasible, *do* it over the next twelve months and compare your experience with not only your reading, but also return to the cards and re-read them afresh in light of the actual experience.

[3] - Resolve to offer a three card reading to someone (either a friend; or online on any Bulletin Board or Forum that has this as an option and to which you are already a member).

Allow the narrative to emerge of its own accord. Remember that this is also an exercise in reflection. Once the developed narrative has been given (no longer than about a page, and perhaps only a paragraph), reflect upon – but do not allow this part to influence you during the narrative itself – the specific metaphysical or eschatological views that appear to therein be embedded. As it can be difficult to *consider* this because we can be as oblivious to our own worldview as fish (or so we popularly assume) are oblivious to the ocean in which they dwell, 'critique' it from the perspective of the Judeo-Christian, Hindo-Buddhist, and Psycho-Physicalist *Weltanschauung*.

What aspects of the reading appear to reflect a meaningfulness or understanding of a situation; or provide for a manner of deeper engagement; or reflects authenticity on yourself as reader, and for the person receiving the reading?

What does the reading tell you about your own engagement in life, your insights, and sense of self?

Again, I would suggest here keeping notes and, if appropriate, asking for feedback from the person to whom the reading was offered.

Card Spreads

Quite early on I suggested 'flipping' cards on a surface until the number flipped was deemed sufficient, followed by looking for flowing patterns, the manner in which cards appeared to relate to one another, and for 'groups' of cards to emerge. I would suggest repeating this exercise at this stage. For some amongst us, the difference between carrying it out all those weeks ago and now may not be great – for others amongst us, however, our careful ongoing observation of individual cards is likely to have already opened further vistas in this exercise.

Yet, this is not a card spread that I would necessarily recommend in most situations. Apart from any other consideration, it is rather unwieldy and perhaps even a little too grandiose and extraverted for many. What is *does* show is that card spreads need not ever be fixed, and that the situation at hand may often suggest its own spread – whether it be seeking a creative solution to a board-room meeting; developing a script for a play or film; or addressing situations a person presents. The specific number of cards, their relative position, and the way in which they may inter-relate can easily vary from context to context.

With that said, in chapter twenty-seven (focussed on XVIII the Sun), I shall also refer to the ten-card 'Celtic' Cross spread. For now, let us content ourselves with *developing* a spread that may be appropriate for different situations.

For example, if writing a story (such as a novel) – the most famous of which is perhaps Italo Calvino's *Castle of Crossed Destinies* – a few cards for each chapter may allow for interrelations to emerge in unexpected ways. The *number* of cards, and their relative arrangement, will probably very much depend on how the narrative develops and weaves.

Let's take the following situation and see what emerges.

A person in charge of a group of people is faced with long-term conflicts amongst them, and would like a reading to both better *understand* the situation and to provide the means by which to better *engage* each in the tasks at hand, remaining *sincere* about her own task (ie, recognising that the conflicts may not be her burden to either carry nor assist in resolving).

Let's begin to develop a spread. And here, a reminder that there is no single 'best' method: for some of us – or perhaps even for each of us in some situations – the most effective method may be to simply draw cards and begin a narrative; for others – or again perhaps for each of us in various situations – it may be more effective to reflect on the type of problem and the kinds of inquiry in order to 'structure' the reading-at-hand.

Let's approach it from this second perspective in this case.

We have a group of individuals who have conflicts, so let's assign an area of our reading surface for that. We also have the person with responsibilities for the group, so let's also allocate her a separate space.

The nature of the reading also calls for means by which to best engage each in the tasks at hand, so let's give that a third space.

Already, a structure begins to emerge:

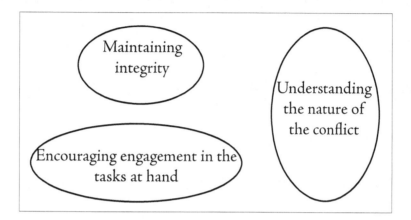

To the right we have a space to strive to *understand* the situation; below and to the left a space to suggest how to best *engage* in the tasks at hand; and the smaller space above perhaps suggestions as to how best keep the person's own *integrity* in the process.

Let's address these one at a time.

In order to understand the nature of the conflicts, perhaps two or three cards may be sufficient. Indeed, in some cases, even a single card may suffice. Developing the narrative as speaking from the cards, the woven words provide the basis for an understanding – without necessarily the specifics being known (which may be either irrelevant or of a more private nature) – of an aspect of the conflict being faced.

We now face the question as to how best *engage* each person in the tasks at hand, for which another three or four cards are drawn, again in part determined by the developing narrative. As can be seen from this chapter's opening three-card spread, it may be that details are weaved back and forth with few cards until the imaginative faculty is given sufficient space in which to allow the ideas to further crystallise.

Finally, a card or two may be drawn to guide the person in charge in terms of her own inner rectitude.

In order to see *how* this spread may look, I suggest actually drawing cards and briefly 'speaking' the narrative.

In this spread, the right-hand cards are very much 'past' focussed in time or existing relation; whereas the others more 'future' oriented in either suggesting potential solutions or in simply being oneself.

I perhaps should note that this is not a reading I had undertaken prior to considering this chapter. In other words, I sought for a situation that has its own freshness at the time of writing, allowing its own specific case to speak of its own accord.

This, and every situation, may at times best be met by in-the-moment spreads that develop with the developing narrative. In other words, the distinction I initially drew in the two methods described earlier are reconciled: the problem at hand structures its own spread in the very act of the narrative, itself in development.

Back to the Noblet

It is pretty evident that this chapter has not specifically focussed on the Noblet, nor indeed on any specific deck. The assumption, however, is that each point raised has been considered with the usage of this deck (even though the same may of course have been said with any deck under consideration).

Where the TdM-type in general, and the Noblet in particular, assume an important role in the above reflections is that, as with our own individual narratives, the very *imagery used* speaks its own assumptions. Some of these we have already met, and more will become apparent in the coming chapters. In some ways, it is in part those internal conflicts we may have between the presented image and our own (at times even perhaps quite significantly) different *Weltanschauung* to Jean Noblet's, as well as inevitable differences in the manner in which we *engage* in the world, that leads us to seek to understand afresh those images as symbolic and relevant to our world some four centuries later than his.

XIII - La Mort

Death

If we consider the death toll of WWI (over 40 million), the 'Spanish' flu (40-100 million), the casualties of WWII (60+ million – including its attendant atrocities of 10+ million), various natural disasters, the continuous wars that have occurred during the course of that same century, and the vast number of deaths resulting from travel, work, and recreational accidents, it's quite astounding how oblivious to death we generally are in western culture.

An aspect that adds to such obliviousness includes a dramatic shift from country or village to city dwelling, in which not only are most people living around us not known, but friendships and community groups may change a number of times over a lifetime. In that context, there may even be a certain unreality to death which becomes psychologically equivalent to someone moving to a place where we are unlikely to see them again – a distancing, rather than a facing of death *qua* death.

By contrast, our forebears inevitably faced death far more squarely: life in village or countryside, and even in former towns or cities, the death of someone was more intrinsically weaved into the life of the departed's kin and, in many cases, the whole community.

There was also a far more intimate knowledge of death *within* family life reflected in two ways: the elderly passed their final years and ultimate transition within the extended familial home; and the likelihood, in most families, of experiencing the death of one or more young children.

In that context, death was not only ubiquitous – as it inevitably continues to be – but also, more importantly, it was (excuse the pun) 'lived with' as normal occurrence. Hence, 'meaning' had to be more readily assigned to death.

That I did not, for example, directly behold the death of another human being until my mid-twenties is perhaps not that unusual in our current culture, yet something simply unimaginable in the context of mediaeval and Renaissance Europe; and, I would suggest, the rest of the world[1].

Yet I am sure that no matter our age, we have all had some more or less intimate experience with the death of either family relation, friend, or in

---

1   I suspect that the poignancy and 'foreign-ness' of Gautama Buddha's experience given his childhood's insulated life is partially lost, in that most among us also live a relatively sheltered life, only never coming to experience what he then had to face as the daily lot of most of humanity.

some cases someone far closer than these terms may perhaps connote.

It has at times been claimed that the tarot image of Death would have called to mind (or even derives) from the various plagues that assaulted Europe. Undoubtedly, when a plague struck a region, this type of imagery, or indeed any other image of Death allegorically depicted, would have been used (or imaginatively 'invoked' and called to mind in stories told). There were (and are), however, sufficient occurrences of death, in various guises, in everyday existence without the need to bring to consciousness a plague in another region or period to account for the image used here. To be sure, *we* nonetheless may want to consider such to deepen our own reflections and gain a broader understanding of Death in general.

Personal view

Before making more general comments on Death itself, however, I would suggest taking a few moments to consider our own views on the matter. This is part of the process and its importance I tried to bring in the last chapter, and trust that, no matter how partially formed our own views, we can each begin to consider not only where we stand, but also be able to consider the great chasm that exists between our own beliefs and the belief of others on this subject.

Take a few minutes to consider your own sense for what happens at death, when the life of the body lives no more. Similarly, consider what happens at birth. And what occurs with the reaping of corn (and I use this word in its earlier sense of any grass seed cereal)?

Looking at the card

Frankly, I cannot see how Death could have been seen as other than proof of life beyond the portal of death. Apart from the numerous writings of Christians and the neo-Platonist, neo-Aristoteleans, and Jewish scholars, Biblical text itself would suggest the same.

And here I shall only refer to a single Biblical passage that seems quite apt:

> In all truth I tell you,
> unless a wheat grain falls into the earth and dies,
> it remains only a single grain;
> but if it dies
> it yields a rich harvest.

Anyone who loves his life loses it;
anyone who hates his life in this world
will keep it for eternal life.

John 12:24-25

The tarot image is not simply an image of 'death' – despite its name. If we consider it carefully, it is one of the few cards in which the main character is in *active* movement, in this case, in reaping with a scythe.

There is also a juxtaposition of opposites common enough for the allegory: the figure of Death is itself presented very much as living. In so many ways, this is quite in contrast to depictions of the process of dy*ing*, in which characters depicted are often sickly and inert.

Let's pause for a moment and consider how the activity depicted in this card contrasts with either the lack of or different activity in other cards.

To my own reflections, this card appears to be only one of *two* that seems to engage the movement of the whole body through one's own volition, the other, which in this deck faces the opposite direction, is the Fou (often called 'Mat', to which we shall refer to in chapter thirty).

Image symmetry with Fou

Looking at these two cards, let's also consider the image symmetry of Death and Fou by placing these side by side in their various possible ways – including mirror imagery[2]:

Let's also, as a comparison of interest, note the differences between our Noblet representation with that of the anonymous 17th century Parisian and the Vieville decks, and the later 18th century TdMs (both type *I* and

2   I have not shown them with the Fou also reversed, so other permutations exist, including arranging these two cards above and below each other.

II) in their Dodal and Conver form:

What is immediately striking is the obvious opposite direction of the figure in the earlier and later depictions. Even the Dodal, a TdM-*I*, has the figure inverted when considered against the Noblet.

We may also take for granted the universality of the scythe; so, for the sake of completion, let's call to mind that it was not the sole allegorical representation used on either tarot cards. Other imagery has included: bow with drawn arrow; or, in the case of the Geoffroy (that brings our previous consideration of similarity with the Fou to even greater magnitude), with shouldered shovel as well as his scythe held in a more 'walking-stick' manner:

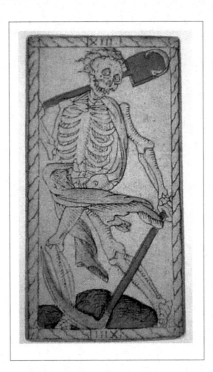

Death as Reaper

What we have, then, is Death represented not as 'killer', but as reaper. Given the context of communities which remained very much dependent on agriculture, the imagery needs to also be seen in light of the reaping of the fields, each autumn, bringing the necessities of life. Death's nature begins to transform itself in the very act of reaping: life is cut short in order that abundance of life may be lived in the hereafter.

Let's also consider what the reaping normally consists of: grains

– whether it be barley, wheat, or any other corn (and here again a reminder that to the European of former times, 'corn' is not, or at the very least is not only, 'maïze').

It is from such reaping that flour is ground from which to bake bread and, with different crops, brew beer: two essential food staples in many parts of Europe (water, without the cleansing benefits of alcohol, was often avoided). Both these 'foods' are, incidentally, yeasted (or 'leavened').

The very act and activity of a full harvest also promises, then, an abundance of sustenance during the long dark season that would follow.

In such a context and given the image, Death literally engenders and preserves life.

Yet the reaping is also of life itself[3].

Reaping of Heads

When I first cast my eyes on the Noblet after many years with other Marseille-type (and non-Marseille-type) tarot, what struck me was the *exclusivity* of the two heads depicted on the ground.

Compare the Noblet with the Dodal and Conver shown above. Unlike on those two latter decks (or on the Vieville, for that matter), *only* the heads, as body parts, are shown: no hands nor feet are on the Noblet – and this, I personally consider, is what one would expect by analogy to the reaping of corn in which only the 'heads' are deemed of 'value', the rest discarded (or rather, discarded as fodder).

This does not mean that we cannot consider the hands and feet as emblematical of our actions and that they too are 'harvested'; rather, it is the symbolic analogy that seems to work with incredible simplicity in the Noblet.

Of note, then, are that two human heads are represented on the ground, one crowned and masculine, the other seemingly feminine.

3   I remain hesitant as where best add the following point, as it 'fits' at the cross-thoughts of reflections on the suit of swords, III the Emperor, XII Le Pendu, and here, especially with regards to the close connection that exists between life and death: 'War is for men,' according to a Vietnam war veteran referred to by J. Glover in *Humanity*, 'at some terrible level the closest thing to what childbirth is for women: the initiation into the power of life and death. It's like lifting off the corner of the universe and looking at what's underneath.' Quoted in C. Taylor *A Secular Age*, p 840.

There yet remains a *third* human head depicted, to which we shall return in a short while; but first, a brief consideration of the scythe itself.

The Scythe and the Sword

Laying out the pips of the suit of swords, imagine each of the stylised scimitars or sabres as the blade portion of scythes.

The clear distinction between a scythe and a sword is not only its intended use, but also who may legitimately wield the one or the other: no noble would normally be able to wield the scythe and, conversely, no peasant the sword.

Consider, then, that each scythe represented depicts either a plot of cultivated land or a peasant working that land, and each straight sword a noble connected to the same field(s).

How is the relation of mutual benefit? How and in what forms can abuse take place – on the part of any of its members? Considering the whole pips laid out as a whole 'country' or region, how does this reflect the inter-communal relations?

Are all crops the same across regions? Are all inter-relations between straight sword and curved similar?

And what of the curved sword without straight ones, how are those to be explained?

Taking some time to consider the above, let's also allow the Death card to enter the scene. How is it reflected, considered and handled in each separate setting? how do adjacent fields respond to the entry of death in one field?

Is Death part of nature?

The very question draws us into considerations that extend beyond death itself. The quote from St John (earlier in this chapter) certainly leads to considerations that the sowing of the grain and its interment into the womb of the Earth is akin to its death and burial and forthcoming resurrection when brought to growth with the waters of life (and, in parallel reflection of this, the move of winter into, eventually, Easter).

There is, however, another view common enough, and clearly illustrating the point. St Ambrose writes:

> Death was not part of nature; it became part of nature.

If nothing else, implying that death is only part of an experiential process in the life of the Spirit.

In some manner, then, the seed may be considered *not to die*, but rather to be metamorphosed into new life, each annual cycle promoting the eternal cycle of life. Such passing into (and hence below) the earth and out again in cyclical motion is well exemplified by the Greek saga of Persephone and Demeter and, perhaps, such would have been brought to consciousness to those reflecting on this card, in some manner more allegorical[4], yet literal, than any other cards so far considered.

Allegory

If we consider the sequence thus far, we have seen stations in life (Bateleur, Empress, and others), representations of life's situations and engagements (l'Amoureux, le Pendu), virtues (Justice and also, in some important manner, the Chariot), and, perhaps by contrast, the Wheel of Fortune as representing life's fluctuations.

Here with Death, however, we have the *personification of an event*. Looking through the deck, this card has this unique quality – though of course this does not mean that image-as-allegory is omitted in other cards.

This is a quality that permits death's ever-so popular caricatured renditions in the 'dance macabre' (or 'dance of death'). Some of the more famous pictorial fragments include images from the Dance of Death from Lübeck (destroyed in WWII but shown in its Tallinn version below). In any case, similar renditions were common enough in manuscript, in various carvings, and in paintings, depicting Death as playfully calling forth its partner to dance, whether it be Emperor, maiden or child. Above are some woodcuts from a source I have misplaced – at the very least, these shows Death in its ever so common form and its inevitability.

A similar *Dance Macabre* is also readily locatable in a quite early book known as the Totentanz blockbook.

---

4   Allegories are characterised in *Meditations on the Tarot* as "figurative representations of abstract notions". To add to the notions of the author of that work, allegories also have an inevitable *symbolic* notion which, as he describes, awakens in us *new* notions, ideas, sentiments, insights and aspirations by the active engagement of the individual studying and reflecting. We can see, of course, in allegory a clear *representation* of something that otherwise remains far more intangible.

Famines, disasters and pestilence

Although the Black Plague had hit Europe some centuries earlier, there would have been only a few generations that did not experience it in Europe even at the time of Noblet and his immediate descendants. However, not every town or region faced the plague in any given generation. Still, disease, poison, and natural disaster were not only common, but feared as a risk that could strike at any time.

In addition, there was the semi-frequent outbreak of famine, the all-too frequent spread of minor disease that had, for many, serious consequences, and the semi-regular outbreak of ergot poisoning (St Anthony's fire).

To give a sense for the frequent outbreak of the plague, consider that Noblet's deck was created not long after the Italian plague and during a great plague in Spain (the 'great plague of Seville'), and only a decade before the great plague of London and of Vienna had taken place.

Not long henceforth, another plague hit Marseille – and these are but the larger-scale epidemics for which extensive records exist.

Death not only was common and pervasive, but also highly visible. Perhaps it is in such a context that the commonality of killings is to also be understood in further reflecting on our previous card (XII).

Consider also that in 1349, in Alsace (and elsewhere – this being more a classic example), Strassbourg had its sizable Jewish population arrested (Friday the 13th, incidentally); and, except for a *small percentage* of about a *thousand* accepting baptismal conversion, they were burned. This followed from earlier 'evidence' (obtained under torture) from Berne and elsewhere that Jews had poisoned wells, causing the plague there[5].

Ars Moriendi

All this certainly also brought to mind the 'art of dying'. If, after all, death is considered not only inevitable and pervasive but also as transition to a new birth into the spiritual realms, then it becomes imperative that individuals prepare and approach death – which may come at any time, young or old – not only properly readied, but also, importantly for the times, with sufficient virtue and religious engagement as to maximise the chances for an existence better lived than the trauma awaiting those destined for purgatory or hell.

No wonder that the life that follows earthly existence would dominate so much attention during the span between the two pillars of birth and death and, as said by Francis Bacon:

> Men fear death, as children fear to go in the dark; and as that natural fear in children is increased with tales, so is the other.

'Mors Janua Vitae'

Or so is claimed to be said by St Bernard of Clairvaux: "Death is the gate of Life".

Similarly, St Francis of Assissi completes his 'prayer of Peace' with:

> Grant that I may not so much seek
> to be consoled as to console;
> to be understood
> as to understand;
> to be loved as to love;

---

5   *Cf* Jacob von Königshofen in *Portable Medieval Reader,* p 174 ff.

for it is in giving
that we receive,
it is in pardoning
that we are pardoned.
And it is in dying
that we are born to eternal life.

It is in dying that we are *born* to life eternal

Let's take a final look at our card and consider it in light of card XX, for by reflective implication, the two are now closely related.

Death and Judgement

Earlier, I mentioned a third head on the Death card, and left it at that at the time. It is of course simply the one shouldered by death itself. What we have in both cards XX and XIII are the images of three distinct individual heads, seemingly of man, woman and 'youth' – even the vibrancy of Death in the *dance macabre* seems to suggest youthful exuberance.

Entering death, there is, then, that resurrected call which awaits us towards the end of the series. In death, the *youth*'s very action becomes the cause of itself – in the same manner introduced earlier by St Ambrose, in that death enters humanity, within this Christian context, as a consequence of humanity's own action. In contrast, the calling forth back to life from the grave comes from the clarion call from a spiritual blast: a carrion awakening by clarion.

A minor note on the title

Mention has been made in earlier chapters that early cards in general were without title, yet it remains also true that TdMs do bear titles – except, in most cases, *this very* card. There are various 'symbolic' explanations given for its omission on other TdM decks, though I would here suggest that the cause may simply be that in image copying (rather than re-creation), important details near the bottom of the card would be lost in this card's imagery by the addition of a panel: both scythe and heads would be covered by the name panel.

It may be that Noblet, unlike many other decks, worked the image within the constraints of those panels pre-decided. In other TdMs, it may very be that the image derives from the copy of a deck that initially bore no titles, and hence would need to avoid such as well for this card. With time, it seems that the titling of the card in most woodcuts was dropped and, as a result, 'symbolic' significance all too often readily offered.

ELEMENTS & ALCHEMY

Elements and Alchemy

This is the second-last of the non-trump-focussed chapters (the final one being chapter 23 on Astronomy), so I also want to take the opportunity of tying a few more-or-less loose ends together, and presenting some (perhaps even) quirky views that I would be only too happy to reconsider with evidence that surfaces.

The term 'elements' has, in the context of this chapter, not only the sense of 'the four elements', but also 'elements' that seem to *influx* into tarot's development. These may at times be quite difficult to unveil or, worse, we may perhaps be mislead into unveiling what was never really there: overlaying and masking what is incongruous rather than rending naked to truth.

I'll start here by what I trust will be read with healthy scepticism, submitting it for further reflection and other alternatives.

Why precisely 78?

This is a question that needs to be considered. Perhaps the answer is no more than 'Accidental, dear Watson!' – for the instant that a set is designed, a definite number of cards within that set will of necessity be determined. If it *is* simply and solely 'accidental' (leaving aside the *significance* of 'accidents' in certain worldviews), it nonetheless has yet to be shown to be so.

Let's recall that the pips appear to be a direct derivative of the Mamluk cards. So we can here say that these are 4 x 10 in number because they likely *derive* from a precursor with that structure. Why did *those* have such a structure? in terms of tarot at least, we can provisionally leave that question aside.

For the court cards, there is, on the one hand, an additional problem in that there is an added card (the Queen) per suit, but on the other hand at least the presence of courtly figures is consistent with the Mamluk cards.

For both court cards and pips, the derivation, even if questions about number are still somewhat suspended, remain clear.

The real difficulties come with the trumps – for which there are various possible replies. So first, let's rephrase the question focussing, this time, solely on the trumps.

Why precisely 22 trumps?

This is, after all, one of the characteristics of not only the Marseille-type decks, but what has come to be tarot in general[1].

Very early decks – what we may call 'proto-tarot', appear to have *less* than 22 trumps. *Trionfi.com* mentions decks with *five* or *seven* trumps in very early specimens (prior to the Visconti-type decks). Perhaps what we have, then, is simply a slow and progressive change that *eventually* stabilises to 22.

Perhaps 22 was settled for no other reason than personal preference of the number by some individual – such as a Sforza count (for which there is some evidence). That it *remained* 22, however, may be for other reasons, including that once some pattern (or number) is established, its inertia and momentum propels its repetition without alteration. In this case, given the potential for symbolic value in the number, additional force would be required to make an alteration.

So what are some of those symbolic values?

This is something that has in some ways troubled me for many years. Certainly I can see that 22 can be variously related to the Hebrew letters, to the number of chapters in *Revelations*, or even to haphazard. What speaks *against* the last two are that I would expect further influx of change should solely haphazard or *Revelation* be at root: the former giving way to some further organising principle, and the latter to image variation to bring it in line (to some extent) with *its* chapters.

There needs to be, I would suggest, a simple and repeatedly found organising principle that commits the twenty-two trumps' stability – and if such is altered or lost, a new one imposed that would again re-organise the trumps' overall structure.

We have seen this in the manner in which the deck saw major re-configuration in, on the one hand, gaming (with double-headed designs and the imagery losing any clear symbolic significance); and on the other in major re-designs by the influences of Etteilla in the 19th century and

---

1   Note should be made that some authors do suggest other number of trumps for a broader view of tarot, such as 16, 20, or 24. Other non-tarot decks, such as the Mantegna, show a 5 x 10 'trump'-like structure (with neither pip nor court cards) – these are *clearly* and unequivocally allegorical in nature.

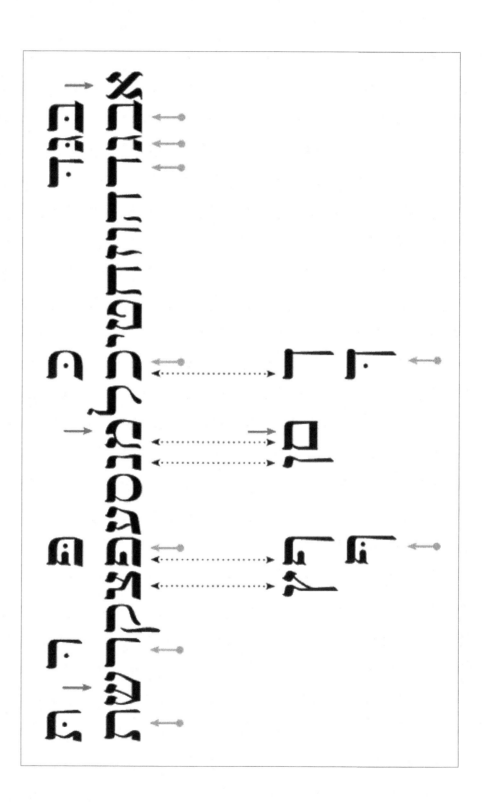

derivatives of the Golden Dawn[2] (such as Waite, Smith, Harris and Crowley) in the 20th: a desire to find anew influxes to ignite the deck afresh.

Hebrew, the 'language of God', *may have been such an influx in early tarot standardisation.* Irrespective as to whether it *caused* a stabilisation to 22, it may have been influential in further minor modifications once such was established.

This is where, from my perspective, the work of Mark Filipas – with specific regard to Marseille decks – bears importance. A sample of his work is available in a past ATS Newsletter (N°4). What he does, beginning with the first letter of the Hebrew alphabet and the first numbered card of the TdM, is posit, in parallel order, plausible relations – describing concepts, words, and imagery found between card and Hebrew word: as he describes it, an 'Alphabetic Masquerade' (perhaps 'alphabetic procession' may be an apt alternative description).

Admittedly, it is possible to list other words that have more or less connections with the trumps in a *different* order to the one he presents, so the consideration is not without unequivocal question. What I personally find of high merit, however, is that here is the first and only (thus far) meta-structure that *accounts* for the TdM sequence as given. And for me, this was what had so far been missing: an account for the sequence as a whole that is held – with whatever creative tension at first seen – as *holon* and with a simplicity easily occluded from view.

If such is the case, then not only would certain elements within card design further standardise, but their standardisation would reflect, when possible, a given Hebrew letter or word. The two cards I have already mentioned in this regard are the Bateleur and the Hanged Man – these being, respectively, the first and twelfth cards having *some* visual similarities to the first and twelfth Hebrew letters Alef (א) and Lamed (ל). Other cards, of course, can be seen in a similar light (observe, for example, the 'scythe' of the 13th letter Mem מ, or the 'upturned legs' of the figure of the 16th letter Ayin ע, or indeed the crustacean-like image of the 18th letter Tzaddi צ). In addition, there are non-visual delineations or indications that are rather *concept*-based or acrostically relevant.

---

2   Not only the Golden Dawn, of course, but certainly, with Papus, Wirth, and Falconnier, amongst the most influential in tarot design for the 20th century.

Whether it be the Hebrew alphabet or something other, it is this kind of organising over-structure that I suspect also played a hand in maintaining design and number.

For those interested in seeing possible connections between the Hebrew letters and concepts in their natural sequence, it may be worth considering the brief pdf-book by Filipas on the one hand, and the work, on the other, of a totally non-tarot related Hebrew letter exegesis such as R. Ginsburg's *Alef-Beit*.

On the next page is the full Hebrew Alphabet – read from right-to-left. The red arrows show what are referred to as *Mother* letters, green arrows point to letters that have a plosive and a fricative sound (for example, 'P' and 'F' are the same consonant), and the dotted lines show letters that *look* different when placed at the end of a word (their 'final' form).

You *may* want to take a little bit of time to simply *compare* trumps in order against these.

Geometrical numbers with base-4

Another quick side consideration is that, except for the total 78 and the total suits of 5 (including the trumps), tarot seems to exemplify a 'four-foldness' – let's look at this rather briefly.

There are four suits of 'basic' cards (ie, excluding the trumps), with each suit having ten pips (which is a triangle of side four – think of arranged pins in ten-pin bowling) and a total of 16 courts (which is a *square* of side four).

So we have the *triangle* of side four for each suit of ten pips; the *square* of side four for the sixteen court cards; and, the next geometrical shape, the *pentagon* of side four gives rise to twenty-two.

This, incidentally, is *not* something that I consider was influential with tarot design, but rather a geometrical consistency that is *discovered* without intended design – even though geometrical considerations such as this were more common then than they are today.

Fire, Air, Water and Earth

In chapter three especially, I avoided discussions related to these elements in connection with the implements and their suits. Hopefully, by now, this will have been seen to be for good reason: first and foremost, the *implements* are to be considered; and the numerals, first and foremost, in their pattern or geometrical presentation.

Nonetheless, in this chapter we also do need to address this important concept of the elements[3].

Within the Occidental tradition, there are four elements that are seen as active behind the curtain of physical manifestation, these having their equivalence in a higher octave as the four 'ethers'. The elements are, in their Alchemical order from most dense to most rarified, Earth, Water, Air and Fire. Essentially, these derive from Greek thought and the formal development of Western Philosophy.

The four elements have been seen to also reflect not only four states or principles or, indeed, substances, out of which matter is composed, but also various psycho-spiritual dispositions or temperaments. Thus we have the four temperamental dispositions: Phlegmatic; Melancholic; Choleric; and Sanguine. How these four humours relate to the four elements has, I would suggest, changed with time as understanding of the temperaments has shifted from a predominantly bodily-focussed approach to a more psychological one.

The four humours , as they were called, are not, in any case, our concern here, save perhaps with considerations in relation to Court cards. Various authors and card designers have made *use* of the four classical Greek elements in either explaining or in correlating tarot's four suits, at times also adding trumps and the fifth Aristotlean element or the quintessence.

The Greek version of the elements dates from pre-Socratic times and persisted throughout the Middle Ages and into the Renaissance, deeply influencing European thought and culture. Let's have a brief look at the grounding of the four elements stemming from Ancient Greece.

Classical elements in Greece

The four elements considered by early Pre-Socratic philosophers were based in part on observation of the world. With Anaximander, two contrasting qualities are suggested: that of heat and of moisture, and their respective absence, cold and dry. Thales had proposed that the

3　　　Some of what follows is modified from an ATS Newsletter I wrote some time back.

world arises from primordial water or moisture, to which Anaximander commented that as moisture does not generate heat or fire, but rather destroys it, heat must be a separate principle.

Modern authors sometimes suggest that each element had its advocate in terms of primacy, and it is commonly listed as: water or moisture, which can exhibit its solid or frozen, liquid, and vaporised states (Thales); air, that can condense to moisture, and further condense to earth (Anaximenes); earth, through a modern perspective the democritean atomistic view is cast back as an instance of the primacy of earth (Xenophanes); and fire (Heraclitus). This last, as an example, is not strictly correct of Heraclitus, who proposed that *each element arises out of the death of another element*. He was advocating a state of the world in perpetual motion, rather than a static one, for which the transforming aspect of fire is the clearest. Yet he claimed that fire arises from the death of air, and air from the death of fire; water from the death of earth, and earth from the death of water[4].

Empedocles proposed that they all existed together in fixed quantities from the beginning. Plato later conceived of them as consisting of atoms with the geometrical shapes of four of the five Platonic Solids described in the Timaeus – these we have already considered, incidentally, in chapter nine. Aristotle adopted these elements, adding aether, as quintessence, in which was held aloft the stellar region.

As we have seen over the past twenty weeks, both the Aristotelian and Platonic views were ultimately in some form or other adopted and accepted right through the Middle Ages and into the Renaissance, and hence prominent at the time of tarot's development.

Just because I prefer to allow for each element to be considered in each and every suit does not mean that interesting insights cannot be gained from considering an element in relation to a specific suit and seeing how it can add further understanding. In such a case, however, the fiery aspect of a sword, or its watery aspect, or its aerial, or its earthy aspects, are not overlooked, but only provisionally put aside.

With that in mind, let's consider each of the suits in light of *each* of the elements... taken one at a time. Let's begin with the most 'solid' element

---

4   cf Guthrie's *The Greek Philosophers: from Thales to Aristotle* for a succinct and excellent overview of the period and its thoughts.

– earth; work 'upwards' to the most rarified – that of fire; then move back to water; and then air. I am here purposefully not taking them in either their 'ascending' or 'descending' order, but somewhat randomly.

Earth

What aspect of the suit of Cups is 'earth'? Looking through each of the ten pips, which appears to have the greatest earth-like quality? Could a cup exist without the element of earth?

What of the Coins: which pip has the greatest 'earthiness', and which the least?

What is the relation between iron and earth in the suit of swords? what would an 'earth-less' sword be like?

In its striving from Earth to Sun, what is the plant or branch doing with sunlight? how is this related to the element of earth?

With the court cards, which of the sixteen figures appears to have the greatest connection to the Earth? is that the same as having the greatest connection to the *element* of earth?

Taking four trumps at random, note each of their qualities of earth.

Fire

What *is fire*?

Which, if any, of the four suit implements does *not* require fire?

Taking *one* trump at random, *one* court cart at random, and *three* pips at random, describe how a fiery quality moves across the scene presented.

Water

Taking the ten of each suit one at a time, *look* at its watery quality - allowing the vision to blur somewhat and wash over the card.

Compare how this is distinct to the *Ace* of *each* suit.

Placing the trumps face-up, allow yourself to be drawn to whichever appears to 'call' more than the others - reflect on its *watery nature*.

Air

What would it take for the air-like quality of the three cups to be transformed into the air-like quality of the King of Bâtons, and then the air-like quality of Death?

Where is the air used within the body? which of the sevens (pips) appears to best reflect an aspect of this?

Alchemical considerations

There are two reasons I want to have a brief look at alchemy: the first is that many of the figures between alchemy and tarot have some similarities that bear mention; the second is that claims periodically recur that tarot is in some manner or other intimately connected to alchemy.

Of the latter, I frankly have yet to find the kind of evidence that shows a sufficient connection as to suggest intimacy. Certainly, figures such as Maria the Jewess can bear similarity to Temperance (to which we shall return in the next chapter), or some figures of the Green Lion to Strength, the King and Queen (Emperor and Empress) as Sun and Moon, some figures to L'Amoureux (the Lovers), even between aspects of an Athanor and the Tower, or *Philosophical Mercury* and the World.

The *key* distinction, however, is that in alchemy the figures, when a set (rather than the rarer single ones) depict a sequence of transformations that are fairly sensible and 'obvious' (to the alchemically aware reader of images). By contrast, even when we 'read' the sequence of trumps as images of sequential transformations, we are doing so from a perspective that *seeks* for, rather than *explains*, such transformative function.

In reference to the former (ie, this aspect of 'seeking' to seeks to see alchemical possibilities into tarot imagery), mention should be made of a more recent PhD thesis by J-P. Jouvin[5]. The thesis makes numerous suggestions of the connection between tarot and alchemy whereby, I would suggest, it seems that the cart is placed before the horse. What occurs is a *re-viewing*, with, admittedly, imagination appropriate for earlier times, but a *seeing* into the deck what may not be there. A similar criticism may of course be made to the earlier section I wrote above with regards to the Hebrew letters.

This does not mean, of course, that *only* individuals who were alchemically oriented considered alchemical figures. Martin Luther, for example, says:

The science of alchymy I like very well, and indeed, 'tis the philoso-

5   *Imagination et Alchimie à la Renaissance: L'example du Tarot de Marseille*, University of Bourgogne (Dijon). I have only had access to some extracts of the thesis, so my comments are solely based on those sections and the absctract.

phy of the ancients. I like it not only for the profits it brings in melting metals, in decocting, preparing, extracting and distilling herbs, roots; I like it also for the sake of the allegory and secret signification, which is exceedingly fine, touching the resurrection of the dead at the last day.[6]

Perhaps that final sentence could be re-read: "*I like it also for the sake of the allegory and secret signification [...] touching the resurrection of the dead at the last day*".

There is of course no doubt that important developments within a cultural setting will bear resemblance to one the other, and that similarities will bear on considerations, reflections, understanding and insight. With alchemy, as with tarot, the dominant particular Christian views of the period would be seen as *ultimate* and central, especially when *transformation* implies, inevitably, the death of an element in order for another to arise. In this, both alchemy and Christian exegesis would complement and support each other, and both would, in that sense at least, be reflected in our Noblet as well as in many other decks of the period and other sequences of imagery found elsewhere (such as Cathedral carvings).

Though, therefore, some of the images found in the sequence of trumps can indeed be considered from an alchemical perspective, I do not think that alchemy was itself a consideration in its design.

For those interested, perusing Adam McLean's valuable alchemical sites may provide further insights in the area, and further refer to the numerous classical and modern texts:

www.alchemywebsite.com

Also of worth is the easily accessible A. Roob's *Hermetic Museum: Alchemy & Mysticism* (published by Taschen).

Alchemical stages

Let's make, nonetheless, a brief note on the sequence of transformative stages presented in alchemical works and note possible equivalence in the *sequence* of the trumps. There are generally three *sets* of transformative steps that are mentioned, grouped in either three, seven, or twelve stages. These sets are not mutually exclusive, but rather like dif-

---

6   Martin Luther's *Table talk*, mentioned on the Hermetic Garden website from a list of quotes prepared by Adam McLean.

ferent ways of more precisely describing the transmutations that occur. Similarly, for example, we could describe the life of an individual in the broader sweeping statements of the three-fold: 'youth, adult, old age'; or divide this same life into a more detailed seven-fold description of 'infant, child, adolescent, young adult, parent, grandparent', noting that not every individual necessarily takes on the descriptive attributes implied by the more detailed division.

Similarly for the differences in descriptive alchemical transformations: a three-fold descriptive division will be more encompassing than the ever-increasingly precise seven or twelve-fold ones that may apply with precision in some processes and not in others.

The three-fold description depicts the stages of blackness (nigredo), whiteness (albedo), and red-ness (rubedo). In the first stage, a formal decomposition, putrefaction, death, and burning down takes place. In the second, a transformation to its 'silver' stage takes place by mixing, binding, and further liberations of extraneous matter; and in the third, its golden purification becomes achieved without residue or dross.

Card sequence

Placing the trumps in sequence, let's consider these three stages as given above. Here, I would suggest that different possibilities can be seen, but let's use tarot's own key markers as exemplifying alchemy's stages: Death for the final achievement of its state of *nigredo*, the Moon for its *albedo*, and the rest (from the Sun onwards) for its *rubedo*.

In the first part of the sequence up to (and including) Death, the imagery depicts various states and stages of living engagement, each part of which is separated until finally death allows all to be reduced to a common state of rancour and rich putrefaction.

With the cards that follow Death, the elements are cleansed, re-bound in different forms, and liberated again until reaching the silvery Lunar stage.

Thenceforth, the final unification of naked king and queen into gold, and spirit's liberation from Earth-boundedness results in the philosophical ascended Mercury or 'stone' (as World), free to be, act and travel as he pleases (as Fool).

Seven stages

Apart from the three stages mentioned above, the most common description is to look at transformations as a seven-fold process. Possibly my favourite image of this comes from Michelspacher's *Cabala*, a work of 1615 - not long before Noblet's tarot was itself created.

The seven steps there depicted are calcination, sublimation, solution, putrefaction, distillation, coagulation, and tincture.

Again, we can begin to consider the sequence of trumps in light of these, though it seems to my own reflections that, as a sequence, we are seeing the distinctness of tarot from these seven alchemical 'steps'.

Pairings and sequence

Whether or not the full sequence of alchemical stages are considered of note, its *process* or transmutation of the individual towards a final integrated state having graced spiritual awakening is reflected in the sequence. Whether this be considered from a Christian or spiritual viewpoint or even only from a psychological one, the *pairing* exercise we started in chapter one also shows an increase towards a state of integration, release, and exaltation.

Pairing the trumps as in that first week, what new insights further emerge *as sequence*? Is there a different pairing, three or four-folding that results in differing insight?

Final comment

I have obviously, in this chapter, gone far behind what may strictly be warranted by the Noblet, rather pointing to some of my own directions of interest. These, and equivalent considerations by other authors and, for that matter, each individual considering the trump sequence, is worthy of reflection in order to ascertain whether or not there is something at play in the trumps that transcends its own imagery.

XIIII - TEMPERANCE

Temperance!

With this chapter we enter the final third of the course, and trust that some time has been taken in ongoing reflection on the past twenty chapters and the work undertaken and, more importantly, your own insights and alterations that may have occurred during this time has intensified. *Temperance* is quite an appropriate card to enter in light of this point: a time not so much for reflection, as for a re-combining of one's own insights, continuously engaged within the stream of other insights gained through one's own effort.

That's probably one of the most important aspects of the image presented: not as much the allegory of Temperance herself, but rather *what* she is doing. So let's have a better look at this.

Mixing of the vessels

Mixing of the vessels... or rather, the intermixing of the *content* of the vessels:

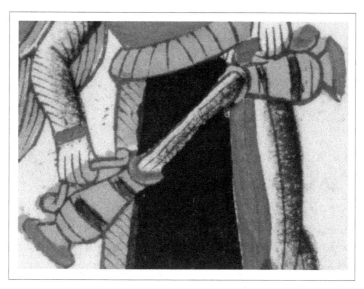

Reflecting on the action depicted, what *purpose* or *function* can this action be put to?

Take a minute or two prior to reading on in order to allow your own insights to emerge prior to four of my own presented in the ensuing paragraph.

There are four instances that come more prominently to my mind when reflecting on the action depicted: the first is that of filling an empty jug from a full one; the second, that of purification; the third, that of dilution; and the fourth, that of dissolution. In addition, a number of other visual interpretations come to mind, such as the 'liquid' perhaps depicting an *upward* flow; or the pulling apart of a more gelatinous substance; or other interpretations that progressively become ever more distanced from the image at hand, though perhaps entirely appropriate for the specific narrative in which the card image finds itself.

Let's begin by separately considering each of the first four that I mention, and then allow these to reflect other considerations in light of other aspects.

The initial reflection that I mentioned is that of pouring from one pitcher to the other, in the sense of the first filling the second. In other words, a situation whereby the waters (here in a general sense) are allowed to be emptied from one vessel and fill a second. The purpose for doing so, and its metaphorical implications, are varied. Certainly what could be called to mind in this reading of pouring from one to the other is what is found in the synoptic Gospels, for example at Matthew 9:17:

> Nor do people put new wine into old wineskins; [...]. No; they put new wine in fresh skins and both are preserved.

Of course, here they are *not wineskins* that are shown, but rather pitchers. Nor, for that matter, does it appear to be wine intended – nor grape juice, but rather water.

We'll return to this aspect very shortly.

My second mentioned reflection is that of purification. If I have a fluid in which residues remain, I can *begin* the process of 'purification' by allowing the particles to settle and then pour the contents into a new vessel, allowing the sediment to remain in the first, repeating the process as often as it takes to have the water as free of pollutants as desired. We'll see this also when we get to the next exercise.

Thirdly, I mentioned *dilution*. Quite frankly, for me this is the clearest and most likely intended meaning: not for the wine to be consumed in its full strength, but rather in moderated form by the addition and admixture of water. In that sense, the wine is 'tempered' – and so are its effects.

The fourth is dissolution. Here, one may consider the dissolution of sugar or of salt. Certainly heating the solution would accelerate the process or, indeed, the repeated movement from one vessel to the other.

I would suggest that time be taken for each of these to be experienced by taking two jugs or water pitchers and actually undertaking the action presented.

Experiencing those various acts

We have each very likely poured water from one pitcher to another. Yet to do it with conscious *awareness*, and reflecting on both what the containers are doing and the movement of the content can here be quite useful.

For example, in the process of emptying one container to the next, I am reminded of the Soul's movement out of one body and into another – whether this be conceived as transmigration or not is, in this instance, less important than getting greater clarity about the *symbolic* emptying of the vessel's content into another.

A metaphorical outpouring of the gift of love could also be apparent, yet the physical carrying out of the pouring does not reflect this gift, for love is poured out from a vessel of limitlessness.

Moving to the cleansing of the waters, add soil (literally) to the water-filled vessel, stirring a little, and allow the residue to settle before partially pouring the top (clean) section of the water into the other vessel, pouring out the soiled remains to leave an empty vessel. Repeating this action, allowing sedimentation at each stage to take place, brings to light deeper insights.

Dilution is, as mentioned before, perhaps the most apparent intent. Each of us have probably already each performed this task: diluting cordial, pure juice, or wine with water. For the purposes of this exercise, I would suggest doing it again with intent, allowing the act to be reflected in consciousness.

Finally, the dissolution of sugar or salt by the process of agitated mixing, in this case accentuated by the pouring from one vessel to the other. This similarly calls to consciousness an activity that we may often perform without reflection.

Moderation, restraint, dilution

Temperance, as one of the cardinal virtues, appears not to have undergone too much change in its general meaning over time. It can generally be considered as moderation in the engagement of the appetites, so that both restraint from excess, and dilution of wine, are seen as representing the virtue.

This aspect of *restraint* also accounts for the second allegorical depiction of this virtue: that of holding the reins of, presumably, passions as implied by animalistic tendencies of the horse – and calling to mind again Plato's allegory of the Soul as we briefly looked at with trump VII - Le Chariot.

What is evident, however, is that in each of these descriptions of the virtue, something '*opposite*' to the other virtues is implied, for temperance is not so much to know oneself and act in accordance with one's inclinations, but rather to allow one's natural inclinations to be reigned in, held back, 'tempered' in order that no excesses result.

If we consider the position of this virtue in the sequence of the cards, it is placed between Death and the Devil. This certainly augurs well its opposite (or vice) as self-indulgence: either towards the self indulgence of mourning; or the unrestrained temptations of the devil.

Let's have a look at this as sequence and consider its possible significance.

Sequence XIII, XIIII, XV

I have placed these in a right-to-left order simply because, as mentioned in a much earlier chapter, we are usually wont to looking from left-to-right: our habitual reading direction has defined how we usually see progression. Yet, by considering this very order, we are also lead to consider that death releases us, that our new state (in death), marked by

a reflection on one's own self-restraints, leads to us facing what has at times been called the Guardian at the threshold.

In Temperance, those activities in which one has not only engaged in during life, but also those that have been properly moderated, become moral forces that have developed within one's character.

Three virtues sequence

It is interesting in this light to also consider that the three cardinal virtues explicitly depicted in the trumps of the tarot are presented in the inverse order considered of importance within the Christian tradition. Normally, we would expect (aside from Wisdom), a descending sequence of Justice, Fortitude, and as lowest Temperance. It is as if the sequencing has been guided by their common *naming* sequence (as I have also just done) rather than placing them in rank with the value increasing with order.

In that light, it is also worth noting that a number of Cathedral carvings added between the 13th and 16th centuries also show precisely these three (and interestingly, not four but only these three) virtues as a set, and in the order mentioned above.

Over the page is one such sequence.

There we have, from left to right, the increase of virtue 'worthiness' with Temperance, Fortitude, and Justice.

It is worth noting that in this image Temperance does not pour from one pitcher to another, but rather from a pitcher to a large dish, showing

that it is not simply the diluting wine that may have been generally implied in the contemplation of the image but also, I would suggest, modesty and cleanliness.

Card vs Petroglyph

Let's carefully compare for a moment that image to the Noblet (and to tarot in general).

In the petroglyph, all are seated. By contrast, the Noblet (and tarot generally) have both Strength and Temperance standing. In each of the three cases, we also have differences in the 'instruments' presented. I have already noted the difference in the depiction of Temperance with pitcher-and-'platter' rather than the two pitchers that may otherwise be expected, and here I simply also bring to attention the broken pillar with a naked or semi-naked allegorical figure (as perhaps 'naked strength'), and also, in this case, Justice with a globe instead of the expected scales.

In regards to Temperance, it also highlights a detail that has long 'bothered' me in the various Marseille depictions, perhaps a detail overlooked, and yet so obvious. Let's compare again the image on the card and that depicted on the petroglyph more closely.

In the exercise earlier in this chapter, I trust that the mixing back and forth between the two vessels has also brought to consciousness how much easier it is to do with one or the other arm raised in the required

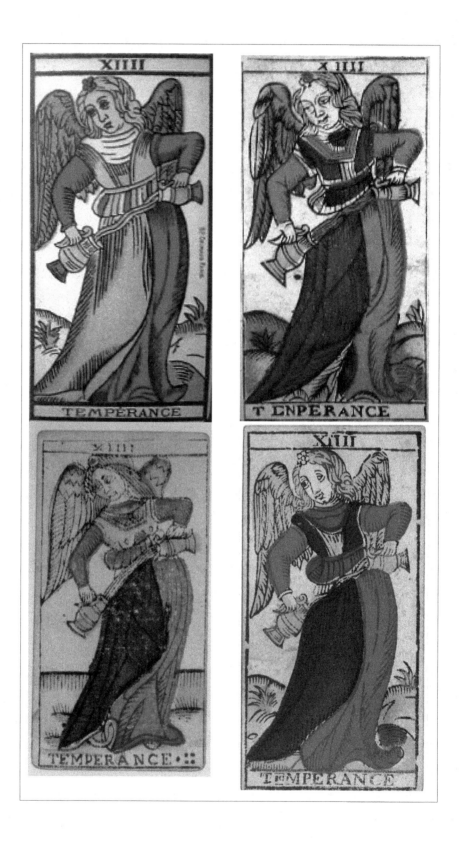

position. What is 'strange', however, is that the *virtue* depicted on the card is shown with her *left arm raised*, and is, hence, pouring from the left to the right.

This is something that is, to say the least, unusual – and yet something quite consistent across TdMs.

For the sake of comparison, let's consider for a while that the image found itself mirror imaged from an earlier model, and gained progressive standardisation – if that is the case, let's also have a look at what the card *would* have looked like with the right-arm raised:

Here the action seems more 'natural' – especially in a world that considered the left-hand ('*sinister*' in Latin) to be less than desirable.

This is also more in line with the earlier hand-painted decks such as the 'Charles VI' and Visconti-type, each painted with *right*-arm raised.

We can, of course, make many interpretations with respect to having one or the other arm raised – the point is more, at this juncture, whether it is an instance of what may have first been a careless error that has

since been re-copied without due reflection. Or perhaps this is an instance where the game of tarot itself lead to an impulse of 'inversed' temperance that manifested in the image of the game over time.

Wings

Another key distinction between earlier forms and the specifically Marseille pattern is the inclusion of wings on the allegorical figure: here we are dealing perhaps not simply with the allegorical feminine, but rather with the angelic state following Death.

This is also where I personally make meaning of the inversion spoken of in the previous section: the inner becomes outer, and in a sense, the 'left' is 'right', and 'up' is 'down' – so the raised left arm is here considered as 'correct', with the flow, however, occurring from the lower to the upper. A kind of inverted-flipped metamorphosis from centre to periphery and periphery to centre.

This is something that can, I suppose, be at first somewhat disorienting, and where one may perhaps *want* to find an anchor upon which to cling. Again, the progression from Death, Temperance, to the Devil.

In the set of trumps, this is also the only *winged* figure that has feet on the ground. Or so it seems, for her feet are generally not visible.

Arête

Let's have a final look at the concept of *Arête*. Calling to mind earlier discussions, *arête* (virtue), suggests a striving towards one's essential being or, as I have seen repeatedly described, as

> a humble and constant striving for perfection and self-improvement combined with a realistic awareness that such perfection cannot be reached. As long as an individual strives to do and be the best, that individual has arête. As soon as the individual believes he has actually achieved arête, however, he or she has lost that exalted state and fallen into hubris, unable to recognize personal limitations or the humble need to improve constantly.

Again, considerations of this description in light of the card's position between Death and the Devil brings to light both the virtue itself and the very risks in striving towards it.

Irrespective of the card presented, her gaze appears relaxed and not fixed on the effortlessness of the task her hands are carrying out. Yet the *aim* of the flow is precise and accurate: drops fall not outside the flasks. And so not only is here a possible implication that the opposite of *arête* is simply *hubris*, but also *hamartia*: the archer who misses the mark by tragic misapprehension or understanding of the situation at hand.

Effortless Precision

Using active imagination, place yourself as the Angelic figure, and allow the flow between the two pitchers to precisely move from one into the other, your attention itself allowed to be reflected in the act. *Sense* into the motion, and the position of your various 'body' parts (including the wings).

Does the motion between vessels require the interchange of raised arms, or not? and what, as an essential characteristic, is it that flows?

Plutarch, Good Will, and Concord

Plutarch has this to say:

> The wise man is blessed in himself, and blessed also are the auditors who

can hear and receive those words which flow from his mouth; and perhaps, too, there is no need of compulsion or menaces to affect the multitude, for the mere sight itself of a shining and conspicuous example of virtue in the life of their prince will bring them spontaneously to virtue, and to a conformity with that blameless and blessed life of good will and mutual concord, supported by temperance and justice, which is the highest benefit that human means can confer.

When doing the previous exercise some years ago, one of the key aspects that I sensed into the very admixture of Temperance is the striving for what Plutarch has described above as 'mutual concord' – something that can only be reached with good will. The very nature of this brings to mind a movement of oneself out into the world with one's control of thoughts, control of actions, and perseverance; and a converse movement of opening oneself to the world with tolerance, impartiality and equanimity[1].

These are easy words to write – yet, at least when applied to myself, I find their ongoing execution especially trying at times when they are undoubtedly the most needed. How often do we control thought? or indeed grasp control of our own actions? or persevere on the road that well well indeed be less travelled (something quite different to blind obstinacy), rather than taking what is ultimately the easier path? Similarly, how trying can be the need for tolerant understanding, impartial engagement, and a deep equanimity in facing and being in the world with all its quirks and difficulties.

Temperance, as self-restraint, seems to take on many other aspects when considered in light of its consequences.

Insights revisited

I opened this chapter with a comment regarding

> one's own insights, continuously engaged within the stream of other insights gained through one's own effort.

The very nature of insights takes on, in reading the works of various authors, including the clear (but admittedly difficult) work by Lonergan[2], a threefold aspect: of experience, of understanding and of reflection. These act in a self-referential manner so that not only does experience

---

1   Similar to what R. Steiner calls the 'secondary' exercises, mentioned, amongst other places, in his *Knowledge of the Higher Worlds*.

2   Cf his wonderful book *Insight*.

bring forth understanding and reflection, but these in their turn bring to light deeper and further experience.

Not only does each successive insight bring with it its own wealth, but it engages with the fluid insights previously gained, in turn altering – for at least some of them – aspects that may have either been overlooked (an oversight, rather than insight) or misunderstood. A 'pool' forever being flushed and admixed with the activity of experience, of understanding, and of judgement.

In that sense, insight is not so much *cumulative* as it is something that *re-organises* and transforms or transmutes existing structures of understanding. In a very similar sense, the tarot narrative or reading does not so much 'add', but assists in providing insights into situations. As a consequence, it provides a leaven by which a person may re-orient himself or herself in a situation when needed.

Using a different metaphor, not only is the reading or narrative provided from the cards itself going to be tested against the touchstone of one's own understandings, but these understandings may in turn be tested against the touchstone of the narrative.

And as this mention of 'touchstone' calls to mind not only the testing of gold, but also of its symbolic value as 'truth', this brings us back to one minor further consideration with regard to alchemy that I did not touch upon in the previous chapter.

Maria the Jewess

In various tests are references to a very early Alchemist, Maria the Jewess. Apart from various instruments she is said to have invented, including the 'bain-marie', she is at times depicted in a manner that brings to mind, due to various similarities, the imagery of Temperance.

Yet, for all its wonderful considerations, I frankly do not see sufficient iconographic resemblences for the comparison to be more than simply 'somewhat similar'. Possibly the most common image of Maria the Alchemist, as she is also known, is the one depicted below.

Certainly there is a feminine figure. And, likewise and importantly, there are two vessels between which 'flow' the contents from one to the other – interestingly in this case in a vaporised and hence upward form.

Though I do not consider this to have been in any manner intended by the tarot representation of Temperance, it does add to our own reflection,

especially when considering the orientation of movement: here, we see that it is not *always* the case that flow is from that which is above only to that which is below, but that the inverse may also take place.

...and also perhaps that

All worlds, the Upper and the lower, are inside man. (Zohar)

Perhaps the wings on our Noblet (and other TdM, of course) Temperance can be re-considered in light of these thoughts.

Plutarch revisited in imagery

Allow me to complete this chapter with one of my favourite images of Temperance, used as an illumination of Plutarch.

One of my favourite, yet not totally reflective of our Noblet, for as in other more standard representations, her right arm is here raised, not her left as on the Noblet, and, again as more typical outside of TdM representation, she bears no wings. Yet it is not to that to which I wish at this point draw specific attention, but rather to the detail of how each vessel is made to represent a quality, and that she stands – or perhaps a better description is that she is *supported* – by the other three cardinal virtues of *Prudence*, *Justice*, and *Fortitude*.

Her Vessels are named in this instance, bearing the titles of *Honesty* and *Decorum*: these two concepts bring us back again to the importance both of these have in the context of the narrative, and how to intermix

them in such a manner that neither the brute force of honesty, nor the false modesty of decorum, presents its imbalance without the tempering influence of one upon the other.

Contrary to all images shown thus far, in this illuminated text, she faces her *raised* arm, not her lower one...

...with that in mind, let's repeat our previous active imaginative exercise, and observe the difference between facing our raised arm as opposed to facing our lowered arm.

XV - Le Diable

The Devil

In European society, it is only in more recent times that a view of the world as essentially spiritual in nature, permeated by spiritual beings, is not assumed or taken as a given. In the context of such a worldview, the reality of Beings of various hierarchies and dispositions – both benefic as well as malevolent – takes on more 'obvious' reality. The Devil, in such a context, is exactly what it claims to be: a being embodying various aspects of ultimate evil. In addition, and in contradistinction to the freeing quality at best claimed by those on the spiritual path, the Devil has elements of chains that bind or tether.

Also in contradistinction to beings of light, the Devil is considered as a Being of darkness and, therefore, of the night. These are some of the elements that I will consider in the context of the image presented before us. In the first case, let us therefore begin by carefully observing the image as presented.

All three beings are represented with horns – reminiscent, at least to my eyes, of antlers. Yet, what is also not entirely clear is whether these are *worn* as opposed to growing as their own. And this detail repeats itself with most aspects depicted: we are never certain if the detail shown is intrinsic to the being to which it supposedly belongs or whether it is an addition that is somehow superimposed.

Let's begin this observation with the two tethered lower side beings, at times called 'imps' or 'minions'. Even with these, we should perhaps first observe that their relative size against the central figure is, perhaps surprisingly, negligible: they are all of similar heights. Admittedly, the central figure is also a little *wider* than the two side figures, but their relative size-equivalence is deceptively accentuated to appear as though the central figure is far larger than is in fact the case.

For each of the side figures, the arms are placed behind their backs. We may surmise that these are bound. We have, after all, already met such binding a few cards back in Le Pendu. Apart from the neck tethering, however, there is nothing that seems to suggest real binding of their hands. They might indeed be holding their own hands behind their backs in an assured and controlled stance... or perhaps they are holding their own fake tail in position, to accentuate the illusion or, perhaps more appropriately termed, the *deception*. That is, after all, one of the key principles by which the devil operates: Deception.

Deception

Let's have a good look at the card with an assumption of as many elements as possible being deceptive.

For the purposes of the exercise, let's consider that the three figures are actually facing the other way, and that what we are looking at are their *backs* which are masked to give the *impression* that they are facing us. With this in mind, let's take the central figure as having a mask covering the back of his (or her) head, a belt with false penis dangling, and that he wears upon his (or her) front a collar upon which is attached the false wings, his left hand raised as we see it. Hence we also see clearly not his knees, but the back of the knees.

With the two smaller figures let us also adjust our viewing so as to perceive them as wearing a mask upon the back of their heads which we see, and their hands in front of their bodies holding a tail to deceive us into seeing their back as front.

We shall return to this way of viewing the image a little later.

Deception itself is closely aligned to lies. It is, basically, an act that prevents proper insights from occurring through the manipulation of perception and feelings. In this, one is encouraged to come to a state that is not that which we have repeatedly seen when considering the virtues: rather than the mean between extremes, it is the extreme (either one) which may be encouraged. This itself becomes a binding that makes one engage *out of character* with one's own self.

Let's for a moment consider these extremes and the different ways in which they hinder, disorient, bind and belie.

Two Extremes

In the context of the mediæval tradition, even considerations of the Devil were never without considerations of the healing or salvic powers of the redemption of Christ. Still, here we shall only consider such redemptive considerations when later making further connections back to the church.

There is a highly interesting woodblock carving from Paris dated 1568[1] – less than a hundred years prior to the Noblet – which seems to suggest distinctions between the gate of Hell as one being, Lucifer as another, and Satan (on the right) as a third and separate being. The description is:

> Title page showing the jaws of Hell with Lucifer and Satan. From the *Livre de la Deablerie,* printed by Michel le Noir.

There are different traditions that refer to Satan and Lucifer as distinct beings. Here, it is interesting that Lucifer, who is sitting atop the 'gueule' or jaws (gate) of Hell, is crowned with a four-pronged crown, as though seeking to be king of the world, and has clawed feet and bat-like wings. In contradistinction, Satan, in the lower-right-hand area, has human feet but that second face on his belly.

Both are horned in a manner somewhat similar to the Noblet, though in this woodcut the horns are a little more goat-like than the antlers on Noblet's depiction of the Devil.

---

1   according to another source, it stems from Cranach's *Passionary of Christ and Antichrist,* which contrasts Christ and the Papacy.

If such a distinction between Lucifer and Satan was known in Paris at the time of Noblet's creation (and it should be noted that the book underwent, though long, through multiple imprints), then the combined figure would have been perceived as not just a simple depiction, but as the representation of the two beings of evil, the one or the other forever seeking to mislead in excesses – but, again, as *two* beings in one.

But what of these excesses? What are their characteristic differences?

The Moral Realm

There are undoubtedly numerous ways in which the extremes may be characterised. I'll begin here with one simple distinction based on alternate 'moral' considerations. In the moral realm, the human being is faced with decisions to action that inevitably have a moral dimension

– whether or not this is obvious or obscured, conscious or not.

Two 'temptations' become central here. On the one hand, a kind of bigoted or fundamentalist view is possible, whereby the 'rule' or previously formulated dogma takes the place of moral consideration, whereby moral considerations are relinquished and abandoned in favour of deontological rulings. In its extreme forms, each generation witnesses this when social movements negate the individual for the 'mob'. A kind of luciferic abandonment of oneself for the claimed kingship of the movement occurs.

On the other is the negation of morality, the claim that morality is no more than individual preference. In recent times, this appears to have been the focus of the 'battle' waged by Pope Benedict XVI against 'moral relativism'. In its extreme form, the individual takes no cognisance of the social fabric or due *care* of others outside their own relatively immediate environs. A call for equivalence of all social or culturally derived views is considered on a par, irrespective as to how its own members are in fact treated, and irrespective as to moral considerations. Ultimately this is a very satanic view that isolates and encourages conceit, for the negation of moral considerations as ultimately *amoral* advocates a superior view of its beholder upon itself.

The extremes can be characterised as, on the one hand, "come to us and become one with our will" and on the other as "do whatever you incline".

The above description have, of course, limitations as being no more than mere caricature of the two opposites. Another manner of characterising these is by considering healthy developments in each: namely as expressions of art and of science. On the one hand, art becomes a creative expression where a loss of oneself in the creative output has similar characteristics to the luciferic stream; on the other, the removed engagement (or even dis-engagement) in order to achieve a claimed objectivity that permits understanding and the development of knowledge as found in science. In their extreme forms, these tendencies give us the caricatured debauched artist and the mad Frankensteinian scientist.

I am reminded of these two extremes by the two smaller figures that are shown tethered – for each of these temptations orients and binds one in some manner or other.

But let's return to our exercise considering the image as inversed.

Looking at the image

Was it in fact warranted to consider the image as though the three figures were facing away from us, with no more than masks and belts deluding us into altering our perception – or was that in itself an exercise in delusion?

When looking carefully at the image, it seems that nearly all of it was indeed feasible... except for some details that appear to negate this possibility. So let's again have a look at the Noblet image.

Bodily details

Each figure has at least one detail that shows that the exercise we did is inconsistent with the image as presented – even if other details permit it. The right-hand figure's leg-bend at the knees suggests that she or he is indeed facing us; the left-hand figure's neck-and-jaw shows the same, and the central figure's hand holding aloft the 'staff' or 'wand' shows it to be his or her left-hand:

The exercise becomes, then, itself one of attempted deception. Yet deception contains within itself seeds of its own undoing once details are not only given their due attention, but allowed to gain their own importance.

Gender

With this, let us consider the gender of each of the figures. Except for the central one with dangling phallus, I would suggest that gender is not altogether clear. Even with the central figure, the leg-shape and hips, together with the depicted breasts, gives the impression of a figure that has both masculine and feminine characteristics – something of a hermaphrodite. This is, nonetheless, more of an imposed interpretation: the image itself appears to make the devil a masculine-type figure. The two side figures, by contrast, and though the genitalia is ambiguously drawn, seem to suggest in both cases feminine forms.

Hephæstus

Aside from his title as the Devil, much of the figure reminds me of Hephæstus. Here is a divine being, born of Hera and Zeus, who was twice thrown down from the heavens: the first for being born deformed (he was lame), and the second for disobedience.

The Devil's feet on the card image certainly appear somewhat lame or deformed, and the item upon which he stands bears a close resemblance to an anvil. His hand, holding aloft that forked wand, hints or somewhat suggests tongs – something that in any case is also often associated with devils in order to tend to the bodies burning in hell.

In the eighteenth book of Homer's *Iliad*, it is mentioned that Hephæstus had maidservants who assisted him. These can be naturally conceived as tethered – or at least recalls the tethering chains he made. According to Philostratus, (*Life of Apollonius of Tanya 6:11*), these maidservants he made as living statues of gold, "in appearance like living young women" (*Iliad* 18).

Though he married Aphrodite, her loathing for his ugliness made her seek instead Ares. Here we also have an aspect commonly associated with the devil in relation to lust, save that in this case it is Hephæstus who is cuckolded by the adulterous relationship of his wife.

Considered as a more Hephæstian figure, the card bears the hallmarks of not only the revenge he sought on his mother for having rejected him at birth, but also of the craftsmanship he develops despite his physical deformities and general ugliness. Here is someone who also suffers and is brought back within the fold of Olympus, the latter only when it is realised he has usefulness.

Of course, Hephæstus takes us away from times with which we are now familiar. Yet it should also be recalled that the Ancient Greek writings were being re-discovered at the time of Noblet and enjoyed relatively wide popularity. Gods and sons of pagan gods were considered either as stories or indeed, especially in this case, as the devil: his fire, his fall from the Olympiad, his making of automata, his enslavement, and indeed even his stature point to possible cross-reference and consideration pertinent to our depiction – even if the Ancient Greek artistic representation is rather distinct (see above).

Bindings of structures

In chapter one I wrote:

> religion points to a blessed life, its structures to a binding.

This was more specifically in relation to suggested pairings between V and XV. Now, however, we can reconsider this statement in light of the card itself.

If some of the considerations that we have made are legitimate, then each engagement in the world has a virtuous mean from which it becomes ever so tempting and ever so easy to deviate. The Church (or indeed any organisation) builds around itself rules, regulations and physical structures by which to not only operate, but also provide both a sense of security and direction.

These become the very same chains that bind us to the Devil's anvil. When, instead of the spiritual to which it points, a religious organisation begins to point to its own perpetuation and structures, it ceases its liberating impulse and instead binds. In the process, inevitably it attracts those who seek of their own volition the false security of those very structures that falsely proclaim the spiritually liberating life.

I do not wish to imply that structures are of themselves evil. Indeed, without such I would be without home, without secure social standing or income, and possibly even without the ability to develop from childhood to adulthood.

It is, perhaps, the question 'whom does the binding or structure serve' that makes of it either effective support or chain.

A structure, however, may as much attract those who seek its secure shelter as attract those who wish to use it with malevolent intent. And this we have repeatedly seen over the centuries, not only with the various religious impulses and their accompanying structures, but also in the political and legal as well as the economic spheres: bindings made of other people by deceptive or manipulative power.

There is another aspect that can here be considered that directly relate to binding and, indeed, its sexual and social ramifications: that of the *agunah* – in Hebrew, עגונה – or the still 'chained' separated woman who is awaiting her divorce, and until such is granted, remains very much unfree and tied to the worse aspects of socio-cultural chains.

From Arete to Hubris

If at numerous times we have been called upon by the cards to consider *Arete* or virtue, here we are faced with its arrest should we falter. And faltering is as easy as coming to a stage where the individual believes that he or she has reached some level of perfection – or at least has gained such confidence in their own abilities or indeed their own virtue (*arete*).

This is what was at times referred to as pride – not in its sense of the gladness one has of one's achievement, but the immodest self-aggrandisation of excessive self-confidence and self-pride.

Lilith

There is another aspect that we may also consider, especially as it re-appears in various guises in discussions of the Devil: that of Lilith.

If there is one aspect of the depiction of the Devil that points in her direction, it is its repeated depiction in Marseille-type decks as having many feminine characteristics. Lilith has various cognates, some of which appear to be early Mesopotamian feminine deities rather than her Talmudic account which, nonetheless, becomes the bearer of developments for Mediæval considerations (especially with regards to her sexual appetite and preying on the unsuspecting).

Irrespective as to how she was perceived, more recently various renditions and archaeological finds that are similar to the following have been claimed as Lilith[2]. What is interesting is of course her similar stance and wings; that she has a pedestal, though in this case either a couple of lions or a double-headed lion; and that two smaller figures, in her case owls, mark the sides.

Of especial detail, from my perspective, are her 'clawed' feet.

Another – perhaps earlier – version has the two 'attendants' as even more directly pertinent, as they appear, instead of lions and owls, as goats complete with horns (cf the second image).

But what of this? Is it likely to have been an influence on the design of the deck?

2   For questions as to this identification, see the wonderful site maintained by Alan Humm.

Whether or not this specific image had any such influence, the concept of Lilith – her voracious sexual appetite, together with a rediscovery of the Ancient Greeks including the *Iliad* and the plight of Hephæstus, mixed with a dominant world view permeated by considerations of not only spiritual beings of light, but also of evil, an evil with whom one may gain intercourse (in both its senses) – is, I trust, sufficient for *us* to consider her as significant in light of our modern worldviews.

Keywords

In reflecting on the various aspects of this card, I would suggest taking some time to note down at least fifteen different words that can be called forth in relation to its principal impulse. I have already mentioned *deception* as one – and in fact have made use of a number of other concepts... but shall leave that as is.

Below I briefly describe my own experience with this exercise, so I suggest doing the same thing prior to reading the next brief paragraph.

… … …

Perhaps it is because I tend to the visual image as bearer of a multi-faceted meaning more easily than the verbal; but myself found I was straining to find terms in this exercise. Sure, I could come up with fifteen words easily, but many, it seems to me, were just alternatives or near-synomyms for earlier ones.

Other decks and tarot images

One aspect I have purposefully avoided thus far is bringing in important imagery from related decks and uncut sheets. I should here also mention that the earliest hand-painted decks – the Visconti-Sforza, Cary-Yale and the 'Charles VI', do not have a card depicting the Devil. Of course, it may simply be that the card from each of those decks has been lost (or destroyed).

Of interest may be the vastly different design on the Rothschild uncut sheet (dating from approximately 1500). Here, we have a far more simple and ferocious design – and yet one which, I would suggest, plays more on the infantile imagination than it does on the more sophisticated

mind: certainly the depiction brings fear to the heart of the believer. Yet, the Devil *deceives* quite some time before he gains the chance of devouring his victim.

Above to the right is the Vieville Devil. Vieville is not only a contemporary of Noblet, but was also based in Paris. Of the various images used in representations of the Devil, it seems that the rather 'benign' version became standardised as the Marseille version. Yet it bears within it, at least from my perspective, the more hideous, in large part because veiled, allusion to what is essential for devilry: a seductive appeal to what becomes a binding.

The two faces revisited

In the little space I have to complete this chapter, let's again look at the image and appeal to the two faces and their relative locations: the head and the belly – with the first calling upon the dryness of thinking as rather distanced and separate from the *engagement* within the world of the second, itself separated from thinking; of, in another way of describing this, the second drawing on the appetitive moistness and yearning, and of the first the coolness of analysis.

These two, without the balancing and healing element of the heart, remain but the two extremes of the belly's fire and the mind's ice.

The sceptre

I have only made one passing reference to the forked instrument he holds aloft – it is certainly reminiscent of the wooden pitch-fork used for hay in former times, and its fork calls to mind the forked tongue of the serpent or viper. Can one come to trust the words uttered by deceit? Or rather, how easy it is to be beguiled!

A variety of images from the times indeed show the Devil with such a pitchfork. Many such images occurs outside of decks. The Cary Sheet (another uncut and in this case only *partial* sheet also dating from around the year 1500) is unique in showing the Devil with the pitch and its rather apparent use:

Some further references

At this point, some of you may also be interested in having a look at the work of Robert O'Neill. For example, his essay on the Devil (amongst many of his other essays) is available at:

www.tarot.com/about-tarot/library/boneill/devil

On a related image, I also wrote a brief paper for the ATS Newsletter (in May 2007): 'When the Devil is not the Devil'

newsletter.tarotstudies.org

A brief mention should also be made that in later TdMs, the 'sceptre' has been replaced by what appears to be a sword blade, its top still aflame, very much calling to mind some more of both Hephæstus as well as the fires of Hell...

...but of course, what is called to mind is first and foremost reflections on the imagery and its embedded spiritual-cosmological framework, in the context of one's metaphysical understanding. These are what allows for deepened insights.

ASTROLOGOS

Astronomy

When I initially prepared notes for this book and decided to constrain it to thirty chapters, there appeared at various junctures considerations about astronomy that seemed sufficiently large to warrant its own chapter, as well as enabling me to relinquish these discussions when considering individual cards.

Unlike the topic on Alchemy and the Elements, astronomical, or indeed, astrological, considerations were not only commonplace at the time of Noblet, but depictions were prominent in both public places and illuminated manuscripts.

In addition, it should perhaps again be mentioned that astronomy formed part of the general education of the times, being one of the seven liberal arts and sciences. More strictly, it was part of the Quadrivium which included arithmetic, astronomy, geometry, and music. These would have followed the study of the Triuvium of grammar, rhetoric, and logic. Such study had been in evidence since late Antiquity and something that was still in common parlance at the time of Noblet's creation.

Even the young count Sforza from the 1400s had a manuscript made for him about the celestial spheres, *De Sphæra*, a book we have already had cause to mention and from which imagery was displayed in the second chapter (on the Bateleur). We'll have another brief look at this book a little later.

What I would like to first consider are the two ways in which astronomical considerations come to bear on the deck. For our purposes, I shall make no clear distinction between *astronomical* and *astrological* details, for in terms of imagery and the night sky personified in asterism imagery, distinctions do not occur – save perhaps that the names and locations of individual stars within an asterism may be deemed more important in the former than in the latter.

So what are those two principal considerations, and how do they bear on the set and on individual cards?

Celestial theory

The first is a general view of the world or universe. Is the world geocentric or heliocentric... or neither? Even within each of these models, there are differences about which 'sphere' is closest Earth, and what their order of distance is from our point of observation?

Can or does this have an influence or impact on card depictions?

These are the types of questions that occur to me, especially when considering the cards that are to come. We have, to use their TdM titles in order, the Maison Dieu, the Star, the Moon, and the Sun. Indeed, we can continue the sequence and notice both Judgement and the World... in case these play into such considerations.

Simply in terms of order, we *may* have instead expected the Star to occur *after* the Moon and Sun, reflecting a more 'natural' world-view for the period, in that the 'sphere' of the fixed stars is seen (from either geocentric or heliocentric perspective) to be beyond that of the Sun.

In fact, the most common astronomical view of the times was the Ptolemaic one, in which the Earth is seen as surrounded by 'spheres' of the elements (water, air, and fire), and then in order the 'spheres' of the Moon, Mercury, Venus, the Sun, Mars, Jupiter, Saturn, and the fixed stars, beyond which are the spiritual realms.

Whether the card of the Star depicts the fixed stars (or specific fixed stars) or the planets in the Ptolemaic order, we could reasonably expect that the card's position be either between the Moon and Sun or, even more naturally, beyond the Sun. At best, and from such astronomical considerations, coming before the Moon seems rather strange.

Even with the Copernican heliocentric view, from Earth's viewing position, the Moon is closest and the order remains more or less the same, save that all the other planets are seen as orbiting the Sun. Still, in that instance, the Star(s), whether as planets or as fixed stars, are placed either between the Moon and Sun or, again more appropriately, *after* the Sun.

Let's take a look at this with some diagrammes and imagery. For those of us who have long been accustomed to tarot's ordering, it may take some effort to even begin to question whether the order that we have makes sense from those standard astronomically perspectives.

Celestial Spheres

Numerous such depictions arise, perhaps one well worth considering arises in Robert Fludd's *Utriusque Cosmi* (second volume), and reproduced in Tarotpedia. Here we have pretty standard considerations, save that in this case Fludd has ensured that *twenty-two* spheres are depicted, reflecting the letters of the Hebrew alphabet:

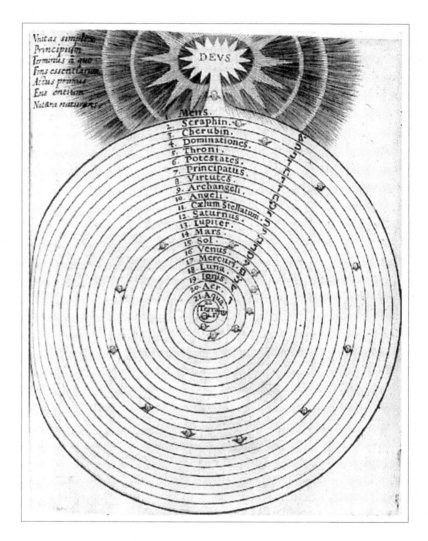

Incidentally, Fludd died just over a decade prior to Jean Noblet producing his deck. Also, though I have called the above 'spheres', they are strictly speaking not depicted as spheres at all, but rather as a *single* spiral.

Ptolemaic view

Though the above is very much based on the Ptolemaic view, it includes considerations from outside of astronomy proper – specifically including the nine orders from the pseudo-Dionysian hierarchies (angels, archangels, etc. up to the Seraphim), as well as, mentioned already, that it is not spheres that are being depicted, but rather a hierarchy of what may be called spiralling 'condensation' or 'densification'.

I would personally see this as quite apt in terms of the various neo-platonic influences on trump imagery, yet the more strict astronomical ptolemaic view is also important to consider:

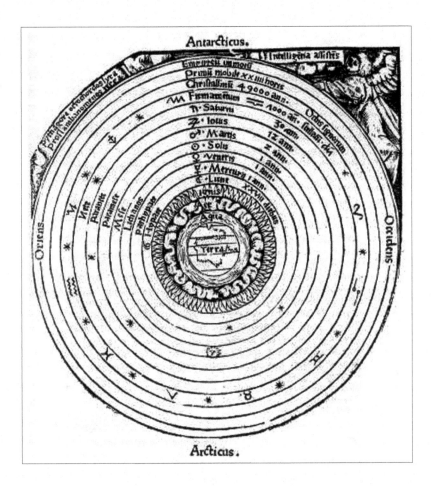

We can easily see here the similarity to the Fludd diagramme. What is perhaps not evident is that its basis is entirely Aristotelian (this image is in fact from a 1519 Aristotle *Libri de caelo*), and that each circle is a representation of a whole *sphere* that successively encloses the one smaller. Following the planetary spheres are the ones of the fixed stars incorporating the zodiacal signs (upon the ecliptic), themselves surrounded by spheres supposedly of crystalline substance, eventually to reach the Primum Mobile.

Perhaps an easier representation is the following:

The Cards

If we consider the cards not only in their sequence, but also solely focussed on their upper segments, we have the following, depicted overleaf with XVI in the lower part of the column, rising to XX at its pinnicle.

Observations of Detail

Here we can perhaps better see what may have been expected had the 'natural' celestial world view been reflected, in that the Stars would naturally be placed between the Sun and the Angel of Judgement. The Noblet (and hence also general TdM order)is thus certainly at odds with normal mediaeval and renaissance cosmological views.

Showing the partial card images in that manner also enables us to see other details that may not at first be apparent.

Firstly, that XVI *seems* to show a meteorite shower, possibly with the depiction of a comet in the top right hand corner. More on the specifics of this will be mentioned when we get to the card in the next chapter. For now, it is the astronomical consideration that we have at hand, and it makes sense in the sequence that such 'showers', either falling to earth or closely seen (and quickly moving), shows their proximity to the Earth.

The next detail that becomes apparent when presented in this manner is the relative sizes of the astral bodies: the one with the greater light is

far larger than the one preceding.

This order is also reflected in common language, as when we speak, even in poetic manner, of (in order) the Sun, the Moon and the Stars. It seems that any other sequence does not quite 'sound' right or at ease. And it is this very speech order that is reflected in many documents, without hinting at astronomical considerations. Still, in terms of *imagery*, it may have been considered that the Aristotelean-Ptolemaic order would have had more of an influence.

This linguistic ordering of Sun, Moon and Stars, of course, is also found in numerous Biblical places – perhaps of especial significance are Luke 21:25-27, Matthew 24:29-30, Mark 13:24-27 (included below as the second quote) and 1 Corinthians 15:41, which reads:

> The sun has its own splendour, the moon another splendour, and the stars yet another splendour; and the stars differ among themselves in splendour. It is the same too with the resurrection of the dead: what is sown is perishable, but what is raised is imperishable.

and Mark 13:

> But in those days, after that time of distress, the sun will be darkened, the moon will not give its light, the stars will come falling out of the sky and the powers in the heavens will be shaken. And then they will see the Son of man coming in the clouds with great power and glory. And then he will send the angels to gather his elect from the four winds, from the ends of the world to the ends of the sky.

Let's allow this last quote to be our first reflective exercise.

Placing trumps XVI to XXI in sequence, re-read that last passage various times, allowing the sequence of words to be reflected in the sequence of imagery.

Greek Cosmological views

Apart from the Aristotelean-Ptolemaic view, there were of course others. Of specific significance here is that of Anaximander, who considered the order of the spheres to be as those depicted in our TdM order: Stars, Moon and Sun.

Though this, and its antecedent Babylonian view are the same as the Noblet ordering, it seems rather unlikely they were an influence as both are anachronistic and in some ways quite unnecessary.

Rather, the linguistic and Biblical references are in themselves, I would suggest, sufficient, and call easily to mind the more dominant Aristotelean-Ptolemaic and neo-Platonic views.

Cycles

Another aspect that emerges from this cosmological consideration are the various cycles that each of the major three astral cards reflect. The first, as fixed stars, the year; the Moon the month, and the Sun the day.

Extending the sequence a little on either side, if XVI is indicative of comet, then this reflects an even longer cycle than the annual one of the star, and, travelling through the sequence towards XX, a literal and symbolic "quickening" can be felt as advance is made towards the spiritual realm.

This *sequence* of (especially) Star, Moon and Sun is certainly something that has fascinating aspects and, frankly, I suspect that much has yet to be found to explain the reason behind the specific order adopted – despite the explanations given by the examples above, and others such as the order of creation in Genesis, reflecting in some ways a descending order and moving from XXI towards XV.

Astrological Zodiacal signs

If the above discussion focusses more on the upper part of the cards mentioned, consideration of the signs of the zodiac tend to be focussed in the lower panel – though in this case considering the whole image is needed to understand both zodiacal and planetary relation.

We now therefore move to the second consideration indicated on the first page of this chapter: that of the asterism as represented as zodiacal sign.

We should, however, maintain also some reservations, for despite similarities, it is not clear that it is a zodiacal sign that is represented. In fact, this can be also surmised by considering an early deck such as the Mantegna, which *adds* to the existing tarot trumps and augments them further with (amongst other things) twelve zodiacal cards – surely not something that would be done were any existing card considered to already form part of the zodiac.

Still, in terms of specific imagery, a number of cards come easily to mind. And once this way of viewing the imagery is started, it becomes relatively easy – perhaps deceptively so – to see how other trumps may similarly reflect such zodiacal imagery.

Some of the following will be picked up again when considering the individual cards in forthcoming chapters, so I shall here remain rather brief.

The first card that really shines forth as potential astrological zodiacal sign is the Moon: here we have not only the astrological ruler of Cancer depicted and named, but also prominently featured is some type of crayfish, 'crab' (its more generic older term) or crustacean.

To my eyes, even if all other cards can be dismissed with regards to their display of intended astrological imagery, this one cannot: the sheer size of the crustacean and direct connection between it *as sign of Cancer* and the Moon looms too prominently.

Let's have a rather brief look at a few others – or at least those that are the more prominent.

In this exercise, it is not so much trying to fit any *sequence* in order to force any correlation, but rather to carefully observe whether the images have resemblance to zodiacal imagery. Strictly speaking, the same could also be extended to asterisms outside the zodiacal belt. For example, (though taking it further than what is simply suggested by the image) Stephen Mangan shows how the Fou reflects an aspect of Orion adjacent Canis Major – for this, see "The Fool, Alef and Orion" in a past ATS Newsletter.

The cards that reflect such imagery appear to be especially those cards that also have astronomical details: the Star, the Moon, and the Sun. Respectively, similarities to depictions of Aquarius, to Cancer, and to Gemini are prominent.

For example, if we compare the following images of Aquarius from

early illuminated manuscripts to the lower portion of the Star card, we have in each case a naked figure pouring water.

There are, of course, also differences between these and the Star *card* image, including that there are *two* pitchers out of which water is poured in the Star.

Two pitchers, however, are also found in various other representations of Aquarius, though I have not as yet seen any of these in which a naked person is also depicted – apart from images in tarot).

Similarly, Gemini as the twins can be found in various places, looking somewhat akin to the pair below the Sun on that card. For example, here are petroglyphs from, respectively, the Cologne and the Amiens Cathedrals:

Again there are of course differences, including the lack of the wall, a detail here omitted that, in constrast, remains consistent in TdM depictions, and to which we shall return when we study the card.

In making astrological or astronomical comparisons we are not seeing whether there is absolute identical representation. There are, however, sufficient iconographic similarity, *especially* with these three cards depicting celestial bodies, to suggest that celestial zodiacal signs would have been called to mind.

The only other trump card that to me *suggests* such asterism is XI Fortitude (La Force). This card, I suggest, calls to mind both the adjacent signs of Virgo and Leo, in this case the former overcoming the latter, as it does metaphorically each year, without effort, by mere passage of time.

Let's look at the image of XI La Force as these two signs combined, with Virgo 'overcoming' Leo. In terms of combined imagery, there are no such images from early times that depict these two signs overlapping in this way – rather, the images of Force tend to be as described in chapter sixteen. The purpose here is more as an astronomical (or astrological) *consideration*, in the same manner that the Fool *can* be seen to have similarities to Orion.

Seasons, events, and manuscripts

Let us finally return to the Sforza *De Sphæra*, begining, specifically, with the pages on the Moon already mentioned in chapter two:

In so many ways, I would suggest that if any type of profession or activity – rather than a social *station* or an allegory – is going to be depicted in card imagery, then it will also be found in manuscripts or other illustrations related to the planets and those activities or professions over which they were deemed to rule. To find, then, an astrological representation of the Bateleur should be less surprising than it may first be for many of us – myself included.

Cathedral petroglyphs often also included not only the signs of the zodiac, but, adjacent to each of these, the activities of the month as similarly shown in the illuminated manuscript above.

In reaching the end of this chapter, let's have a brief look at some of these and call to mind various cards within the deck. In this way we are therefore not any longer looking at the card images and seeking to find therein similarities to astrological or astronomical detail, but rather its opposite: are there details that, given a person familiar with such common imagery of the period, are likely in some manner to be called to mind when looking at trump imagery?

Here are three from the Wolfegg Mediæval Housebook: the Moon, Venus, and Saturn:

If in the Moon the Bateleur can yet again be easily seen, I would suggest that with Venus the procession of young couples in the lower-right hand section calls to mind trump VI L'Amoureux, and that Saturn clearly brings to mind not only old age and the Hermit, but perhaps more significantly the tortures that were not only ever so prominent, but so accepted, and brought to mind in chapter 17 on Le Pendu. In fact, there is even a hanging, and a wheel of torture, atop the mount depicted just below the representation of Capricorn.

These are not, of themselves, astrological. Rather, the planetary rulership calls to mind, and thus connects, these figures with tarot trumps.

Over the coming chapters, some aspects of these astrological considerations will be further explored.

XVI - Maison Dieu

La Maison Dieu

I looked forward to writing this chapter, in great part as this is probably the card that has cost me the most, both in terms of personal effort in pursuing a specific image, as well as leading me far more into historical considerations. Not that other cards did not: indeed, as I hope the past chapters have already shown, there is a wealth of historical context that needs to be untangled and discovered to support one's own preferred interpretations.

With *La Maison Dieu*, I was struck by two comments made by Fred Gettings in his 1973 *The Book of Tarot*, a book that I obtained only in the early-1990s following its republication by Chancellor Press as *Tarot: how to read the future* – admittedly a title that, were it not that it appeared to focus a little more on historical considerations, I nearly passed over.

There, on page 87, is a petroglyph from a 'lumiere' Cathedral, hence ante-dating tarot by some centuries, clearly in line with the card's most important details... though we'll visit as well those aspects that are *not* in the petroglyph later. The caption Gettings gives is:

"Illustration to the Golden Legend. Reims Cathedral".

Unfortunately, *both* these attributions are incorrect! The story he mentions (to which we shall soon return) I could find nowhere in the *Golden Legends* (in neither an English edition and a complete French edition I later also purchased in case the English book I had read was an edited or partial version), and the image is nowhere on Reims Cathedral.

How do I know this latter? In 2000, about six years after having seen Gettings's book and madly searching through countless books in local University libraries for imagery from Reims Cathedral (recall that this was, effectively, pre-internet days), my wife and I had the opportunity of paying a visit to the region. In bursting wind gusts and some lacerating rain-drops, I searched, and searched, the whole building to which I had access. I then also asked not only the tourist office, but also guides, about this image which was supposedly on the Cathedral *somewhere*! All to no avail.

We left Reims with me rather disappointed. It still had not occurred to me that perhaps Gettings had referenced the Cathedral incorrectly – other than perhaps there being another Cathedral (or church) in the township, but to no avail. I am certainly ever grateful to my companion for putting up with what must have appeared a unicorn or wild turkey hunt!

It was not until we returned to Melbourne on the other side of the globe that I happened to come across a *similar* quatrefoil petroglyph... surely both must have been from the reference therein mentioned: not *Reims* to the East of Paris, but rather *Amiens* to its North!

From thereon, it was not too difficult to confirm and eventually find the image, though it would be another five years – in Autumn 2005, that I was able to again travel and discover, with the joy of beholding firm confirmation with first-hand experience, the ever so evocative petroglyph displayed on the next page.

By that stage and before heading to France, I had also referenced another, thought different, image of similar import from another region, this one in Moissac, a location in the South of France and near where we had rented a house a couple of weeks after our Amiens visit... and so I was also looking forward to seeing it *in situ*.

The number of images on 'lumiere' or Gothic and on (and in) Romanesque religious buildings is astounding not only for their variety, but also, I would suggest, there constant presence due to these being part of the daily life and reflection of a city's or town's residents, and this until quite recent times. And even now, despite the overwhelming images with which each citizen is faced, the petroglyphs presented on the outer walls of what are still large and centrally located churches, Cathedrals and other religious buildings are near impossible to avoid.

Weaving across France from north to south, most trump imagery can be found, bearing either exact or similar elements. It is in such an image-rich landscape that our ancestors played (in whatever fashion) with those cards which would have inevitably called to mind, whether consciously or not, similarities with petroglyph designs.

I will present much later another petroglyph when we reach the last chapter on the Fou.

For now, let's return to the specifics of the Maison Dieu.

Infancy pseudo-Gospels

It is not in the *Golden Legends*, a compilation of the lives of various Saints, that the story mentioned by Gettings is to be found, but in one of the various pseudo-Gospels that told the story of the life of Jesus not covered in the canonical works.

In one of these, the *Infancy Gospel of Pseudo-Matthew*[1], the story is told of the events that followed after Mary and Joseph, with their baby Jesus, fled Judeah due to Herod's threat to their infant (this is prior to the Judea's destruction and simultaneous creation of the region into the Roman province of Palestine).

After various miracles performed *en route* by the infant, the story continues:

> While they travelled on, Joseph said to him, "Lord, the excessive heat is cooking us; if it pleases you, let us go by the sea, so that we can travel, resting in the coastal towns." Jesus said to him, "Fear not, Joseph, I will shorten your journey, so that what you were going to travel across the space of thirty days, you will finish in one day." While this was being said, behold, they began to see the mountains and cities of Egypt.

> Rejoicing and exulting they came to the region of Hermopolis, and went into one of the Egyptian cities called Sotinen. Since they knew no one in it from whom they could ask for hospitality, they went into the temple which

1   reproduced in *The Other Bible*, ed. by W. Barnstone, HarperCollins, 1984. The story is also included in the earlier *Arabic Gospel*, and in many later works.

was called the "Capitolium of Egypt." There had been placed in this temple three hundred and sixty-five idols, to which, on appointed days, divine honor was given in sacrilegious ceremonies.

It happened that, when the most blessed Mary, and her child, had entered the temple, all the idols were thrown to the ground, so that they all lay flat, convulsed and with their faces shattered. Thus they revealed openly that they were nothing. Then that which was said by the prophet Isaiah was fulfilled: "Behold, the Lord shall come on a swift cloud and enter Egypt, and all the idols made by the Egyptians shall be removed from his face."

[...] Then all the people of that city believed in the Lord God through Jesus Christ.

Evidence that this is indeed the story, or one of its forms, depicted in the Amiens image is clear when the image is taken in context, and consideration given to numerous similar depictions from illuminated manuscripts flourishing at the time.

On the Amiens Cathedral, the context is in a *series* of quatrefoil petroglyphs. On the Moissac Abbey Church (image on next page), it is far more scenically presented. In each case, however, it shows that the infancy stories were far more part-and-parcel of a culture that, in the

21st century, seems ever so remote and foreign.

Both these depictions, from Amiens Cathedral (in context) and from Moissac may also be seen in larger resolution on my fourhares.com site.

General form of the story revisited

Let's look again briefly at the general sense of the story and consider how its overall meaning and imagery may also have been more popularly understood.

Basically, we have the Jesus infant who, when entering Egypt, had its false idols (and, I would suggest in the minds of mediæval and Renaissance listeners, also idolators), fall. It is perhaps worth recalling that at the time of both the petroglyph depiction and early trump design, Egypt was already a dominantly islamic country, with islamic rules and customs.

At the time of the construction of the Cathedral petroglyphs, as seemingly suggested by the carved imagery, the 'false worshippers' of first century Egypt would have been anachronistically conceived as contemporary moslems, with the figures falling seen as from minarets with, therefore, 'idolators' instead of *idols* conceived as in fall. This is suggested on both Amiens Cathedral and the Moissac Church as the figures falling appear far more like *people* than statues.

In the tarot sequence, following the card of the Devil, this card may even have been seen as linked to the Devil: here is the worshipping house of false gods – with its worshippers obviously deceived by the Devil that nonetheless cannot withstand the powers of even the *infant* Jesus.

For the many crusaders of former times and in the stories recalled by them, as well as from then contemporary visits to places under either former or current islamic control, the fall of a minaret would have been considered as a liberating of the population from its deceptive shackles. And it may be worth bearing in mind that in Christian Europe, one of the 'names' of the Devil was 'Mohamed'.

Liberation

With the above in mind, let's have a look at the card and consider its possible meaning in the context of a reading as both 'liberation from falsehood' and 'liberation from those who seek to bind others to their will or world-view'.

Placing the Maison Dieu on a reading surface, draw two other cards, placed below, to narrate how an individual may liberate themselves from any binding situation. Whether this reading is for another person, for yourself, or as part of a fictional narrative is, by this stage of this work, very much up to you. The focus is to deepen one way of understanding this card by seeing how various situations not only bind, but also often show their own path towards liberation from such binding.

One of the consequences of having idols fall is that the worldview promulgated remains full of false promise. False because they are ineffectual; or, perhaps even worse, falsely and deceptively effectual.

Here, then, is a symbolic image that is full of promise: from past social hoodwink to liberation towards the light of truth.

Tower of Babel

Numerous tarot books suggest that this card depicts in some manner or other the Tower of Babel. Quite frankly, I find the suggestion at odds with the tarot image in terms of its general depiction and in terms of what is known of both Babel Tower and what we now know of the then popular infancy gospels.

Its sole common feature with Babel is the fall of its workmen as they seek to ever raise the ziggurat. And ziggurat the card image is not.

For the sake of seeing the difference, a couple of Tower-as-ziggurat are worth perusing, and include below both the now famous Bruegel painting as well as a different depiction from a Book of Hours for the Duke of Bedford, this latter complete with falling figures.

What we can see in both, however, is that the ziggurat, no matter how far removed from its Biblical pyramidal structure of the region and time, still maintains its important structural spiralling ascent.

Compare these, by the way, to a Mesopotamian ziggurat:

The usefulness in making this comparison is not so much to discredit or diminish the European Babel tower images, but rather to lend further credence to the idea that local knowledge and views on structures influence how they are imagined – whether these be ziggurats, Egyptian temples, idols, or North African minarets.

Babel and Minarets visited

Although I dismissed all too easily an understanding of the tarot image as the Tower of Babel, there are various significant aspects to be kept in mind should we wish to pursue such line of thought.

One of these is that both a mosque (with minaret as its most distinguishing feature) and the Tower of Babel are, each in their own way, falsely attributed 'House of God' (or *Maison Dieu*). Falsely in two senses reflecting the understanding of the time of Noblet: in the first instance, as God did not grace his presence therein, for its worshippers (and builders) did not meet 'in his name'; in the second instance, as even the worshippers or builders did not consider such as a place for the presence of *God*, but rather a space for the presence of worshipper (in the first instance) or seeker of ascent towards his throne (in the second instance with regards to the Tower of Babel).

'Maison Dieu'

The titling of this card as 'Maison Dieu', then, proves in many ways problematic, unless taken to itself be suggestive of an *idolator*'s naming of the same. Nonetheless, even with this explanation, it is something that, for myself at least, and despite various suggestions made over time, has not satisfactorily been solved[2].

Perhaps, as I personally do not place much importance on card titles – instead considering that these are 'unfortunate' additions – it is not something that seems to *need* as much investigation.

Infancy gospel and details

I have already shown what I consider the more important image similarities between the Maison Dieu and the pseudo-infancy Gospels. Let's, however, have another brief look at these and observe also some of the key differences between card images and infancy story.

2   it may be worth noting that the title 'Maison Dieu' was later also used to refer to a charity house, hospice or hospital. None of these, however, seem pertinent to the card image, especially if the title is considered in its ambiguity.

In many other depictions, the style is far more 'Roman', in that the idols are shown on pillars from which they fall. In many of these, it is clear that the falling figures are indeed of stone or clay, rather than living figures.

Others, of course, repeat the form shown on the petroglyphs, and the figures appear far more as human, usually in pairs, as per the TdM depiction.

Let's look at one final image of the type as we compare these (and the petroglyphs earlier shown) to our tarot card imagery.

What is evident in all these and the petroglyphs is that in the Noblet not only are the central figures of the escape to Egypt (ie, Mary and Child) missing[3], but also, and importantly, that in the *tarot trump* three other details are different: the top of the tower is afire; a large shape is in the right-hand corner; and the scene is filled with what appears to be a shower of large stones.

These details are too consistently different for the card image to only have been influenced by the infancy story. I would nonetheless suggest that the infancy story played a crucial role in the way in which the card image was perceived and understood.

Three card images

If we consider card imagery from the three different decks of the period (and the same region: Paris), it is evident that whatever the allegory or intended narrative, it had not stabilised to a single representation.

Let's briefly look at these, in the form of the anonymous Paris deck, the Vieville (respectively left and right below), and the now familiar Noblet – each, it should be recalled, from *circa* 1650 and from Paris.

---

3   though that can in part be 'explained' by reference to the Amiens petro-glyphs that separates out various sections into different images, with the fall from the tower being only *one* such panel.

What is of course striking are their differences. Yet, in many ways, these are perhaps not as dissimilar as may at first appear. The Vieville very much depicts another scene from the same story, as can be seen from another petroglyph of the same series on the Amiens Cathedral. If anything, this *difference* in imagery, given the context, is further evidence for the infancy Gospel.

...but still those stones are missing.

'Baetyls' (meteors) and Comets

Natural but rare events are always something to behold, and meteoric showers, lightning bolts, and the portent of the passage of a comet can all be experienced as extraordinary events coming from the sky.

A meteoric shower – an effective plundering and destruction from the heavens – could easily be seen as a wave of devils riding forces of destruction, and this is something that appears to be depicted on the Paris deck shown earlier.

Even in our time, a comet's passage is an awesome sight – as it was for those of us situated in regions where the spectacle of the 2007 McNaught Comet was visible, a magnificent testimony.

The Noblet (and other TdM) card details appear to show the combined impact of what is perhaps a large meteorite object, breaking on entry into the atmosphere, yet reaching various localities with destructive ferocity. A number of images from various periods show something of the kind, as the following mid-15th century depiction illustrates.

Here we have not only the destruction of the town, but also of its population, with all those elements of a comet as well as the downpour of a meteoric shower, missing from the infancy narrative. There are a number of reports of such observations from the late 16th century, so it is likely an event did take place at that time[4].

The Will of God as Punishment

Combined, the various aspects of the card image seem to show the will of God and the punishment of evil-doers – a concept well formed and maintained in mediæval and counter-reformation times, and bringing to mind its Biblical antecedent in the destruction of Sodom[5], rather Europeanised in its image and at times depicted in tones clearly reminiscent of tarot-like imagery:

---

4   There is a modern equivalent in the November 1833 Leonid shower, for which, it is recorded: 'The Meteors fell from the elements the 12 of November 1833 on Thursday in Washington. It frightened the people half to death.' (Cf 'Brief history of the Leonid shower')

5   detail from "Lot and his daughters", attributed to Lucas of Leyde, 1520, located in the Louvre in Paris (h.34 x w.48 cm)

Cleansing

In each of these examples, whether as the liberation from shackles or destruction, what occurs to reflection is that the image is of a cleansing, and I shall close the chapter on this concept.

XVII - L'Estoile

LESTOILE

Rather than using the old French form, perhaps I should head this chapter more simply as '*L'Etoile*'. As a minor point of linguistic interest, many words that were formerly spelled with 'es' near the beginning or middle of the word are now rendered 'é': 'estoile', 'este' (or even earlier 'æstæs') and 'estampes' as now, respectively, more usually 'étoile', 'été' and 'étampes'.

The title of this card as presented and without regard to its attached image, and by homophony (or the 'language of the birds') also gives us: 'Les Toile' – the Cloth or Web (though in its written form the singular of 'toile' works against the plural of 'les'). In a way, this is similar to a word such as 'bank', which would bring to mind differences of meaning were it a caption for an image of either a river, a building, or an aeroplane in flight.

And here, the image is clear: no cloth nor web is implied. Simply, instead, the Star and its details.

Overall image design

Two chapters back on astronomy, I mentioned that in a general sense the design here appears to be of Aquarius: we have a figure below a stellar pattern pouring water from, in this case, two vessels.

The stellar pattern above certainly seems significant and various suggestions have been made as to its likely intent.

Of the figure, we can note a number of various details, including that the water is being poured on land as well as what appears to be in a river. This calls to mind the astrological poetry of Marcus Manilius, a Roman writing during the 1st century BC, compiled in his *Astronomica*:

> And young Aquarius pouring out his stream
>
> Here spreads a watery, there an earthly beam.

His book (or remnants of his book) were collected and published in 1473 (by Regiomontanus, a giant in the history of Astrology), and then again in Paris by Scaliger *circa* 1580 and in Leiden some twenty years later. I mention this not because we shall focus on either this or other poetry or texts of the times, but as an example of the numerous astrological references that formed part and parcel of the period, and which had its place in everyday life.

Later in this chapter, we shall also briefly consider some non-Aquarius related motifs. For now, however, let's enter this aspect a little more, for rather broad considerations emerge. Considerations, I would suggest, that have direct bearing on understanding the image as it may likely have been seen in former times.

So let's consider some further evidence for at least the popular eye *seeing* the card image as Aquarian in model.

Aquarius

Let's begin by re-considering one of the images shown in chapter 23, recalling that I also mentioned that at this stage I still lack an image of a naked, kneeling figure pouring from two vessels.

In many places in which either *lumiere* or Romanesque religious buildings stand, we witness that the cycle of the year and its various community activities are depicted. These petroglyphs are in addition to numerous others that focus instead on biblical scenes, lives of saints and the pseudo-infancy gospels (mentioned in the previous chapter), and pairs of virtues and vices. In quite a number of places, the annual cycles are depicted with the inclusion of the 'months' shown as zodiacal signs, adjacent which are depicted, often in another panel, daily activities. For example, the Amiens panels of Capricorn, Aquarius and Pisces are rendered in the following manner:

The most similar representation I have yet seen between a rendition of Aquarius and the trump card comes from the Bedford Book of Hours (*circa* 1414-1423). Here we have Aquarius with two vessels (as well as trees), without, however, the other details of water poured on both water and land, nor kneeling, nor, of course, the centrality of the stars themselves.

If we consider these – amongst the hundreds that were both visible in major public places (such as Cathedrals) and smaller and more private collections, it seems all the more reasonable to 'see' the lower portion of the card image, especially in light of its sequentially successive cards also having astrological and astronomical imagery, as a representation of Aquarius.

So let's look at that part of the card, and then consider what the identification of the card as Aquarius would bring to mind for a person of the 17th century, as well as, importantly, equivalent modern considerations.

Noblet image

If I can include a small note of critical reflection on Jean-Claude Flornoy's reproduction: note the colouration of the body (relative, for instance, to the hair) from a scan of the original and one of the deck we are using.

February

If this is Aquarius, then foremost is that this is generally the coldest time of the year for those living in temperate zones of the Northern

Hemisphere. This is undoubtedly obvious to those living there, but less consciously so for the many living in latitudes further south – or indeed in the Southern Hemisphere.

Here is a time that food supplies are, on the whole, solely from crops that have been stored; from fruits that have been conserved in various ways; meat and fish that have been salted, smoked or in other ways cured; milk that has been cultured into cheeses; and all prepared and consumed at a time of *extensive* darkness. Though the nights have by then for some time begun to shorten and daylight slowly increase, nights are still vastly longer than daylight.

And the cold is blistering.

In fact, Europe (and the world) was to experience what has been referred to as a little Ice Age that peaked only decades after the Noblet was produced, and that by Noblet's time had already had some major effect on crops that were no longer able to be grown in more northern latitudes. For example, grapes, which, only a century earlier, were even growing in England[1], were by then restricted to more southernly latitudes.

The depiction of water poured from those vessels, then, also calls to mind how reliant the period was on the whims and fluctuations of the seasons, and how famine was ever only around the corner: perhaps next season would share abundance... or misery.

The waters from heaven became not only a necessary part of what was required for growth, but they also signalled many dangers that we have forgotten: stagnant waters which harbour disease; floods or torrential rains that may call to mind the destruction and wreckage of the previous crop; and the hope that the new year brings with it falls that bring a healthy restoration (or continuation) of crops for the next harvest still many months away. And yet, when best to have this brought to consciousness in the Northern Hemisphere than in *February*, when, but for wood-chopping, some public festivals such as Oilmec[2], and various inevitable works of maintenance, indoor activities are paramount. In terms of its annual social cycle, Oilmec is reminiscent – of sorts – of the North American "Groundhog day" which, though still clearly winter, at the same time announces the ending of the bitter cold, and looks forward to the inevitable Spring in the not *too* distant future.

1   See, for example, B. Fagan's *The Little Ice Age*
2   also named Imbolg or, in its more pertinent form, Candlemas.

As Candlemas, the feast celebrates the fortieth day following the birth of Jesus, at which time Mary brought the infant to the temple. The festival, during the middle ages (and beyond, of course), brought townspeople together who circled outside the church with an effigy of the infant and then arrived at its door.

If we consider the two dominant 'Winter' Christian festivals, the first opens with the birth of Jesus at the birth of Winter[3]. After many cold days combined with, however, *hope*, itself marked by the slow increase of daylight and the diminishment of long nights, achieves the *peak* of its annual cycle of bitter cold with a celebration marking the end of the worst of Winter with the celebration of Candlemas.

If the time of Aquarius marks the bitterest cold, it also ends in renewed hope for both humanity (given its religious significance) and for the seasonal alterations already beginning to show forth. Aquarius already sees within its time the beginning of the melting of the coldest snows, and, importantly too, signs of renewed life with various late winter flowers delicately making their way through the cold white blankets, and blades of green shooting through both ground and what is otherwise bare flora.

And so it is winter... but a winter breaking and giving rise to renewed hope. Unless, of course,

"if Candlemas Day be bright and clear, There'll be two winters in the year."

Hope

I have at times pondered on the reasons why the Star has been linked to Hope. Hope is certainly one of the three 'theological' virtues (with Faith and Caritas, mentioned in much earlier chapters).

The considerations just made about Winter perhaps show one aspect to consider with regards to hope: the hope that Aquarius brings during a time that is otherwise bitterness-filled. There is, however, another consideration that adds credence to the joining of the symbol for Aquarius with the Star as 'Hope'.

The *Star* bears an etymological connection to *Hope*. In *Imaging Aristotle*, a book previously mentioned, Oresme is described as having produced a celestial book titled *Traitié de l'espere* (rendered there as meaning *On the Sphere*). '*Espere*' has, then, a twofold connotation: as, on the one

3   some countries have in living memory decided to officially begin the 'season' by the *first* of a given month rather than by the equinoxes and solstices.

hand, stellar; and on the other as esperance or hope.

There is, of course, another and perhaps more 'obvious' connection between a significant star and hope within the Christian story: that of the Star of Bethlehem.

If the previous card (La Maison Dieu) can in part be seen as incorporating the image of a comet, there is a contrast that emerges between that comet as a 'star of fear' and our our current card under consideration as its opposite: the Star of Hope leading the three Magi to the adoration of the newborn child.

An early uncut sheet[4] (now in the Louvre in Paris – see top of next page), dated *circa* 1500, shows the Star card in this manner. Admittedly, this is not a pattern that has made it to any of the major stabilised decks. It shows, nonetheless, interesting that very concept of the Star may have traditionally brought to mind a variety of considerations – including both the adoration of the Magi and, by analogous thinking that simply links the various considerations so far presented, the festival of Candlemas, the dual senses of 'espere' as Star and as Hope, and the month of February and Aquarius.

4   referred to as the Rothchild Sheet

The Stars

But what of the stars themselves?

The central and main star appears to be an eight-pointed star with, admittedly, another eight 'shadow' points interspersed between the main beams. As such, it may symbolically call mind baptism, as baptismal fonts are classically eight-pointed (though in that case as two intelaced squares), and symbolic of regeneration and redemption. Given the figure is also naked by a stream, this aspect of baptism may be significant. I have not, however, found any similar images representating baptism, so I mention this more as exegesis of the elements of the card starting, in this case, from the dominant star.

We have, to be sure, also already mentioned the possibility of the central star as the guiding light for the three Magi or Kings. Let's now consider other more or less obvious connections.

The first of these is simply a nonspecific grouping of stars; the second, somehow related to Aquarius; the third, to the Plæiades; and finally to Sirius.

A nonspecific grouping of stars, yet one which, by the very fact that a *group* is shown, forms an asterism, calls to mind all stellar patterns. Frankly, most of the time I personally consider that the card's stars are just this: *an asterism without specific reference*, despite what I write below.

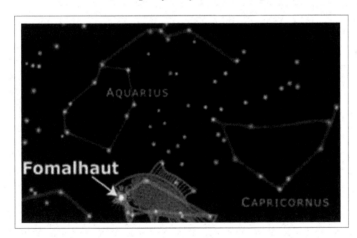

Aquarius and Fomalhaut

The depiction as an asterism on the card is simply too different to that of Aquarius for it to be what was intended. Yet, I must admit, there is an aspect of the constellation of Aquarius that is brought to mind. There are a number of stars in the night-sky that are dominant for navigation purposes and one of these occurs in the mouth of the whale or fish[5] just *below* Aquarius. Interestingly given the numbering of this card, Fomalhaut is also the *17th brightest* star in the night sky.

This star, though strictly not directly within *Aquarius*, remains one of the more important ones and a central one for that region of the sky[6].

Amongst sailors, perhaps, this connection may have been made, but I find there is simply insufficient support for this to have been the intended depiction on the card. It remains, for myself at any rate, a highly interesting connection that may be made in various narrative contexts, but no more.

The Plæiades

Similar conclusions can be made for assuming the depicted asterism to have been intended as the Plæiades. Yet let's also consider these.

This is again a group of prominent stars – and undoubtedly one of the more important clusters that has a long history in the mythologies of numerous cultures spanning the globe.

 The Plæiades[7] is located between the asterisms of Aries and of Taurus.

5   note: *NOT* Pisces, but rather the 'Southern Fish'

6   the other three dominant or 'regal' stars each being within the other three fixed signs of the zodiac: Aldebaran in Taurus; Regulus in Leo; and Antares in Scorpio.

7   whose modern astronomical name, for reference's sake and to make sense of the image presented, is the poetic "M15"!

Certainly, with these stars we have something of ancient significance. If, however, the Plæiades were *intended* on the card, then, I would suggest, a more definite depiction of the seven sisters would have formed part of the central image. However, in light of the apparent shift in the depiction of the gender of the main figure from a more Aquarian-masculine figure to one, over time, that has feminine breasts (though more on that later), the perception of the group of stars as calling to imagination the Plæiades is, among some, also very likely.

If that is the case, then the Greek version (rather than its numerous world-wide variants) would be prominent. So let's consider briefly these seven sisters and their allusions, the latter part of which will take us further afield into, eventually, the land of Egypt.

The Seven Sisters of the Pleiades

First, the seven sisters, below rendered as the *Dance of the Pleiades* by Vedder.

Whether as rain-bringers, protectors against storms, or their invoked protection against the call of sirens, they are generally considered a quite benign influence, calling to mind, in so many ways, a similar positivity and call to hope previously mentioned about this card.

There is, however, another aspect that appears to be directly connected with the Plæiades which has, it seems, mostly disappeared from general consideration, and that is its connection to a different sense of the sensual (and sexual). For this, let's again return to Manilius's *Astronomica*[8]:

> "The Pleiades, sisters who vie with each other's radiance. Beneath their influence devotees of Bacchus and Venus are born into the kindly light, and people whose insouciance runs free at feasts and banquets and who strive to provoke sweet mirth with biting wit.

> "They will always take pains over personal adornment and an elegant appearance they will set their locks in waves of curls or confine their tresses with bands, building them into a thick topknot, and they will transform the appearance of the head by adding hair to it; they will smooth their hairy limbs with the porous pumice, loathing their manhood and craving for sleekness of arm.

> "They adopt feminine dress, footwear donned not for wear but for show, and an affected effeminate gait. They are ashamed of their sex; in their hearts dwells a senseless passion for display, and they boast of their malady, which they call a virtue. To give their love is never enough, they will also want their love to be seen".

Here we have not simply the transvestite, but also what calls to mind the androgyne.

And with this, let us move to considerations of Sirius, and thence return to some of our original considerations.

Sirius

If Fomalhaut can be considered in part as one of the brightest of stars in the night sky, Sirius, part of the Dog constellation (*Canis Major*, located near Orion), is the brightest. Like the Plæiades, it too has a long historical record and usage. Of these, it marked the coming of Summer for the Greeks, and the flooding of the Nile for the Egyptians, and it is with this latter consideration that we shall take a short diversion.

The overall image of the Star trump certainly can bring to imaginative reflection how the rivers of the Nile are augmented at the time of the Star showing itself, with increased waters both on the land and within the river itself – in the case of the card, seen symbolically by the pouring of additional waters from the pitchers.

Of additional interest is that the God of the Nile is Hapi, the full-breasted god whose task it was to render the lands fertile by the Nile's annual inundation.

---

8   Passage quoted on gay-astrology.com

In both this, and in the Manilius extract earlier quoted, we have aspects that bring together the masculine and feminine elements. In the case of Hapi – and though the depiction can be explained as an aged man with drooping breasts – it is as likely that he is representative of someone with XXY chromosomes: having masculine external genitals, whilst also developing full breasts from adolescence.

Looking at the image of the trump, we can certainly consider here a depiction of the Nile (the water shown on the left of the card), Sothis (Sirius as the central brightest Star above the figure), and Hapi (as feminine breasted male) pouring the additional waters necessary for the Nile's flooding[9]. 'Necessary', and annual, bringing to the surrounding lands the nutrients and soil for the rich hoped for harvests – harvests that the Roman Empire also cherished.

Even if, as I would suggest, a direct reference to Hapi is anachronistic and unintended, the development of the image on this trump leaves this

9   Given the previous reference to February, note should be taken that the Nile's flooding occurs *circa* August.

aspect as one quite consistent with the overall meaning upon which we can reflect – despite the differences in geographical region and farming needs.

Homage to thee, O Hapi.
Thou appearest in this land
And thou comest in peace to make Egypt to live.

Thou art the Hidden One
And the guide of the darkness
On the day when it is thy pleasure to lead the same.

Thou art the waterer of the fields which Ra has created,
Thou givest life unto all animals,
Thou makest all the land to drink unceasingly
As thou descendest on thy way from the heavens.

[Hymn to Hapi, 18th or 19th Dynasty]

Concern for the gifts from heaven

In each possibility and interpretation at which we looked in relation to this card, one central issue came forth: that the natural cycles, which of themselves guarantee a source of food and health, are provided in a timely fashion by the hands from above.

This is more than the work that humanity has endeavoured to widen in order to be able to mitigate against natural calamities. For example, building reservoirs of both water and grains (and other food supplies); diverting waterways (canals and aqueducts) and developing farming methods that ensure higher yields. Each of these, though they of course mitigate against the more extreme cycles in weather conditions, still show that we remain dependent on the blessings of rain and sunshine, each in doses that are moderate for harvests to be successful and life to continue.

Woodcarving exercise

Finally we come to an exercise that I have delayed until this card – for a variety of reasons, in part as I wanted an image that allows a segment to be selected relatively easily.

There are three media I would suggest for this exercise: either use a piece of relatively soft wood (for many tarot woodcuts, pear-wood is used); or a piece of lino (craft shops should have pieces for lino-cuts); or simply, as we did when I was a child (and it works wonderfully!), a rather large and not too starchy potato (cut in half for a flat surface).

Choose either the top section of the card only (the stars) or, if wanting a challenge, the whole card. Either draw the image *in reverse* on the surface with a 2B or 4B pencil, or trace the image and then, turning the paper over, rub it to transfer the image onto the surface.

Now comes the careful carving around the lines made so that the area *where no lines appear* is hollowed (a little). Once completed, apply either paint or liquid ink with a brush or small roller to the block, and imprint the image on paper.

Actual woodblocks for a whole deck were, however, not made as separate blocks for each card, but rather allowed either the 78 cards to be imprinted in one swipe, or a large number of these. Below is part of the 1760 TdM-*II* Conver (from Marseille) woodblock.

Spiritual Current or Impetus

Let's briefly return to card spreads to complete this chapter. In considering a spread, a common version is to view, for example, three cards as bringing to light something of the past in the situation at hand, the present, and the future, this last in terms of its momentum.

Another manner of considering three cards is to reflect on a *force, current* or *impulse* that seeks to make itself manifest. Whether this is to be understood in a psychological manner or as a spiritual embodiment is something which I leave here for reflection and to which we shall return.

XVIII - La Lune

La Lune

Before we consider the aspects pertinent to three-card readings on which we closed the last chapter, let's take a careful look at the composition of the card and its difference with other TdMs.

There are various ways in which to divide the overall composition, so the manner in which I do it below is one among others – some of which we shall also consider later. I have edited the images that follow in order to remove elements from each 'panel' of the card. Specifically, the towers have been removed from the top section, the droplets from the middle section, and the lower portion of the right-hand animal from the bottom panel.

This not only elongates the overall image, but brings to clarity distinctions between the dominant three parts of the card.

Let's proceed, then, by looking carefully at each part and allowing these to bear on various considerations that come to mind.

Top panel: the Moon and droplets

The Moon itself is composed of three distinct parts: its face centrally facing us; the crescent upon which it rests; and the dual rays depicted gold and red.

This is of course not the only manner in which the Moon is depicted across TdMs. For example, TdM-*II* decks are distinguished from this model by having the Moon's face look to the left, as in, for example, the Chosson:

Strictly from an astronomical perspective, the difference is striking. In the Chosson and other TdM-*II* decks, the Sun's location is to the right or the left of the depiction – right or left depending on whether we see the *face* as reflecting the light, or the red crescent doing so.

In the Noblet especially, but also more generally in TdM-*I* depictions, the face is shown as lit-up, with the lower crescent darkened. This shows it to be astronomically opposite the Sun, and hence as *full Moon*. Having said this, however, I should point out that various people prefer to consider the depiction as being of a Solar eclipse, with the rays behind described as those of the Sun. Though in the context of a specific reading such interpretation may emerge, in terms of the *depiction* this frankly seems rather unlikely: apart from considerations that emerges with other parts of the Moon card itself, the Sun is separately depicted on the next card.

Taking the Noblet as showing a (near) Full Moon, then, it also therefore depicts the time of the cycle during which much of the night has sufficient natural light for quite a variety of activities, including hunting. In fact, in terms of deer hunting, night periods surrounding the full Moon may have provided optimal hunting – especially for those full Moons occurring nearer the end of the year as Winter approaches. Not only would hunting have been possible, of course, but also fishing. Whether or not the catch was (or is) in fact bigger than other times (as popular lore would have it), it seems that the engaged activity was considered by its participants as of greater merit.

Social evening activities were also more likely to occur during or near full Moons – and there are still, for example, some Freemasonic Lodges that meet on a day close to this time for the (formerly) very practical reason of having light by which to return home, whether on horse-back or carriage. In contrast to other Moon phases, then, this tends to be a far more active one.

Even though we have only considered the top section of the card image, it already seems that much of the rest emerges 'naturally', if the phase is considered to be full. Yet, of course, there are decks from amongst the earliest that show the Moon to be in its more classical rendition as crescent – as does, for example, one of the hand-painted 15th century decks: the 'Charles VI' deck, shown overleaf, depicting not only what appears to be astronomers, but more specifically of Arabic dress and hence, we can presume, Arabic cultural heritage.

Moving to the 'droplets', this is the first instance we re-encounter them since we looked at the pips in chapter three. There, we referred to them by their heraldic name of '*gouttes*'. I would suggest that there are two ways in which we can see these in this card: in the first instance as, indeed, 'droplets' of 'moisture' and, hence, as *ascending* towards the Moon; in the second manner, however, as 'arrow-heads' of 'light' shooting *from* the Moon towards the Earth. Although our modern eyes are more likely to see these as droplets ascending, I would suggest that the second suggestion is perhaps more likely the manner in which these would have been perceived. Also, these arrowheads of course recur in both the Sun and Judgement, and are pictorially distinct to the *gouttes* that are shown on the Aces of Baston and Sword as moving 'droplets'.

Unlike the 'balls' of card XVI (which are more likely *Baetyls* or asteroids), the 'arrowheads' of light seem to depict an influence far more benign and regular; whether it be, as in this instance, from the Moon or, as in the ensuing two cards, from the Sun or accompanying the trumpet blast from the spiritual realms.

Despite the fact that many TdMs have these 'arrow-heads', not all do. Variety exists, therefore, both in terms of the orientation or *phase* of the Moon, as well as whether or not the astral figure has 'arrow-head' additions.

As an interesting note, the variety exists not only in the TdM, but also amongst various Besançon decks. These, characteristically, have replaced the Papesse and Pope with, respectively, Juno and Jupiter. Aside from that, however, they tend to on the whole reflect details of either TdM-*I* or *II*. For example, the Blanche Besançon shows a more TdM-*I* type depiction of the Moon, with details that we shall also use when considering the two lower sections of the card.

Middle Panel: Towers and Beasts

I've long wondered *why* specifically two towers make their appearance on this card. One can always suggest artistic balance or the 'accidental' whim of the designer that subsequently gets copied. It seems, however, to be rather a strange detail to have been retained, especially given its intricate design for the woodcarver.

Furthermore, unlike the beasts – which do not appear on the Cary Sheet (shown on the next page) – the human-made structures appear to

be included. Let's pause here a moment, consider this last statement and look again at our sequence of cards, in this case looking specifically for instances of human-designed objects, even if held by an allegory (such as Justice) or spiritual being (as in Judgement).

For myself, it is especially when considering this card that *human* design and construct gains some kind of conscious significance: were it not for the towers, the entire card design would be of the natural world.

Perhaps similar thoughts may have risen to consciousness beforehand with, for example, only the vessels held by the figure on the Star depicting human-made objects. But for me, and perhaps it is simply because I took all instruments depicted until this card for granted, or as part and parcel of the activity of the symbolic representation, those two towers somehow seem 'odd'.

Perhaps the card originally depicted a specific location that has since been forgotten. A couple of years ago, discussing this with Robert

Mealing and Paula Goodman, images of Verres (in the Aosta region in northern Italy near both France and Switzerland) brought the possibility to mind:

However, the towers remain a detail for which I have yet to find or read a satisfactory explanation[1].

As well, let's note that the Cary Sheet image of the Moon card has no beasts, and it is likely, I would suggest, that these were added later.

I have called them, thus far, 'beasts' rather than 'dogs', as there are various possibilities as to what they specifically depict – even, I would suggest, on the Noblet.

Allow me first to *consider* some of the less likely candidates. We can see, for example on the Blanche Besançon image previously shown, that the animal on the right-hand side is far more ambiguously depicted than that on the left. The ambiguity remains, though less pronounced, in the Noblet: it's as if the right-hand animal allows for various other possibilities.

If we consider again for a moment the earlier discussion of hunting by the light of the full Moon, then it becomes at least feasible that what is depicted are hunter and hunted. In the fashion of the times, hound and

1　　It is worth considering that a city-state may had used something similar for its coat-of-arms; as does, for example, the modern city of Haifa in Israel.

hare.

It is perhaps strange to see either of the beasts as rabbit or hare – we are so used to the furry-bunny variety, or a realism quite at odds with what is presented on the card. Yet, see below the reproduction of a 16th century print from France of a '*lapin*', ie, a rabbit:

When compared to the image of the Noblet animal on the right, especially given its paws, there is sufficient ambiguity for readers at the time of Noblet's creation to have 'seen' therein a rabbit or hare. In addition, there are numerous references in tradition to not only Hound[2] and Hare together, but also to both of these having some kind of connection to the Moon.

For some time I have also reflected on the differences in Christian symbolism between these two animals that have closely matched names in their Latin form: *Lepus* (Hare) as pure and innocent; in opposition to *Lupus* (Wolf) as symbolic of evil. These, again, are both closely connected to the Moon in common lore in France and other places, with the former said to be depicted on its face, whilst the latter is often depicted or considered as howling at it.

2   Cf Iamblichus *Theurgia*, ch. 12: "the powers […] of animals, such as the dog [...] are assigned to the Moon".

The light of the full Moon, however, calls to mind the light conditions of dusk and dawn. I was reminded through a post made by Stephen Mangan of a phrase my grandmother used for the period: 'entre le chien et le loup' ('between dog and wolf'), derived from a phrase describing dusk (and pre-dawn) that makes more complete sense:

"quand l'homme ne peut distinguer le chien du loup"

"when man cannot distinguish dog from wolf"

This phrase dates, supposedly, from at least the 2nd century, and was common in France from the 13th onwards.

And with this phrase concepts enter into considerations, concepts that have made their mark in various exegetical ways, including ideas about the difference between the wild and the domesticated; fear and trust; ravager *versus* companion.

The sense of *difficulty* in *distinguishing* between one and the other, on the other hand, adds an element to the frequently mentioned quality of the Moon card as delusory.

Lower Panel: the Crustacean

Finally we come to the crustacean. As a symbol, and given its context with the Moon, it is clear that it is depicting Cancer. To revisit briefly an image presented in chapter 23 (on Astronomy), Cancer, which to our modern sensibilities is represented by a Crab, is here shown by its more common depiction as *any* crustacean – and yet specifically, also, as crayfish or yabby (crawfish). This does not of course mean that the Crab wasn't also used: the Amiens Cathedral petroglyph clearly shows it was. Rather, the crawfish and its cognates were far more common in lands that are non-maritime.

Let's consider for a moment both the crab and the crayfish as animals, for they are remarkable. Specifically, let's first consider the depiction on the card, and ask:

in which direction is the crustacean moving?

Crustaceans are strange in that way, in that the crab moves with greatest ease side-to-side, and the crayfish, when swimming, appears to be going *backwards* from our perspective. Given that the card depiction shows it to be in water, its movement, by the use of its tail, is *downwards* to, literally, ever profounder depths.

Another aspect of this part of the card is its dormant water. Here is the water is not moving, unlike the earlier image of a stream or river. The depicted body of water appears more that of a pond, lake or marsh: *still or 'stagnant'* water.

We have, with Moon and this stilled water, reflection upon reflection, for each reflects the light. Though not depicted as such, to our own reflections within the confines of our minds, we can imagine that the Sun is reflected upon the face of the Moon, which itself becomes reflected upon the surface of the water. Each reflection, of necessity, loses some essential quality of that which it reflects, yet it simultaneously reveals the same.

It is with this consideration that we return to the closing paragraph of the previous chapter.

Previous Chapter's end Reflection

The previous chapter ended with the remark that:

> Another manner of considering three cards is to reflect on a force that seeks to make itself manifest. Whether this is to be understood in a psychological manner, or as a spiritual embodiment, is something which I leave here for reflection [...].

Let's flesh this out a little more.

Another manner of describing one aspect of this is to talk of 'drives'. Not only are there numerous drives that seek to find expression within us as individuals, but there are, similarly, 'drives' or impulses that strive to see the light of day in social groups, broader society, or even globally.

In a spread such as the popular Celtic Cross, we may consider the six cards that specifically form the cross to be reflective of, on the one hand, a (horizontal) sequence of manifested expression through time (past, current, future); and, on the other, as (vertically) an expression of a drive or impulse seeking to find expression.

For example, a narrative may develop that reflects a past situation [1] transformed into a present one [2], apparently heading into a further direction [3].

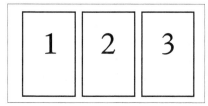

A person may have engaged in some event that results in a current circumstance that appears to be heading, by its own inertia, in a specific direction.

The remarks I made a little earlier also suggest that different, yet also revealing, impulses are at work simultaneously.

Here, it should be noted that card 5 is often placed at right angles over card 2 which, among other reasons, also allows both to be simultaneously seen.

The sequence in this case may narrate the drive or impulse (card 4) that lead the person to engage in some activity in the first place, and the ongoing motivation for such to keep going. Card 5 here shows how this drive interacts with the situation as it manifests currently in the

world. Inevitably, a tension is created, for the pure drive cannot find its fulfilment as pure drive, and instead finds the constraints of the world a medium through which to find partial expression. Card 6 may here indicate in the narrative how the drive may be transformed in a creative manner for the individual living in the stream of his or her environment.

Psychological considerations

Returning to the Moon card itself, there is an overall structure to the card that seems to mirror well aspects of our own psychological makeup: above is a dominant light that reflects the light of something still brighter; in the middle are not only our animal instincts and soul qualities, but also the constructs we build for ourselves in part for 'protection' of ourselves; and below are the waters of what remains not only often unconscious, but its very beings surface only to move rapidly back down at any sign of danger.

For those who have specific psychological-model preferences, titling these parts with those of the theory becomes an exercise that may well reflect the human psychological condition.

Plutarch

It's worth considering another aspect of the overall image in light of comments by Plutarch in 'On the face of the Moon' in his *Moralia*. I do not have the space to quote at length the whole section, so will here focus on one small part:

> In the composition of these three factors earth furnishes the body, the moon the soul, and the sun furnishes mind to man for the purpose of his generation even as it furnishes light to the moon herself. [...]

> [...] All soul, whether without mind or with it, when it has issued from the body is destined to wander in the region between earth and moon but not for an equal time. [...] For many, even as they are in the act of clinging to the moon, she thrusts off and sweeps away; and some of those souls too that are on the moon they see turning upside down as if sinking again into the deep. [...]

> First they behold the moon as she is in herself: her magnitude and beauty and nature, which is not simple and unmixed but a blend as it were of star and earth. Just as the earth has become soft by having been mixed with breath and moisture and as blood gives rise to sense-perception in the flesh with which it is commingled, so the moon, they say, because it has been permeated through and through by ether is at once animated and fertile and

460

at the same time has the proportion of lightness to heaviness in equipoise.

The Moon is here described as being of Star and Earth – of partaking of both the dense, and the volatile. It is certainly a different manner in which to consider this nearest of celestial bodies. To add, in a manner that perhaps Plutarch would not have accepted, it may be suggested that the Moon is able to reflect the light of the Sun as it shares in its own nature, however removed, in a similar manner that it can be said that we have the ability to have thoughts reflected within the confines of our minds by sharing in essence something of the transcendent qualities of which concepts and ideas take their form.

Vertical Card Structure

As I mentioned towards the opening of this chapter, there are other ways in which to consider the overall structure of the card, and one of these is by considering its central *vertical* elements: that of the direct relation between Moon and Cancer.

In considering the card in this manner, another aspect emerges: the figure of the crustacean becomes itself 'mirrored' at a 'higher octave' (or perhaps more appropriately, if I am to use musical terminology, as *canon* or *fugue*) within the whole card, with the head the Moon, the claws the beasts and towers, and the lower portion of the body. A mirroring silhouetted exponentially.

XVIIII - Le Soleil

Le Soleil

Of all card images, I find this one of the most difficult to discuss, yet in so many ways also the easiest. Perhaps it is because it has an aspect that appears to be benign, so 'pleasant', and reminiscent of so much that is joy-filled, loving, and enriching; relaxed, yet active.

I quoted Matthew 5:14 in chapter 14 whilst discussing the Hermit, and it may be apt to repeat it here in a far more literal context:

> You are light for the world. A city built on a hill-top cannot be hidden.

There is also something absolutely simple in the depiction – and something that is mentioned by Jean-Claude Flornoy in his little booklet accompanying the deck (p38), where it is called to mind that here is a walled garden, a concept that originally stems from ancient Persia and commonly referred to as Paradise. Such depictions of walled gardens were common enough in Europe just prior to Noblet creating his deck. They depict not only images of the Garden of Eden as paradisiacal, but also the mythological times of the Golden Age – whether conceived as in the distant past, or in the distant future.

Let's have a brief look at some images of gardens prior to looking at the card image itself.

Walled Gardens

The first feature to note of walled gardens is that they are artificially constructed, or in other ways depicted in a manner opposite to the wilderness of that which appears beyond the wall. In the case of the Persian context, it is the wilderness of the encroaching dryness of the desert and the dangers of wild beasts; in the context of Europe, the difference between careful cultivation and the dangers of the forests, considered as nature rampant. Within the walls, even when seeking to replicate 'wilderness', nature is not left but 'properly' managed by the cultivating hand of humanity.

The walled garden brings to light a gentle sophistication of comfort and support, where it seems that the travails of labour are nonexistent. Perhaps it is in part this that is brought forth in my opening paragraph.

Certainly the labours that would have gone into the construction of the wall or the tendering of the garden itself are not apparent in the following depiction of the Garden of Paradise, *circa* 1415, by a Master of Oberrheinischer.

What is also brought to one's attention is that the garden's focus is not on its plants – though it is richly laden – but rather on the space it provides for the people therein represented. No such space would have extremes of weather. Instead, we may very well expect that the day is sunny and pleasantly warm, yet not scorching; the light is bright, yet not overbearing; the soil and grass is abundant and soft, yet not overgrown.

The idea of a walled garden, without the attendant idea of sunlight, is in this context rather senseless: the one calls to mind the other, even when the garden concerned has far more horticultural reasons for its existence.

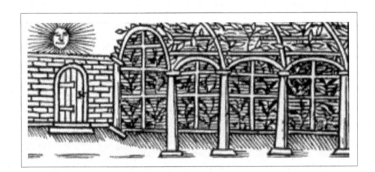

In the Noblet – as in the TdM in general – we are faced with something that is also quite specific, in that two individuals, naked except for the loin cloth, are presented. Here is where I consider the Noblet to have retained clear gender differentiation, whereas many (except for some that have regained the depiction) other decks appear to have lost it.

Let's compare, for example, the Payen, Dodal, Chosson, Conver, and Blanche (admittedly, this last is a Besançon, not a TdM) – starting with our Noblet.

Though we certainly *can see into* the non-Noblet images two people each of separate gender, they are as likely to seem to depict two masculine figures – something that is of course consistent with various renditions of the twins Castor and Pollux (or Remus and Romulus) that later writers consider in light of the imagery – and to which we shall also briefly turn to later.

It is the Noblet, however, and other decks more closely akin to its image, that appear to better 'justify' the wall behind as that of a *garden* wall, above which the Sun sheds its benign influence. And it is this wall, which in many ways is in itself perhaps the least important of the three key parts of the image (with the Sun and the human couple of more import) that nonetheless provides a central interpretative pointer to the image's likely intent.

Here, it is Paradise that seems depicted – whether as lost, or found again, or as future state, or as heavenly realm – but paradise, and with it, a realm of idealised human interaction and freed pleasure. We can sense into both its aspect for a nostalgic past and hopeful future that, within a Christian context, begins with its loss in Genesis, and attains its possible redemption by the death of Christ. Taking into account the sequence with the ensuing card of Judgement makes this image all the more poignant and pregnant with hope and salvation to mediæval (and later) Christian sensibility.

Even depictions of Hesiod's[1] 'Golden Age', in the following example by Lucas Cranach (the Elder), *circa* 1530, bring to light how not only this more general sense of the card image may have been seen far more 'naturally' then than for us, but also how innocence itself, yet obvious sexual intimations, are juxtaposed (see next page).

Of course, this image's titular reference also calls to mind the Sun through its association with gold.

If the idea of the pair within the garden brings forth this aspect as edenic and paradisiacal, its innocence similarly brings forth its very opposite:

---

1   The sequence of Ages from Golden, Silver, Bronze and Iron make their way from Hesiod (*circa* 700 BCE); Virgil (*circa* 30 BCE); and Ovid (*circa* 7 CE). These classical authors are amongst the most influencial in European culture. With Virgil we also have a connection *via* his *Eclogues* in which the Age of Saturn is rather referred to. *Cf* also Charles Taylor's *A Secular Age*, p339, for mention of this and the importance of the sense of 'Arcadia' in pre-18th century thought.

one cannot imagine either the above depiction, or indeed the Adam and Eve within Eden, without the consummation that will, at some not-too distant future, complete the awakening. Even there, of course, there is the influence of the Sun hovering as benign protector.

Alchemy and Psychology

With the consummation, however, we enter different ideas that are removed from the image as we have it, instead moving to the directly sexual and more common themes in alchemical texts: that of the 'marriage' of King and Queen; of Sol and Luna; of opposites, in order for an inner metamorphosis that transcends separateness and leads towards an integration as Philosophical Mercury (this is an aspect which I also mention in chapter 20, with the image from Michelspacher's *Cabala*). Here, the more directly pertinent point is the joining of the two figures in 'alchemical union', from separateness to unity. Let's begin with another from the series from Michelspacher[2], as here too the couple is within a paradisiacal Garden together, in this case, with the trinity.

---

2   See Adam McLean's www.levity.com/alchemy/amclglr18.html for co-loured renditions of the set. In the image above, I only show the top segment of plate 4.

The joining of the King and Queen, Sun and Moon, masculine and feminine, leads us to the following type of images:

From union, to integration into what is at times referred to as the *Rebis* (Royal two):

In all this, we have of course moved rapidly from the original image to reflections taking us into alternate realms. Yet, I would claim, there is in the paradisiac image an intimation of something akin to this process of reflection that would have in earlier times seemed far more natural than perhaps for us now. Whereas the reflections may then have moved from that of innocence, to its loss, to its recuperation via the sacrifice of Christ, and from thence back to innocence, for many in the 21st century the work is considered from a more psycho-spiritual perspective: leading towards a wholesome integration within the individual.

Polysemic 'Paradise'

The subheading used here, 'polysemic "paradise"', is itself multi-variate, and here I wish to return to an aspect that has been touched upon in numerous chapters without detailed nor direct focus. And yet, it is something that the use of the imagery inevitably brings to mind: *allegorical imagery has multiple layers of meaning.*

Before we get into this a little, a brief mention that if the term 'Paradise' is a garden (or orchard), it was used as an acrostic in Hebrew to denote a fourfold exegesis, and that this same (or very similar) fourfold reading and interpreting of both text and image had its equivalence in Christian exegesis – though usually applied only to the Bible.

פרדס '*PaRDeS*' (remembering that in Hebrew vowels are not usually shown by letters), by its very connection to the fertile enclosure suggested by the word itself (as garden), suggests the following four levels of interpretation, each of which 'builds' on the previous level, without which there would be no meaning. It is a little like considering the various layers of a garden consisting of its soil and nutrients or *ingredients*; its dimension and *location*; its *produce*; and its *uses*. In fact, reflecting on those four aspects analogically can help to show the similarity with allegorical interpretation, as we shall see.

Let's return to פרדס '*PaRDeS*':

The 'P' (פ) – for 'Pashat' – is its literal or 'simple' meaning. Much of these chapters have focussed on this aspect of card imagery: before *interpretation*, let's *look* at what's *actually* depicted.

'R' (ר) – for 'Remez' – is generally considered the contextual or implied meaning. For example, the figure of Justice is, as to be expected, 'hinting' or pointing to Justice, rather than to a woman holding out sword and scales. Again, much of these chapters have sought to see how the 'hints' or contextual understanding would likely have been understood in the context in which they were presented.

'D' (ד) – 'Derash' – begins to become a little more removed from the image or text itself, without losing its intimate connection to it, a little as the flower is 'removed' from the root of the plant, yet remains intimately connected. What I am doing in this very section is such: we saw that the image is of a couple in front of a stone wall below the Sun (the literal or Pashat); hinting at consideration of paradisiacal illuminations (its Remez); and here other appropriate metaphors and uses are being considered: 'paradise' calls to mind not only its rich and harmonious cultivation, but also, by its acrostic, manners in which to understand and delve into text and imagery.

'S' (ס) – its 'Sod' value – is both its most difficult to adequately consider and, when discovered, its undoubtedly most sublime: it is its 'secret', mystical, and anagogical value. Yet here is where one must be careful to unveil this as *exegesis* and not be tempted towards *eisegesis*[3]. Is, for example, the Sun's '*Sod*' meaning in part the sublimity of the consanguinal act and the close ties amongst the family of humanity?

To be sure, the above fourfold interpretation according to *PaRDeS* is a *tad* different to the mediæval *Christian* fourfold exegesis. Of these we are reminded, for example, by Dante's letter to Can Grande, in which he writes:

> For me [to] be able to present what I am going to say, you must know that the sense of this work is not simple, rather it may be called polysemantic, that is, of many senses; the first sense is that which comes from the letter, the second is that of that which is signified by the letter. And the first is called the **literal**, the second **allegorical** or **moral** or **anagogical**. Which method of treatment, that it may be clearer, can be considered through these words: "When Israel went out of Egypt, the house of Jacob from a barbarous people, Judea was made his sanctuary, Israel his dominion" (Douay-Rheims, Ps 113:1-2). If we look at it from the letter alone it means to us the exit of the Children of Israel from Egypt at the time of Moses; if from allegory, it means for us our redemption done by Christ; if from the moral sense, it means to us the conversion of the soul from the struggle and misery of sin to the status of grace; if from the anagogical, it means the leave taking of the blessed soul from the slavery of this corruption to the freedom of eternal glory. And though these mystical senses are called by various names, in general all can be called allegorical, because they are different from the literal or the historical. Now, allegory comes from Greek *alleon*, which in Latin means *other* or *different*.[4]

In general, and for the sake of a little more accuracy, exegesis normally took as its second step a linking between textual documents, usually by relating the given text to either Old or New testaments. In the case of each trump, such level of exegesis would search for an appropriate topological equivalence in the Bible. Though it is something that may indeed have taken place, it remains only at times, from my perspective, apt. A good example of its irrelevance already looked at is trump XVI

---

3   '*eisegesis*' normally refers to seeking to read a text in such a way that not only one misinterprets it, but such is done in a way that one's own preferred views are overlayed thereon, causing oversights and mis-readings.

4   Para. 7 of Dante's epistle (or letter), which otherwise talks of his *Divine Comedy*. My emphasis of the key terms.

which, though still intimitely Christian in origin, was more likely to have stemmed from non-Biblical texts (in this case the pseudo-infancy gospels which have been previously referred).

Reading tarot as exegesis

I would suggest that in the process of reading a spread of cards, something akin to these four aspects, perhaps even considered *steps*, are often taken: the card sequence can first be spoken or described in its literal form; out of which an integrated narrative emerges; from which is then allowed to develop an enriched consideration which at times *explains* its significance and ethical dimension; resulting, ideally, in a *shift* that permits new insights and understanding into the situation at hand, the whole transformed and integrated in a healthy and fruitful manner.

With this in mind, let's continue the work we began last week with six cards, and complete what has come to be known as the Celtic Cross sread – and I of course here present but one of many possible ways in which the basic pattern can be viewed.

Celtic Cross Spread

We have already worked the first six cards of the Celtic Cross, albeit in a manner that is undoubtedly a little different. There remains to be drawn four cards, placed as a sequence in a column to the right.

Why this spread[5]? In so many ways, it has established itself as a spread pattern that seems to capture something that is both quite extensive and yet simple. In earlier chapters, we have also used other sequences for the purpose of developing a narrative. With the Celtic Cross, we can make use of more precise positional meaning and its influence on the developing narrative. There is certainly neither historical link nor intrinsic reflection between the Celtic Cross and the Noblet or the TdM in general – rather, it is developing familiarity with a common spread that lends itself to its usage for the purposes of the development of narrative development.

I would advise looking at last week's chapter with regards to the first six cards, using the suggested positional factors mentioned there[6].

---

5   It was suggested to me that I should also include within this course a spread I developed a number of years ago called the *Dynamic Hexagramme Spread*. It is now therefore included in chapter 29.

6   Many authors, I should point out, have the first and second cards drawn

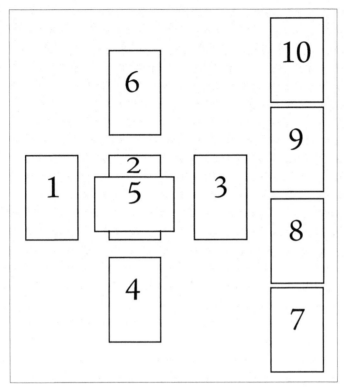

Let's take two different and quite specific situations in order to further practice the development of a narrative. In the first instance, let's imagine somebody considering moving residence; later, let's repeat this exercise considering how to complete a task one is undertaking (in my own example at the time of writing, it may very well be the completion of these chapters).

First the 'moving residence' narrative:

The first three cards will show how things have happened in the past, the present, and how they appear to be heading. The next three some of the root impulses at work that are key to the move, and how this is playing out in the present situation, and ultimately seeking to manifest.

Now for cards 7-10.

For 7, what is it about the individual (or family, or couple) concerned that seems to also be reflected? With card 8, what are some of the social or friendly advice and directions being given? Card 9 is usually described as 'hopes and fears' – let's ask instead what are some of the false impressions that are being received or playing themselves out in

---

in what are here numbered, respectively, 2 and 5, with appropriate adjustments to the ensuing four cards.

the overall understanding of the situation? With card 10, what is a useful step to take to resolve the overall situation?

Here, I would suggest that card 10 be seen as a *practical* resolution taken in light of the creative manner of resolution in card 6, the future direction of card 3 also taken very much into consideration.

In a similar manner, card 1 shows something of the past that is still living in the person(s), and 4 the impulse at work, that hints also at how card 7 seems to be experiencing the situation at hand. Cards 2 and 5 also, in some manner, elucidate aspects of cards 8 and 9. Visually, the rapport may be considered in the following manner (other consideration may also be made, of course):

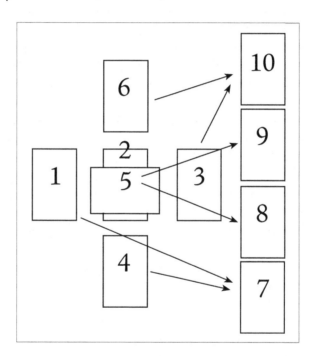

The second task – considerations pertaining to completing a task one is undertaking – I shall leave without further description. What is important, however, is the transformation in the narrative from simple (or literal) description, towards an ever increasing multifaceted and *integrated* understanding of the imagery and its polysemic allusions.

Gemini

Let's return, before completing this chapter, to the imagery itself, and consider its rather explicit representation as Gemini – all except for the wall, for which reason the earlier reflections are, from my perspective, quite central to the overall image.

Mediæval images of the zodiac, as already shown in previous chapters, are many; Gemini is generally exemplified by the two figures in various forms, including two more-or-less genderless individuals, as well as, at times, two people that are clearly masculine and feminine.

In addition, the position of Gemini in the heavens, at quite a steep angle relative the ecliptic, can suggest the sexual representation encountered when considering the alchemical union of King and Queen. Below, the image is simply of Gemini, depicted on St Lazare Cathedral, in its astronomically appropriate inclination relative the ecliptic:

City of the Sun

There are two final and minor considerations I shall also briefly mention in light of the imagery of the card – both relating to what has been called in different times by different people the 'City of the Sun'. If we consider the wall to be symbolic, what may have been called to mind is not only the paradisiacal Eden, but also city walls and, as city walls, given the card, the fabled and various 'cities of the Sun'.

Two of these are found within the fertile crescent: Heliopolis (in Egypt) and Palmyra (in Syria), this latter also referred to in the Sybeline text[7], ch.XIII, in a pertinent manner:

> The *city of the sun* shall offer prayer;
> And round about her shall the Persians dare
> The fearful threatenings of the Phœnicians.

7   Interestingly re-published merely 50 years before the Noblet by Johannis Opsopus (John Koch) in Paris.

But when *two chiefs*, men swift in war, shall rule

In addition, there is also the important and influential early 17th *c.* utopian work by Tommaso Campanella, *City of the Sun*, which, though radically different in content, certainly comes to mind often when I consider this card. And if for myself, given the popularity of the work, perhaps for some of our forebears also.

XX - Le Jugement

Judgement

The general form of the image, outside of tarot and in the everyday environment of the populace, would easily and instantly have been recognised along with that of 'The World' card, as forming pretty much standard depictions of the Last Judgement. We'll return to the ensuing card in itself in the next chapter. For now let's, however, look at *both* of these, cards XXI as above XX, in relation to some of the numerous representations that can be found in illuminated manuscripts, paintings, petroglyphs, and woodcuts.

The 'full' version of the Last Judgement imagery is somewhat more elaborate than the card version; yet this is where, as in various other card depictions, that the economy of image selection manages to capture the essential characteristics of the overall scene. On the page after next is Weyden's 15th century polyptych, now in Beaune. We have not only the calling forth by 'trumpet' blasts, but also what follows: judgement and its repercussions leading either to heaven or to hell, with Christ shown above.

I would suggest that even though Michael is himself not shown on the card image, to the eyes of our forebears, he is implied as part of the overall understanding, or visual setting, upon which our 'zoomed in' or 'cropped' partial tarot image captures.

In any case, the import here is of the Judgement itself following the clarion call and resurrection of the entombed. What is, however, meant by this?

Here we have two aspects to consider: firstly its eschatological sense, and secondly reflections on its more general meaning.

Eschatological considerations

In chapter 18, reference was made to eschatological considerations with regards to one's own belief. With this image we are faced with a worldview that dominated the then Christian European world. The Last Judgement brought to mind not only apocalyptic thoughts, but more importantly the day of *one's own* reckoning.

To get a sense as to how this very concept was considered, allow me

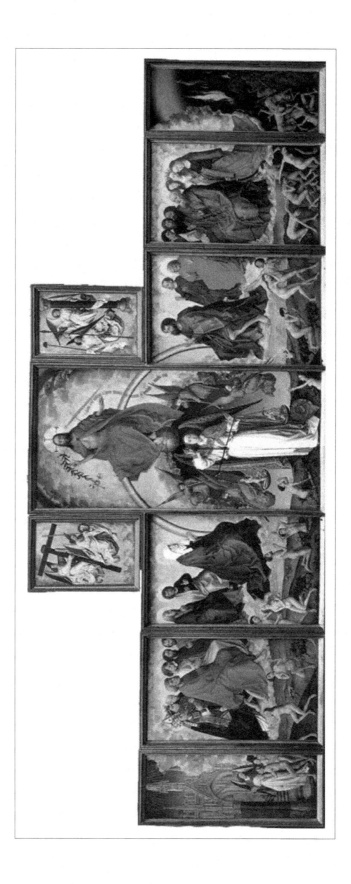

to quote a summary from D. Stone's *Outlines of Christian Dogma*, 1903 (p.266):

> [...] The bodies that are raised will be essentially the same as the bodies of the present life. They will be in a greatly changed condition, incorruptible, glorious, powerful, spiritual.
>
> After the resurrection there will be the general judgment. The grounds of the judgment will be the deeds of this life. At the judgment past lives will be revealed. [...] The result of this judgment will be the division of mankind into the saved and the lost.

I am certain that amongst us there is quite a wide variety of metaphysical and eschatological views, and that the above may appear either strange and removed, or, at the other extreme, quite familiar. It is towards this latter end of the spectrum that those living during tarot's emergence tended, and how, I would suggest, the image is to be considered.

Irrespective of the eschatological view one may have, the section of the quote I highlighted above brings a whole realm that needs to be considered: "The grounds of the judgement will be the deeds of this life". This is further exemplified in the 15th century one-act play *Everyman*, whose plot concludes thus:

> As the journey continues, each of his companions leaves Everyman. Beauty is the first to go, since beauty fades quickly as man approaches death. Next Strength departs, for as man's health fades, physical strength is also lost. Next Discretion leaves, and then Five Wits abandons Everyman. Finally, Knowledge departs, and only Good Deeds remains for the final journey. An Angel greets Everyman to escort him the remainder of the way, where only Good Deeds can speak for him. At the play's conclusion a Doctor of Theology appears to remind the audience that all men must make this journey and that only their good deeds will speak for them at God's final reckoning.[1]

Life's Deeds

If we consider for a moment what this implies, we are faced with deep ramifications for each act, no matter how small, we either do or omit to undertake. We shall consider in a short while *intentions* – at this stage, however, it is not *intent* that is being considered, but actual *deeds* or acts.

Take the time to undertake a number of meditations on the ramifications and the consequences of holding in your hands that Noblet deck,

1   Cf the 'Plot Summary' at Answers.com

beginning by reflecting on all that needed to be achieved in order for this particular deck to have reached you. These reflections undertaken on not only the engagement and times of those involved in its design and manufacture in the 17th century, including: the production of paper at that period; the cutting of the pear tree for the woodblock; the distribution of the various decks in that time until one found its way into the National Library in Paris; and the deck to be considered sufficiently important by Jean-Claude Flornoy (and others) for him to redraw and redesign images; to have these imprinted on a massive press in Eastern Europe requiring various inks, each having their origin in different parts of the world requiring mining and the production of electricity, and for these to be eventually cut and packaged and delivered to yourself. In addition, at most of these junctures, finances changed hands (and passed across countries) in various ways – it's quite an astounding set of interweaved and amazingly impact-filled set of circumstances.

I am reminded of the modern saying (fast becoming a proverb): think globally – act locally. The thinking globally allows us to begin to have an intimation of the vast network of ramifications each of our acts have upon not only our immediate environment, but for those who live in places we shall never see during this lifetime.

The *deeds of this life*. Where every deed has thought-out, as well as unthought aspects, consequences and ramifications.

The question 'Am I aware of what I am doing!?', therefore, takes on new shades of meaning when considered in such light. And yet, of course, we do not have this fuller or complete sense of awareness of the interweavings of our actions.

Is the deed the pressing of a button, or its explosive consequences?

Thoughts and Deeds

The question immediately above raises others in reference to deeds, for surely it does seem that *awareness* of the consequences of one's actions somehow ought to be taken into consideration when reflecting on and judging deeds. In fact, the whole ethical dimension raises anew its spectre, for here again the deed will need to be considered not simply in terms of its consequences, but of its intrinsic merit: the grounds of the judgement will be the deeds of this life.

From this perspective, thoughts are indeed deeds, and moral deeds require an insight into their very essence. Furthermore, for each deed to be able to be judged accordingly, an implicit freedom is required, for only the individual who can act out of his or her own self has a deed by which to be judged.

This calls to mind some radical considerations that may have been quite differently thought of during former times. Yet, *freedom* is also a concept that was far more commonly thought of during Christianity's formative period than it was post 1650, and especially since the modern development of Newtonian Science and Kant's dominating deontological views.

I shall here simply quote from one of the books I personally consider foremost in its ethical dimension, Steiner's *Philosophy of Freedom* (1894), (Ch. 9):

> Kant's principle of morality – Act so that the basis of your action may be valid for all men – is the exact opposite of ours. His principle means death to all individual impulses of action. The standard [must] be what, for me, is to be done in each individual case. […]

> When Kant says of duty: 'Duty! Thou exalted and mighty name, thou that dost comprise nothing lovable, nothing ingratiating, but demandest submission,' thou that 'settest up a law ... before which all inclinations are silent, even though they secretly work against it,' then out of the consciousness of the free spirit, man replies: 'Freedom! Thou kindly and human name, thou that dost comprise all that is morally most lovable, all that my manhood most prizes, and that makest me the servant of nobody, thou that settest up no mere law, but awaitest what my moral love itself will recognize as law because in the face of every merely imposed law it feels itself unfree.'

> This is the contrast between a morality based on mere law and a morality based on inner freedom.

Under such an understanding, certainly errors can be made – and may at times be made as a result of lack of insight into a situation but, importantly, the *specific individual* situation will be the one considered, and the most appropriate deed undertaken. The *deed* is judged on its merit, and presumably not according to deontological considerations[2].

Heaven or Hell

Re-considering the context of the Last Judgement, one of its

---

2   Much of Steiner's *Philosophy of Freedom* considers the interrelationship between deeds and freedom in relation to knowledge and ethical insights, and into which the 'I' penetrates.

consequences is that the person would be sentenced to be either rewarded or punished. Dante's trilogy from the 13th century (*Inferno, Purgatory, Paradise*) calls to mind that here was not only a motif well used, but that considerations of heaven and hell was never far away in an environment in which death was much closer than it is for us.

In the words of the Franciscan Thomaso di Celano, also from the 13th century, the whole aspect of the Last Judgement brought to heart that one's Earthly acts had serious consequences:

> "Ah! what terror is impending
> When the Judge is seen descending,
> And each secret veil is rending.
> "To the throne, the trumpet sounding,
> Through the sepulchres resounding,
> Summons all, with voice astounding.
> "Sits the Judge, the raised arraigning,
> Darkest mysteries explaining,
> Nothing unavenged remaining."

Card details

In considering these aspects, we moved, instead of from card details to broader perspectives, from first considering the greater tableau in which the card image itself normally forms part, and into considerations of how this is to be understood. Let's return to the card's imagery and consider its two dominant parts.

The first is the top section, itself consisting of an angelic being bursting through a cloud, blasting a 'trumpet' to which is attached a flag emblazoned with a quartering blue cross (image on next page).

The trumpet here depicted is far closer to the ancient Greek salpinx, though if we consider that in most representations the clarion is curved upwards, the image angle may in fact present such, with the horn curving slightly towards the viewer – though saying this, I acknowledge that the bell-end seems as downwards pointing as the rest.

Clarions and the like were quite common not only in depictions, but in actual use in *announcements*. So here we are seeing, by its very use, that the judgement and pronouncements are still to be made. The clarion call is to announce that such is imminent, yet not quite as yet here.

The angelic being, despite numerous attempts to link it to various specific names, simply lacks precision of iconographic rendition. Certainly, as mentioned earlier, Michael would be *present* at the scene. However, presence does not lead to identification with a 'lower' task – any more than the idea that just because Christ too would be present the angelic being is Christ himself. The angelic figure, I would suggest, is simply one from countless unnamed messengers.

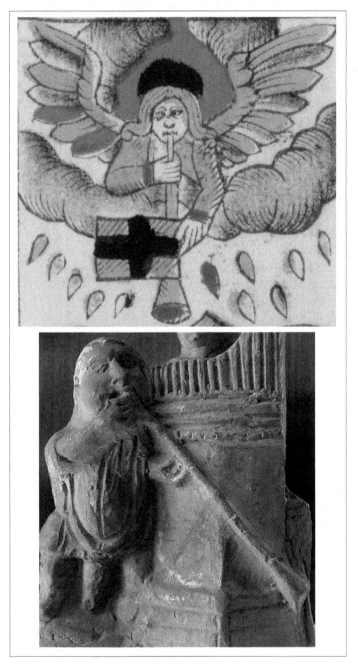

It is a messenger, however, from the heavens, which are clearly opening behind and above the figure. And here it can be surmised, given the standard imagery, that indeed above, unseen (unless placing card XXI there), would descend Christ.

Rending of the Veil

This 'rending of the veil' is presented in three different manners throughout the deck: with clouds parting or through which appears a figure; a stellated opening (trump VI) or stellation with rounded effect (aces of Bastons and Swords); and the 'aureole' of card XXI *in* which appears the figure.

Though there are other cards that we can consider have such 'piercing' light, for example card XVI, it the Judgement card and L'Amoureux that stand out as most clearly showing a division between the earthly and the spiritual realms in a combined depiction. Furthermore, these two specific card images have other aspects in common – though of course the differences are distinctive. In each case, we have a 'heavenly' being performing an action that has an influence on the figures below, and in each case these lower figures are three in number.

One of the *distinctions* is that whereas in card VI the impact will be between human interaction, with card XX, the impact is as an awakening towards the spiritual realm: the contrasting focus of the figures between cards VI and XX remains distinct.

Here, I personally like to think of this 'awakening to the spirit' as having different ramifications for the self-judgement of one's own actions – not so much those of one's past, but rather *henceforth*. This, of course, is entirely anachronistic, for the Last Judgement focuses on one's prior deeds; yet, in my view, there is consistency in that our ancestors for whom such was a living reality would have believed their current and ongoing actions had inevitable post-*mortem* personal consequences.

Halo

There are few figures in the deck depicted with halo, with only this and the ensuing card showing these. In each case, the halos shown are elliptical or circular. Though this may seem like a rather straightforward point in our modern day, in former times this showed a more precise meaning, for *three main* types of halos were common: the circular, square, and stellar.

The square halo only ever appeared on people still living at the time. Relatively few such depictions survive (though still numbering in their hundreds), as for example this image of St Theodora (in Rome), painted during her lifetime:

Though the square halo does not figure in any deck of which I am aware, the stellar form does, and is usually restricted to allegorical figures – and usually those depicting some Virtue or other. Here, the 'Charles VI' deck stands out as an exemplar that shows that such details add another dimension when *reading* the whole image, distinguishing allegory from other symbolic referents.

The rounded halo, lastly[3], depicts beings (people or angels) living in the spiritual realms only – so either already dead (as in the depiction of most saints), or simply of the angelic hierarchy. In this card, there is a clear implication that the three figures raised from the dead are therefore not saints: they lack the halo.

Flag

The flag itself is peculiar, in that it is quartered, something we may well expect in order to render a cross, but its *blue* colouration, and the quarters alternating red and yellow suggest that perhaps there was some specific 'ownership' to which reference was being made. Of course, it may simply have also been the very opposite, being careful to *not* depict a known or used emblem.

The closest I have seen is the 17th century Russian marine mast flag or *Bushpritnyi* flag, though there, and though the blue cross is similar, the quarters are red and white, not yellow and beige.

What is curious, in any case, is that such a flag is included in the first place: it is neither common on depictions of the Last Judgement (though not totally absent – for example, Giotto includes flags), nor seemingly needed for the overall rendition.

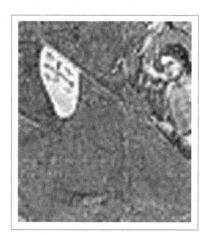

Perhaps it is simply that, as the key figure who judges is not depicted within the overall image, it is to remind the viewer that the angel who blasts the trumpet is not doing so on his own accord, but rather as representative of him to whom the flag may rightfully belong or represent.

---

3   'lastly' for us, for other shapes had also gained precise meaning, such as the triangular and the cruciform halos.

Lower panel

Clearly three individuals are shown, and in that sense, as already mentioned, the image bears similarity to *L'Amoureux*. On the right is clearly a bearded man, but the other two figures are unclear, though from other depictions we can confirm our sense that the figure to the left is feminine.

The central figure – and the only one depicted clearly as arising from an actual tomb – has various ambiguities. On the one hand, there is a sense of a 'smaller' body, and thus the implication that perhaps here is a child, for not all who have died and will be resurrected are, of course, adults. The small 'tonsure' upon the back of his head perhaps also indicates this aspect of youth. Yet here is a detail we have met before, many weeks ago, when considering card V (chapter 8): could this also be the mark of clergy?

Let's return for a moment to one of the key biblical references that gave rise to the popular depiction of this scene.

1 Corinthians 15

In 1 Corinthians 15:44-54[4], St Paul writes:

> If there is a natural body, there is a spiritual body too. So the first man, Adam, as scripture says, became a living soul[5]; and the last Adam [ie, Christ] has become a life-giving spirit. But first came the natural body, not the spiritual one; that came only afterwards. The first man, being made of earth, is earthly by nature; the second man is from heaven. The earthly man is a pattern for earthly people, the heavenly one for heavenly ones. And as we have borne the likeness of the earthly man, so we shall [or 'we would be able to'] bear the likeness of the heavenly one.

> What I am saying, brothers, is that mere human nature cannot inherit the kingdom of God: what is perishable cannot inherit what is imperishable.

> Now I am going to tell you a mystery: we are not all going to fall asleep, but we are all going to be changed, instantly, in the twinkling of an eye, when the last trumpet sounds. The trumpet is going to sound, and then the dead will be raised imperishable, and we shall be changed, because this perishable nature of ours must put on imperishability, this mortal na-

---

4   I am quoting from the *New Jerusalem Bible* [*NJB*] translation, with my emphasis.

5   The note within the *NJB* reads: 'something that is alive because it has a psyche giving it a merely natural life, subject to decay and corruption.'

ture must put on immortality. And after this perishable nature has put on imperishability and this mortal nature has put on immortality, then will the words of scripture come true: Death is swallowed up in Victory.

There are whole dimensions to this quote that have richness beyond what may at first be surmised. For example, I am reminded of the Pythagorean (and importantly neo-pythagorean) view that equates (and perhaps equivocates) the tomb and the body, which in Greek are closely related (*soma*=body, *sema*=tomb), giving a whole new sense to considerations of the incarnation of the spirit within the body, and the latter's transformation. And this aspect brings to light another important consideration: that of initiation.

Initiation

If initiation can be considered in any manner relevant here, we should perhaps first reflect that it has long been considered an event through which an aspect of the ceremony may include the symbolic death of the individual, and his or her rising from this state, newly awoken to previously unknown insights or faculties.

The image presented to us is quite remarkable, in that, as already mentioned, precisely *one* sarcophagus or coffin is shown, and that without the expected lid shown (it is at times shown moved to the side, or forced open).

Initiation can sometimes take the form of quite a prolonged isolation. For example, anchorite monks may endure prolonged solitary confinement in order to achieve a kind of awakening that pierces into the spiritual realms.

Without heading to such extremes, somewhat similar initiatic states may be embraced by regular meditative practice, and an experience of voluntary solitary confinement (in its positive aspects) experienced through sensory-deprivation chambers. In each case, what is also significant is not only the experience within the state entered, but also re-emerging into the world following such depth of state.

In the quote from I Corinthians made earlier, line 51 (the first line highlighted in red) makes such possible initiatic reference even clearer by using the term 'mystery': an initiatory secret is possibly revealed – and what better description than the one given in this part of 1 Corinthians!

In the card's depiction, considered in this light, what we face is also the raising after initiation of the central figure, to which the other two may only be observant or assisting. Only in such a state is the individual able to perceive beyond the veil of the physical realm.

In arising from the tomb, what we again have is a *liberation* of the person from the confines of entombment, from the confines of the body.

Awakening into Seeing

If the Last Judgement is to be considered in symbolic terms, it shows, in my view, that here is not only an awakening to insight into the fullness of one's own everyday deeds, but also an awakening into seeing aspects of our lives and the world that are all too often missed by simply not being observant – this applies even more to our everyday engagements than it does to major events.

Deeds and actions, undertaken in freedom and in light of individual moral intuitions, become imperative for the truly free human being.

Dew Droplets

A final point before we close: as with the other two previous cards, this one too shows those 'arrow-droplets' emanating on all and sundry.

Here, if stemming from the spiritual realms, they are shown as again beneficent and aiding, prior even to the awakening, if only we remain open to their blessing.

XXI - Le Monde

Le Monde

Beginning from where we left off in the previous chapter, let's at first consider the image as that of Christ, itself part of an overall panel, below which is depicted the last Judgement.

Considered in this way, *The World* is not a depiction of some past event, whether Christ in Ascension or a representation of his Assumption but, rather, it is a representation of a *future* event. It is a promise of things to come, of his second coming, and not by rebirth or re-incarnation, but by direct descent from the spiritual regions.

We'll return to an aspect of this in a while. First, however, we need to consider the image itself and consider the central figure's gender.

Central figure

The central figure appears with cape, long hair, a wreath of leaves around his rather more masculine hips, and what are clearly feminine breasts.

We have previously considered that feminine breasts do not necessarily imply a feminine figure, as in the case of the Egyptian God Hapi (which we saw when considering XVII the Star in chapter 25). Here, however, we have quite distinct considerations at hand.

Firstly, there is the ambiguity of gender in the Greek version of the New Testament (from which other translations derive) in especially[1] Revelation 1:13, in that the Greek uses '*mastos*' for breasts, the word normally denoting *female* breasts (in distinction to 'stethos' for 'chest'). Numerous translations have been proposed for the section, and here is mine, somewhat concocted from various possibilities, yet consistent with the original:

> And among the lampstands was one like a Son of Man, clothed with a robe reaching to his feet, girting a golden girdle below his female breasts.

I would suggest that some of the mediæval imagery that depicts or describes Christ with breasts justifiably does so on this passage alone. In the context of the Last Judgement, it becomes even more pertinent as the event is found in the same book: i.e., *Revelation*.

There was also, by the time of the Noblet, another influence possible in the writings of the 14th century mystic Julian of Norwich, where she (and others) speaks of 'Mother Jesus' and suckling the living waters (or wine-milk of the Word) from his breasts.

In 'From Folklore to Scientific Evidence'[2], the authors say that:

> Contrary to modern days, Jesus Christ has been often portrayed as having feminine qualities in medieval times. This includes both having physical feminine attributes such as lactating breasts as well as religious ones, such as Christ lactating his believers, reversing the role of Mary and Christ-child to Mother Jesus and the child-like soul. Others have connected the wound in Jesus' side and breasts full of soul-sustaining milk or used breast milk symbolism to illustrate ideas of the motherhood of Christ versus the fatherhood of God.

---

1   Too many, in discussing the Greek used, primarily reference St Paul's letter to the Galatians 3:28 "there is no longer male and female; for all of you are one in Christ Jesus". Personally I do not think this latter is the source of the androgenous nature of Christ's representation.

2   Lia Moran and Jacob Gilad, 'From Folklore to Scientific Evidence: Breast-Feeding and Wet-Nursing in Islam and the Case of Non-Puerperal Lactation', *International Journal of Biomedical Science* 3:4 Dec. 2007. Cf also C.W. Bynum's *Jesus as Mother: Studies in the Spirituality of the High middle Ages*, 1982.

Of the late Mediæval Lyric 'In the Vaile of Restles Mynd', Hill mentions that 'lines 107-12 depict him [Christ] as a tender nursing mother'[3]. One final quote before moving on, this time by St Bernard[4]:

> Suck not the wounds, but rather the breasts of the crucified. He shall be as a mother to you, and you as a son to him [...]. So you, Lord God, are the great mother.

Still, despite these statements, it continues to be relatively difficult to find images that clearly illustrate feminine breasts upon Jesus. One exception to this is the following anonymous 16th *c.* painting[5] generally known as 'Lamentations around the body of Christ', though in all other ways distinctly different to the figure we have on our tarot depiction:

Feminine & Masculine

In light of the above, I would suggest that the imagery of the Noblet is indeed of Christ – but a Christ that has striking and important feminine qualities that has long vanished from the popular imagination within both Christianity in particular and the Western mind in general.

---

3   T.D. Hill 'Androgyny and Conversion in the Middle English Lyric, "In the Vaile of Restles Mynd"', ELH 53:3, 1986.

4   A thank-you to Stephen J. Mangan for this reference.

5   Again a note of thanks, this time to *Spoonbender* who attached the image to a post on tarotforum.net in reply to a comment I made. The breasts had been painted over and only restored in 1993, located in Notre-Dame de la Rose in Lessines. How many other images have been so altered!?

F. L. Carvalho, in 'Representations and Images of Mary and Christ in Early Christianity', writes:

> In early Christianity images of an effeminate Jesus, which were sometimes confused as images of Mary, were so represented as to denote his role as nurturer of souls. The feminine look of Christ in early Christianity have been detected in statuettes and mosaics where Jesus is usually represented with a round soft beardless face, encircled with light and extravagant hair that falls on his shoulders. As Matthews observes, the image of Christ has been taken to be an image of the Virgin given to the fact that Christ lacks any masculine vigour. Christ's shoulders are narrow and sloping and his hips are broad. Early Christianity art often shows feminine aspects of Christ such as swelling breasts that are 'noticeable in sarcophagi of the 5th century in Ravenna'.
>
> It seems that Christ is given breasts to mark the crucial difference between him as his apostle colleagues. However, the key point is that representations of a feminine Christ foretell the pivotal place occupied by Mary in the centuries to come when Christ's sexual ambiguity was repressed and split between images of Christ and Mary. Thus, feminine representations of Christ in Early Christianity cannot be taken as accidental or as a transitory or regional development. Such images were not only widespread in Gaul, Rome, Ravenna, and Thessalonica from the mid 4th Century to the beginning of the 6th century, but were also displaced and re-articulated as the body of Mary from the Renaissance onwards[6].

If, since the Renaissance, we have increasingly, or even singularly, lost the femininity of Christ in Christian writings and iconography, there has nonetheless also been a converse expression in the development of tarot's imagery on this card, with a general loss of his masculinity and a near exclusive representation of the figure as feminine[7].

Depicted as such, she also calls to mind Christ's role as *Wisdom*. And here, a harkening back to various Old Testament passages that the Middle Ages have linked to Christ adds to this connection between Wisdom and Christ.

Platonism and Sophia

6　　Cf F.L.Carvalho, 'Representations and Images of Mary and Christ in Early Christianity', *Australian eJournal of Theology*, August 2005, Issue 5, ISSN 1448-632

7　　Admittedly, to be sure, many have *talked* of the trump's figure's androgynous character.

As soon as we talk of Wisdom, what is called to mind is not only one of the four cardinal virtues that we have touched on at various times in earlier chapters, but also the sense of *Sophia* as feminine. If any of the Platonic texts were considered in reflecting on the imagery, I would surmise that his *Timæus* would inevitably have come to mind – *especially* within a neo-Platonic context – showing a feminine figure in aureole (and hence spiritual) within a quartered four elements.

Though the Timæus (especially §32-37) gives in detail a particular world view, it is the general image that is called to mind in the context of the card image, especially with the four beings at the points of what would be an 'X' if connected.

Through this, again, given the Christian context of the development of the imagery, another connection to Christ would have been brought to mind to our forebears.

Sophia is here not only *Sophia* as wisdom, but also the *Anima Mundi* or Soul of the World, 'diffused throughout the body'[8].

Diffused and Connected

In light of this sense of the World Soul diffused throughout the whole world, one reflection this card may suggest is one's own sense of connectedness. Perhaps a different description may also be 'integrated' – though in each case never implying a loss of self, but rather a heightened sense without an artificial *personæ* (or mask).

It is in reflecting on this 'meta-personal' aspect of inter-connectedness that some sense of one's own state can also be gauged. The following questions have, in the original Survey[9], a reply scale from 1-7. I would suggest reflecting on these one day, and the next rating them.

1. _____ My personal existence is very purposeful and meaningful.

2. _____ I believe that no matter where I am or what I'm doing, I am never separate from others.

3. _____ I feel a real sense of kinship with all living things.

4. _____ My sense of inner peace is one of the most important things to me.

---

8   Timæus 34. Also see Proclus on the *Timæus*.
9   Teresa L. DeCicco and Mirella L. Stroink 'A Third Model of Self-Construal: The Metapersonal Self', *International Journal of Transpersonal Psychology*: 26 (2007), p 97. The questions form part of the 'Metapersonal Self Scale Survey'.

5. ____ I take the time each day to be peaceful and quiet, to empty my mind of everyday thoughts.

6. ____ I believe that intuition comes from a higher part of myself and I never ignore it.

7. ____ I feel a sense of responsibility and belonging to the universe.

8. ____ My sense of identity is based on something that unites me with all other people.

9. ____ I am aware of a connection between myself and all living things.

10. ____ I see myself as being extended into everything else.

Once completed, re-look at these in light of the overall imagery of the World card.

The Four Evangelists

The four figures at the corners have long been representations for the four authors of the Gospels[10]: Matthew; Mark; Luke; and John. Matthew to the *Man* (or Angel); Mark to the *Lion*; Luke to the *Bull*; and John to the *Eagle*.

The Biblical sources for these are various, but, again, dominantly in Revelation (4:7), and in this case harkening directly back to both Daniel (and mention of the four winds) and, more importantly, Ezekiel 1:10. Revelation[11] has it thus:

The first living creature was like a lion, the second like a bull, the third living creature had a human face, and the fourth living creature was like a flying eagle.

The *order* of these four in various tarot representations is similarly not fixed, though they have generally become standardised within the TdM tradition in a manner that I personally find the most appropriate (and I'll return to that very soon). Let's have a brief look at *three* of these various

---

10   Generally, St Jerome's version has become the most established one. So though what I write is generally firmly established by the time of the Noblet, there *were* variations as to which Evangelist was associated with which figure – for example, St. Irenæus of Lyon connected the Lion with John and the Eagle with Mark; St. Augustine had the Human with Mark and the Lion with Matthew; and Pseudo-Athanasius had the Lion with Luke and the Bull with Mark. What is significant in terms of imagery is that irrespective as to which one was which, the four were seen as the four Evangelists, normally surrounding Christ.

11   *New Jerusalem Bible* translation.

orderings, both in the world of tarot and outside trump representations.

Yet, by presenting it in the manner in which Noblet chooses, not only are the two 'earth-bound' representations (Bull and Lion) below the two 'sky' or 'heaven'-bound ones (Angel and Eagle), but their respective positions reflect the modern view of the corresponding locations of the four *fixed* signs of the zodiac, with which they were also from a relatively early date connected: Taurus in the lower-left; Leo in the lower-right; Scorpio (in its 'higher' Eagle representation) in the upper-right; and Aquarius in the upper-left. This has an economy of scale that hints also at its plausible cosmic connections, and calls to mind at least one image from various Mithraic/Phanes representations:

The Initiate

I mentioned last week that an aspect of the previous card could be seen in reference to initiation. If that is the case, then here is not only the initiate, but the very being of the *initiator*. Whether as Mithra, Phanes, Christ, the *Anima Mundi*, Sophia, or Orpheus – all of which were at some point or other equated with one another with, usually, Christ as key or central consideration – the image brings to light the state to which the candidate for initiation aspires.

Within the Christian tradition, this becomes the *imitation of Christ*[12] and, ultimately, one's own deification or Theosis. In the words of Athanasius of Alexandria, "The Son of God became man, that we might become God".

If we consider the past twenty-eight weeks of study through these chapters, what I would hope to have shown is that the card's images have a depth that may assist in not only developing the imaginative faculty, but also quicken one to the spiritual, and, in time, awaken us to ever deeper insights into our own nature and the being of others – whatever this may be.

Brief Overview of Card Variation

Given the diversity of the manner in which this card is depicted, and in light of the above discussion, it would be useful to also keep in mind that within the variety that does occur, there nonetheless, on the whole, appears a persistent and increasingly common form: a metamorphosis moving from globe with Christ as masculine, to Christ as androgenous, to what becomes akin to the *Anima Mundi*, perhaps even foretelling the coming 'Age of the Spirit' foretold by Joachim of Fiore.

---

12   An intended reference to Thomas a Kempis's 15th century text of the same name.

    The cards that precede are, in order, from the 15th *c.* (the 'Charles VI' and Cary-Yale) through to the *circa* 1500 Sforza Castle engraving, onwards to an early Flemish deck, and thence to (above) the 18th century with the Chafard (which combines woodcut *lines* of a TdM-*I* with a red *drawn* band in a TdM-*II* style), and finally the Conver TdM-*II*.

With a number of similarities we can find numerous images that suggest common sources – though we will here focus on only three such images – all showing, perhaps by now to be expected, Christ, somewhat, to be sure, feminised:

The two images on the next page (amongst hundreds of like division) perhaps also explain how the aureole or *vesica piscis* has acquired a fourfold 'binding' on the Noblet – though interestingly omitted from the Sforza Castle card and TdM-*I* decks in general, yet also found in the image of *Philosophia* with which I end this chapter.

Christ as YHShVH

I have mentioned earlier that the four evangelists or their representation by the four living creatures are also representative of the four fixed signs of the zodiac. They also form, by reflective exegesis, the 'revealers' of the Tetragrammaton, ie, the four-lettered name of God found in the *Torah*: YHVH. Since late Mediæval times, a relation was established between this name and that of Jesus's: by placing within the

fourfold name the 'fire' of *Shin*, 'YHVH' (Yahweh) became 'YHShVH' (Jeheshuah, or Jesus).

This aspect again calls to mind the discussion in Plato's Timæus of the World Soul placed within the centre of the four-fold elements. Whether such, however, would have been considered in the context of the image, though quite consistent with various other considerations, is relatively unlikely – except perhaps for early image makers in a specific context.

Reviewing earlier cards

In light of the two images above (those in the left-hand column), let's look again especially at cards II the Papess and III the Empress. I am not suggesting that either of those images derive or reflect Christ as here presented. Rather, the skin tone is here 'feminised' by its paleness, the general body shape is also feminised by its shoulder proportions, and, in terms of the Empress, the transverse pillows that I mentioned in chapter five are here and finally shown in appropriate form.

As we look through the numbered series and consider that we have arrived at the last numbered card in the trump sequence, it is worth reflecting on the journey thus far in the context of not only what each calls forth, but also what the 'calls' ultimately seek.

For myself, the sequence shows itself to be a journey of transformation that leads towards integration and deification, at each stage requiring all previous stages to be integrated and allowed to be reflected in their proper light.

Staff or Sceptre

The one detail I have as yet omitted is the staff held which, at least in the Noblet, recalls that of the Empress's and Emperor's, in each case surmounted with a globe divided into three parts (similar to the Flemish deck image and Christ with the Earth as his footstool – both shown on the previous page), itself surmounted by a Cross.

Dynamic Hexagramme Tarot Spread

There are numerous spreads in existence, hundreds, in fact, and we have already visited a number of variations on the three-card spread, throwing cards at random, and, more recently, one version of the Celtic Cross spread. What I tend to generally prefer are spreads that allow a very open and actively dynamic interaction between the cards at hand. Of course, any spread may be used in that manner. Having in the past also used the I-Ching, I have always found one particular manner of looking at 'thrown' hexagrammes highly instructive, and decided to develop a spread using an aspect of its hexagrammes: its 'dynamic' aspect, if I can call it that. The similarity to the I-Ching lies more in the way in which outer and 'invisible' trigrams included *within* the six are used in the narrative.

The Spread

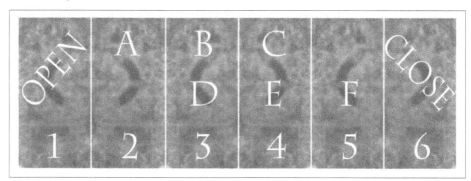

The Reading

Once the cards are layed six-in-a-row (as above) they may be read in the following manner.

Opening Card

The opening card (card 1) gives what is present as an underlying impulse in the situation at hand, whether this be a relationship, a work situation, or whatever it is the reading is about.

It may also indicate what the reading is actually about in cases where either there is no specified question, or where the ensuing reading seems to address other than the supposed question.

Central cards (2, 3, 4, 5)

Cards 2 and 3 can first be looked at as part 'clarification' cards for card 1.

Then, the situation at hand is described as it manifests in ABC (cards 2, 3 and 4). This is basically a three card reading which may show forth various pertinent aspects (financial, physical effort, psychological, etc).

The situation is of course never static, but in a permanent state of transformation. This is what DEF (cards 3, 4 and 5) now show as a 'new' three card reading.

The suggestion sees the sequence ABC transformed to DEF.

Closing card (6)

The Closing card (6) gives an indication for the manner in which the future pulls the situation into its sphere. Again, here, cards 4 and 5 can be looked upon as clarification cards for the final or closing.

Wheels within wheels

In a nutshell, the six-card spread has the dynamic virtue of the manner in which an I-Ching Hexagramme may be read. Here, the basic 3-fold readings pattern is repeated:

firstly as Opening ⊠ 2, 3, 4, 5 (as a group) ⊠ Closing;

secondly as the convergence of impulses from the past (1, 2, 3) meeting impulses from the future (4, 5, 6);

thirdly, as the manner in which the situation ABC is in the process of transformation to its new state DEF; and

finally (for now), the way in which this situation (ABC ⊠ DEF) has its two forces playing in from the opening and closing cards.

Some further remarks on the spread

As perhaps is by now obvious, I personally do not advocate a strict position = 'specified meaning' type reading, so the above is to be read, if taken as intended (of course anyone adopting it will transform it to their own preferred style), as dynamic and very much influenced and re-worked according to the specific cards layed out, and as to whether or not other mitigating factors (such as the preponderance of a particular suit, or figures, or colour, etc) play into the layout.

Boethius and Philo-Sophia

I cannot pass by one of my favourite non-tarot images that calls to mind this very card. To reach the heart of *Philo-Sophia*, a ladder of nine rungs has to be ascended, starting with *Phi* Φ (beginning the word 'Philos' or Love), and ending with *Theta* Θ (beginning the word 'Thanatos' or Death).

LE FOU

The end of the beginning...

It feels like a rather long journey coming to a close, only to find that the end is but the beginning of further travels, perhaps even a re-visiting of the work of the past 30 weeks, re-imaged in personal ongoing transformation.

Le Fou

Before we finish, of course, let's take some time to look at this our final card, and perhaps also compare him to some of the divergent extremes he has not only become in many decks, but also the manner in which the image also diverged in quite early depictions.

'Fou' means not only 'fool', but also 'mad' – in its two common senses of 'crazy' and 'angered'. As a general term applied to someone, it would normally refer to someone who is either, on the one hand, quite a simpleton or fool, or, on the other, afflicted with madness or crazy.

Looking at the figure, he appears as a fellow walking with a small load attached to a carry-stick, with a quite peculiar walking stick with carved head, wearing again quite specific clothing.

We'll just, for now, leave aside his dangling jewels and the pain he is about to likely endure. If it wasn't for his companion and the manner in which the image has over the centuries acquired additional shadings, the depiction seems quite clear: he is dressed as would be the Feast Fool, replete with 'crown', bells, 'puppet-headed'-wand, and even a jester's colourful over-shirt, covering what must be quite simple peasant clothing: a shirt; roll-up tights (or rather, the *chausse*), and simple shoes.

What is clear is that he does not wear the also expected short-like 'underwear' *braies* (acting a little like suspenders) that helped to support the *chausse*[1], and that his gown, which would be expected to reach down to cover his genitals, is obviously too small for his build. The exposure of his genitals adds to the sense that here is perhaps a 'simpleton' upon whom has been given the privilege of bearing the day's crown, adding indeed to the many excesses beyond what would at other times been considered indecorous or unseemly.

His hat is, again, pretty standard in its depiction, and very likely evolved with the ambiguity of a cloth 'crown' with the two side points increasingly coming to depict an ass's ears, and the single dropping rear one

---

1　　From which, incidentally, is derived 'chaussettes' or 'socks'.

symbolic of its tail.

I would suggest that to those of former times, here was not some strange character, but rather a very precise depiction that recurred annually during the feast of fools, with not only its crown king, but an environment that saw, with ever increasing playful ruse, friend sending friend on a fool's errand – to pick up, for example, a dozen rooster's eggs from a neighbour's farm. Or, to reflect on a modern equivalent we associate with April Fool's day (a poor derivative of the same, it seems), to seek spaghetti pickers for the over-grown and ripening spaghetti vines.

Here is the fool, then, not only clearly dressed in his garb as fool, but also clearly on a journey – a true *fool*'s journey: sent on a meaningless errand for which no possible completion can be satisfactorily accomplished.

Pilgrimage

That he holds a knapsack also calls to mind that here his errand may even have required some small travel or pilgrimage, for which he may even need guidance along his way. Such details were frequently depicted in various places, both as a reminder to be wary of guidance at each juncture or crossroad, and also to remind one of the necessity to use discernment. As Proverbs 14:15 puts it,

> The Fool believes everything, but the prudent man will follow the right path.

The image below shows the kind of guidance that deceives: the hand emerges from the rear of the post, such posts commonly having on the front an image of Christ or Mary, on each side those of saints, and hidden behind, forever there for the unwary, a devil:

These, incidentally, are still to be found in various places in France – the following images are from Tarau in France[2]. The tarot card image, by

---

2   There are two villages called 'Tarau' in southern France, each close to the other. The images are, from left to right: the left-hand side; *recto*; *verso*; and right-hand side.

depicting some travel made by the Fool, even on an impossible errand, would remind one that such false or deceptive advice is forever present.

My reason for mentioning these, even though removed from the image as we have it, is to suggest that such cross-road depictions would not have been far from the thoughts of those who at the time of Noblet's creation (and earlier as well as later) beheld the card.

Whether as pilgrimage or errand, life's voyages have pitfalls that call for a presence of mindfulness beyond that of the ordinary fool's.

Simplicity and innocence

If the 'laughable' is an aspect of the fool, there is also its complementary quality: a rich innocence that bespeaks reverence and awe, as well as calling to mind St Paul who, in 1 Corinthians, writes:

> [1:20-27] Where is the wise man? Where is the scholar? Where is the philosopher of this age? Has not God made foolish the wisdom of the world? For since in the wisdom of God the world through its wisdom did not know him, God was pleased through the foolishness of what was preached to save those who believe. Jews demand miraculous signs and Greeks look for wisdom, but we preach Christ crucified: a stumbling block to Jews and foolishness to Gentiles, but to those whom God has called, both Jews and Greeks, Christ the power of God and the wisdom of God. For the fool-

ishness of God is wiser than man's wisdom, and the weakness of God is stronger than man's strength.

Brothers, think of what you were when you were called. Not many of you were wise by human standards; not many were influential; not many were of noble birth. But God chose the foolish things of the world to shame the wise; God chose the weak things of the world to shame the strong.

And perhaps even more importantly a little later (3:18):

If any one of you thinks he is wise by the standards of this age, he should become a fool so that he may become wise.

How does one become a fool in order to become wise!? By, I would suggest, a willingness and ability to even behold what may be paradoxes without the assumption that an answer will be found at this time. A kind of radical frankness of one's own ignorance and situation – something not only akin to Socrates, but also, as previously mentioned in chapter 14, to Diogenes:

During a discourse in the Craneum, Diogenes observed he lacked an audience, and so instead began to whistle and dance to attract attention. People soon flocked around him, leading Diogenes to exclaim "fools! you lack interest and pay no attention to wisdom spoken, yet rush to observe foolish display!".

His astuteness against self-deception called for a kind of response to life that, in colloquial terms, requires 'balls':

> "Diogenes, why do students leave you for others, but rarely do they leave others for you?"

> "Because", replied Diogenes, "one can make eunuchs out of men, but no one can make a man out of eunuchs".

And our Fou is certainly no eunuch!

There are undoubtedly a number of aspects about the Fou that bring to mind Diogenes the cynic, not least of which is his general lack of decorum and his characterisation with a dog (or dogs). Yet, I would here claim that it is especially that sense of radical and simple honesty with which the Fou is imbued that powerfully reflects our remembrance of Diogenes.

Though the philosophically inclined may have perhaps been aware of Diogenes, and he serves us well in considering the liberating power of those who may perhaps accept his radical frankness and Fool-like qualities, there is in his character something that is quite remote from innocence and, instead, a state that has its social dangers. Even if awake to others' slumber, arousing others may have dire consequences.

Beauty and Ugliness

There is often an aspect of ugliness or deformity that accompanies depictions of fools, yet tarot is, apart from much later decks, on the whole very benign to the character, seemingly at worst depicting his simpleton aspect. This does not prevent, of course, various depictions of taunting and sheer cruelty, as both the 'Charles VI' and the Ercole D'Este images show (next page).

They both show, incidentally, the medieval *braies* mentioned on the first page of this chapter. For the sake of completion, the Visconti-Sforza shows both *braies* and *chousses* (below other two images).

There is an aspect of this taunting cruelty that seems to similarly be captured by depicting the animal (whether dog or lynx) jumping at his genitals. Such is a painful experience (to speak lightly!) that will likely give great laughter to the casual observer – unless empathetic to the victim... and generally a fool is *not* someone for whom there was much such empathy. In our contemporary time, this has metamorphosed with the acts and 'pain' of the clown, another aspect of the

jester-*cum*-buffoon-*cum*-fool.

In some ways, the animal looks more lynx-like than dog-like: both its ears and claws seem to suggest the wild cat. Something that would be, indeed, far more of a painful experience than the paws of a dog – and it is its paws or claws reaching for this genitals rather than its teeth.

Indeed, the markings and colouring of its fur seem to suggest the (short-tailed) wild European lynx. Yet, to be honest, I remain unconvinced as to whether the intent was that of a dog or of a lynx: the lines, especially of its head, seem more canine-like than feline.

Contrast to St Roch

It is not only in garb and intent that the depiction of the Fou is here hence distinguished from that of St Roch – a figure so common on the numerous French pilgrimage routes as to render his image clear and obvious to those of earlier times. With St Roch, the dog is always not only clear, but also far larger than the animal depicted on the card, and clearly his *companion* – something that seems unlikely for the Fou.

For many amongst us, however, the striking similarity – including the suggestion of a common 'gash' on St Roch's thigh – brings this figure also to reflection when considering the Fou. Here he calls to mind again not only pilgrimage, but also, in his case, the healing qualities against what the mark on his leg shows: the plague – and a reminder that all of us are prone to the numerous assaults that mark our bodies which are, in a different context, to be cared for as temples of the spirit.

'Mat' and 'Fou'

Though the Noblet clearly uses the more common French term 'Fou', I previously mentioned (in chapter 19 on Death) that this card is often also called 'Mat'. Undoubtedly unintended by the early card-makers, a connection has come to be made by various more recent authors between this un-numbered card and XIII-Death – a card that often remains un-named (though the reason for this is very likely due to the nature of the figure in early decks, which would have otherwise seen the scythe partially hidden by the lower panel). 'Mat', in Arabic (and hence also in chess use) means 'death'.

Reflections on the 30 weeks

Let's leave our Fou here and consider what we have achieved in the 30 weeks thus far.

Encapsulating the work in a rather brief summary, we have firstly looked at the cards as meaningful bearers within the context in which they emerged. Tarot, in my personal view, stems very much from a central core that iconographically cleaves to the TdM-*I*. This does not mean that newer and differing forms cannot emerge: on the contrary such will continue to take place. Rather, each impulse for change needs to somehow reflect both the flow through time to capture some centrality of the impulse at work, as well as being able to somehow reflect the fluctuating present.

It is in better understanding the details that are found in what has emerged as the core around which tarot develops that other decks can similarly be critically appraised in terms of their 'tarot-ness'. The historical context and the rich Christian, neo-platonic, neo-pythagorean and aristotelean foundations of the deck, in the context, additionally, of a broad historical canvas that sees particular socio-political reflections adopted and taken for granted, informs some of the dimensions the images present.

A number of years ago, I introduced a term on Aeclectic's tarotforum that has, I believe, been radically misunderstood – or rather, understood in a manner I certainly never intended: that of Ür-tarot. My sense of the term is derived, and intended, in a somewhat similar manner to the way in which Goethe applied it to the plant-realm with his *Ürplanzt*: it is not something that refers to an antecedent specimen, but rather a 'form' that is perhaps more reminiscent of a platonic archetype. Tarot, in that sense, has its archetypal 'being' that sees at each stage or times various embodiments.

Over the course of the centuries, these have taken numerous forms, usually intermixed with not only the fluctuating social mores of the period, but also with influx from other sources: in the 19th century the once dominant Etteilla-pattern in especially continental Europe; and in the 20th the Waite-Smith in especially the Anglo-Saxon world. With each influx comes also a spreading of the world of tarot both geographically as well as in terms of its acquired attributes, many of which will be later dropped as a close investigation into the realm of tarot unveils core attributes whose wealth was perhaps even reduced by the change. For example, we now generally consider Etteilla's suggestion (following De Gebelin's 1780s *Le Monde Primitif*) that XII Le Pendu be 'uprighted' and standing on one foot as a symbol of *prudence* as somewhat missing something that is central to the tarot impulse (this does not deny considering it as such in the context of a specific narrative or reading). I would suggest that, similarly, the renditions of the Fool by (to use three vastly different and divergent views) Wirth, Falconnier, and Waite-Smith, are likewise 'missing' something, and in the process, of course, also adding and seeking to re-create not only the card-image, but also its sequence.

In that sense I very much see tarot's impulse as a river flowing with not only inlets that continuously invigorate its living waters, but also with outlets from which various forms take shape.

It is by carefully looking at not only the various TdMs, but also considering the wide variety of decks available and the context in which they arise that this metaphor of a central impulse and stream will be judged to either be a somewhat accurate reflection, or found wanting. This is where, whether coming from myself or any other person striving to understand what is central to tarot, each one has to make his or her own carefully considered judgement and exercise discernment.

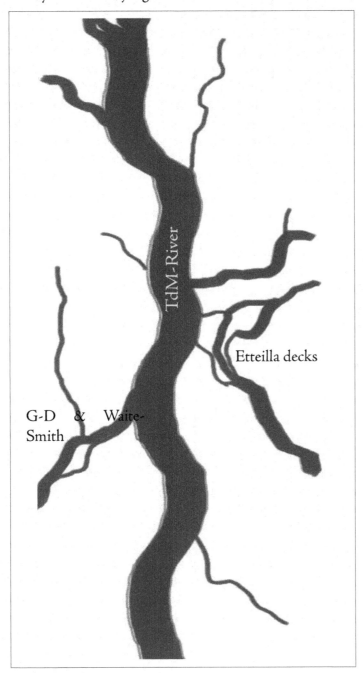

Further reading

Where does this leave us at this stage, with 30 weeks completed and much about tarot not covered? Firstly, allow me to make a very small list of suggested further reading that primarily focus on tarot's historical development:

Decker, DePaulis and Dummett *A Wicked Pack of Cards: the origins of the occult tarot*, Duckworth, 1996

Stuart Kaplan *Encyclopedia of Tarot* (especially vol. 2, 1986)

Robert O'Neil *Tarot Symbolism*, 1986 (ATS, 2004)

Christine Payne-Towler *The Underground Stream: Esoteric Tarot Revealed*, Noreah Press, 1999

It is inevitable that new books will emerge even as I write this. For example, the works of Ross Caldwell, Andrea Vitali, Michael J. Hurst – amongst others – will hopefully see the light of day in published form or, in the case of Vitali, translation.

Also of note are both some past (and future) Newsletters from the *Association for Tarot Studies* and its Tarot History Resource page, listing many of the main sites that will be of use.

As can be seen from these chapters, however, it is obvious that many resources belong outside of the specifically narrower realm of tarot: they consist of studies others have undertaken and published in history, art, philosophy, mysticism, comparative religion, mathematics, psychology, politics, and architecture. And not, I would add, simply from the past. Rather, these fields (and others) provide ever-deepening insights into those 78 images that have come to us enriched beyond, I would suggest, the wildest imagination of its creators, who were, after all responding to the needs of the time, in the context of the times, with the tools and symbols of the times. As we in turn have similarly undertaken in each of our private work over this course.

In this vain, I cannot omit to mention one additional book:

Anonymous *Meditations on the Tarot: a journey into Christian Hermeticism*, 1967 (Penguin-Tarcher, 2002)

Let's finish off by undertaking a quick review of the cards themselves by an exercise we undertook near the beginning of the course and, if you took the time to do so, your own notes from chapter one.

Pairings

Taking the trumps, pair them I with XI, II with XII, etc, leaving XXI and the Fou last. I initially wrote that, in terms of giving a suggested meaning, I would leave this final pair for later. It is now occasion to revisit such and present *its* 'paired' meaning:

The integrated being of XXI presents itself to the outer world as a cowardly fool.

On both the Paris and Amiens Notre-Dame Cathedrals is represented in pairs, courage and cowardice, with the latter depicted in similar fashion to that of the fool: the coward drops his sword and runs away from a rabbit jumping upon his rear leg.

Could it be that our Fou is similarly being depicted with *rabbit*, though the attendant narrative was half-lost and forgotten even by the time Noblet created his deck; and this, even though the *image* was common enough given the Cathedral image that Noblet himself, located in Paris, would have seen?

It remains for us all to keep our eyes open to detail that enriches our own myriad adventures through tarot's 78 astounding gifts!